Unhuman Culture

Unhuman Culture

DANIEL COTTOM

PENN

University of Pennsylvania Press

Philadelphia

10   9   8   7   6   5   4   3   2   1

Published by
University of Pennsylvania Press
Philadelphia, Pennsylvania 19104-4112

A Cataloging-in-Publication record is available from the Library of Congress

ISBN-10: 0-8122-3956-3
ISBN-13: 978-0-8122-3956-0

For Julie Green

Contents

Preface

"Just imagine," Nedko Solakov entreated us in *This is me, too . . .*, a 1996 mixed-media installation:

What would happen if I were to start to live as an ammonite, as a stuffed duck, as a rock crystal, as a snowflake, as the color spectrum, as the material that this very floor (on which you are now standing) is covered with . . . ?

Normally everybody dreams to be "somebody else": a famous actor, a brave knight, a rich hero.

I want to be "a something else"—"something" which I know from my old school books, from the natural history museums' collections, or just from inanimate nature.

Who knows—maybe in this case, with me as an ammonite, as a stuffed duck, as a snowflake, I could establish a more suitable relationship with the society around me.

At once comic and earnest, nostalgic and utopian, Solakov's words represent the eminently human desire to be unhuman. Everyone is familiar with this desire to move beyond the "weariness, the fever, and the fret," not to mention the "sorrow/And leaden-eyed despairs," that all too often may seem to sum up our condition, just as John Keats suggested they did.[1] Typically, as we sit and hear each other groan, we identify this desire with art, which is that species of thing through which humanity imagines another species of being for itself.

It was out of just such a sense of art that Friedrich Nietzsche wrote when he offered us his report about an unhuman creature capable of speech. This animal boasted, "Humanity is a prejudice with which we animals at least are not afflicted."[2]

In its very conception, before it even says a word, Nietzsche's talking animal dismisses the prevailing conception of humanity. In this respect it is akin to the talking vultures in Zora Neale Hurston's *Their Eyes Were Watching God* (1937), which "mocked everything human in death."[3] Following centuries of literary tradition, the artifice of Keats's immortal bird, Solakov's stuffed duck, Hurston's birds of prey, and Nietzsche's mocking creature captures humanity in the act of radically transforming its conception of itself. Nietzsche's animal might even lead one to say, with Theodor Adorno, that art in general "is loyal to humanity only through inhumanity toward it."[4] Once one recognizes—and who does not?—that it belongs to the human condition to be preoccupied with the unhuman, one can also recognize "art's asociality" and its "anticultural character" as its most vital qualities.[5]

So much is well known. It is well known, too, that the role of the unhuman in the definition of humanity is a topic of great concern in many forms of contemporary thought. It appears, for instance, in the thematization of "the Other" in philosophical, psychoanalytic, anthropological, and postcolonial studies. It also appears in the "antihumanism" popularly associated with figures such as Martin Heidegger, Michel Foucault, and Jacques Derrida, as well as in the advent of a "posthuman" age analyzed by critics such as Judith Halberstam and N. Katherine Hayles. Its genealogy might be traced, as Sigmund Freud proposed, to the Copernican, Darwinian, and psychoanalytic revolutions that displaced humanity from the center of the universe, the summit of natural creation, and the foundation of consciousness. Alternatively, as Karl Marx, among others, was influential in suggesting, one might emphasize the displacement of human identity from the presumed centrality of the individual. Identity then would appear to be wrought by the impersonal agencies of economic, technological, political, and ideological forces and structures, in relation to which the so-called individual would appear as a peculiar kind of historical fiction. The critique of universal notions of humanity by way of the categories of race, gender, and sexuality, among others, would then logically follow from the aforementioned lines of thought.

The unhuman does not necessarily signify the inhuman, in the sense of conspicuous or extraordinary cruelty. Rather, it encompasses everything that comes to be asserted, in particular contexts, as being foreign to the definition of humanity and thus, through this assertion, paradoxically necessary to that definition. The extrinsic that yet proves to be intrinsic, the unhuman marks the alienation of humanity from itself in the very act of positing itself. It is through the unhuman that we may come to face the idealization of destruction vital to humanity, along with all the rest of our self-constituting self-deceptions. It marks the beginning and end of the image of humanity; the borderlines of and contradictions within what is supposed to be human sovereignty; the unimaginable presumption that makes humanity imaginable; and, most important, a perennial and perhaps inescapable tendency to underestimate the art in humanity and to overestimate the humanity of art.

However one may approach this issue of the unhuman, questions as to the nature, extent, or even existence of a distinctively human agency come to the fore. In fact, it becomes increasingly clear that any responsible form of cultural criticism today must try to confront all that humanity is defined against and through. We must face not only the superhuman, as with Nietzsche, but also the supernatural, the demonic, and the subhuman; the supposedly disjunctive animal, vegetable, and mineral kingdoms; the realms of artifice, technology, and fantasy; that which is termed chance, necessity, and death—and so on. In doing so, we must confront the role of art as humanity's alibi, serving at once to confess and deny humanity's unhuman constitution. We may then begin to understand why art is as resistant to categorical definition as it is to progress, never getting any better and invariably making fools of those who believe otherwise. In other words, we may begin to come to terms with the necessity of art, which is the necessity of misanthropy.

Today, however one may regard it, the role of the unhuman in the definition of humanity crops up in a wide variety of contexts. It plays a role in theoretical discussions of the sublime, personal memoirs of the Holocaust, aesthetic reflections on technology, political analyses of modernity, economic discourses on globalization, navel-gazing editorials on developments in science, moral and theological musings on evil, and popular accounts of terrorism, to name just a few. Whereas it once may have seemed that the concept of culture always, by definition, pertained to humanity, it now may seem impossible to avoid the realization that we must look at things differently. It is not only art, in the narrow sense of that word, that we must recognize as being unhuman in its implicit distinction from and potential disturbance of whatever is assumed for the moment to figure as the commonality of humanity. For better or worse, ours is now an unhuman culture.

Nietzsche is sometimes credited with having first diagnosed this modern cultural condition, which he saw as calling for a new approach to philosophy and the arts. Crucially, in the workings of language, consciousness, culture, and civilization, this approach calls on us to recognize the violence intrinsic to institutions people traditionally have held sacred. Thus far, at least, I follow his example. Studying the agency of the unhuman in the human requires that we focus on the violence of definition through which we image humanity to ourselves. Accordingly, in this book I write not only of art but also of terrorist acts, imperial presumption, demonic horror, war, iconoclasm, massacre, sacrifice, and mutilation.

In this approach we see that misanthropy is a force constitutive of social life rather than an attitude logically excluded from it. Although it is supposed to be the exceptional, extreme, and uncharacteristic appearance of the unhuman within humanity, we see that misanthropy is the agency not only of humanity's treasured art but even of its common sense. The literary works I bring in to bear witness to this consideration range from medieval saints' lives to the plays of Christopher Marlowe, the *Maxims* of La Rochefoucauld, *Gulliver's Travels*, Gothic novels, *Frankenstein*, and works by Franz Kafka, F. T. Marinetti, Samuel Beckett, and Angela Carter, among others. I also examine the cultural resonance of certain events, including the coronation of Napoleon, suffragette iconoclasm, the Kent State massacre, and 9/11. The artworks that come into my argument range from Pieter Bruegel's *Misanthrope* to Francisco Goya's *Disasters of War* and the performances of the contemporary artists Chris Burden and Orlan; the works of philosophy I discuss include writings by Plato, Thomas More, René Descartes, Thomas Hobbes, Denis Diderot, Nietzsche, Søren Kierkegaard, Martin Heidegger, Adorno, and Jacques Derrida.

As I trust will become clear, then, I do not see my concerns here as exclusive to a modern, postmodern, or Nietzschean epoch. To think through the unhuman nature of culture we need to disabuse ourselves of the impression that its discovery is peculiar to our era. Misanthropy takes distinctively contemporary forms, but we cannot begin to understand its necessity unless we try to look beyond the selves and societies that we presume, in all the violence of our love, to be our own.

Introduction: To Love to Hate

When Chris Burden fired a pistol at an airliner taking off from LAX in 1973, he committed an artwork of terrific suggestiveness, one that helped win him a prominent place among his contemporaries. Perhaps most obviously, *747* (Figure 1) evoked the cliché of the hero going to any lengths for his art. Here we have the isolated individual doing battle with the world, attacking its materials—canvas, stone, plastered ceiling, even the infinite heavens—with a passion bordering on madness. Simultaneously, and maybe even more strongly—judgments will vary— he recalled the antiheroic image of the *poète maudit*. From this other perspective, what we have here is a reckless immoralist so devoted to aesthetic sensations, in both senses of the word, that he is heedless of the human consequences of his pursuits. "Burden's work *is* terrorism," one critic has said, approvingly.[1] We might be reminded of the surrealist dictum, carried over from the Dada gang, in which the random firing of a gun in a crowd was seen as the exemplary aesthetic act.

Then again, we might say that Burden made reference to these other images while also portraying the artist as an utterly abject figure, a bad boy *manqué* whose futility does not even rise to the level of Don Quixote tilting at windmills, so vulgar is it and so lacking in authenticity. Or, more degrading yet, in this moment we might judge him to have been the artist as anachronism. Then we would see a degenerate publicity hound pathetically trying to get with the program of popular culture, as represented most centrally by the movies. From *The Great Train Robbery* (1903) through gangster dramas, film noir, John Wayne, James Bond, and the *Lethal Weapon* franchise, we will remember, the movies have offered us as the image of their compelling power the iconic figure of a man shooting a gun. Or, in yet another alternative, either outweighing or to some degree interrelated with all these contexts, *747* might be seen as offering us the image of the male artist heroically, diabolically, abjectly, and anachronistically, not to mention hysterically, trying to assert himself at a moment when the feminist movement was dramatically challenging the phallic brush and genius no less than the gun.[2] This context in turn would lead us to others relevant to the appreciation of

Figure 1. Chris Burden, *747* (1973). Photo courtesy Chris Burden.

this artwork, including the state-sanctioned mass murders of the Vietnam War, which were still fresh in people's minds at the time.[3]

There is yet more to this work, of course. For instance, it might be viewed as a reflection, both homage and send-up, of the muscular gesture in "action painting" of the 1940s and 1950s. It would then be an act comparable to Robert Rauschenberg's famous erasure of a drawing by Willem de Kooning. The whiff of wimpiness in Rauschenberg's *Erased de Kooning* (1953)—he obtained the Ab Ex master's permission before he flourished his eraser—is also in keeping with Burden's behavior in using a handgun rather than some more formidable weaponry of the sort accessible to terrorists and, one must presume, sufficiently motivated artists. Burden has never really been a terrorist, after all, even though he has deserved to be called "one of America's few really scary artists."[4]

Burden's *747* is an art object that existed as such only in a vanishing instant of time now memorialized in its photographic and textual documentation. Consequently, his pistol points out two directions, into performance and the simulacrum, that beleaguered "high" art has taken from the 1960s to the present day. The emphases in this work on art as a conceptual act, on the human body as integral to the work, and on the artist's personal identity indicate three additional directions that have been pursued. Yet we are also guided elsewhere, farther into the past, as into the tradition of landscape art and, more specifically, the aesthetics of the sublime.

The Burden of *747* then becomes a latter-day wanderer from the canvases of Caspar David Friedrich, posed against the melancholy horizon, seeking to penetrate its mysteries. The disproportions of scale between the puny human and the transcendental airliner call to mind the Faust legend in its Romantic interpretation, in which it tells of the danger of overreaching the bounds of one's nature by desiring to know too much, and also in its more modern or post-Frankensteinian reading, in which scientific knowledge and its characteristic product, technology, are the most profound temptations to the human spirit. If you want an image of Martin Heidegger's *Dasein*, Burden gives it to you.

Even from this perspective, however, Burden's performance leads us into further equivocation. If his was in some sense an act reaffirming the divide between technology and spirit, science and art, impersonal knowledge and human vitality, and all the other oppositions appertaining to these, it was also an act that solicited our epistemophilia, in the most basic empirical terms. Is the photo "real"?[5] (This question becomes all the more pressing if one thinks of the uncanny reversal of Burden's work in a hoax that was widely distributed over the internet almost immediately after the September 11, 2000 attacks—a photograph of a man on the observation deck of the World Trade Center, oblivious to the plane bearing down upon him.) Did Burden "really" shoot the gun? Was the plane close enough to him at that moment so that it was within the realm of empirical possibility that he might have hit it and, if he hit it just right—just wrong—forced it to crash? We can learn, if we are so inclined, that Burden was visited by the FBI but dismissed from its consideration, evidently because he was out of range when he fired his gun.[6]

Like truth, beauty might also be an issue here. As a young man Burden was not, by any ordinary measures, an extraordinarily attractive hunk of humanity, and in the snapshot of this event he looks small and scruffy as he stands in his undistinguished clothes in an equally undistinguished landscape. If we cannot call such a perfectly conceived act "beautiful," however, then of what use can that word be outside of the inverted commas used to terrorize the taste of those who still believe in a regulative ideal of aesthetic judgment? Much the same question might be asked of all the other terms through which we are accustomed to evaluate art, including *morality* and *value*.

Through its symbolic erasure of the line commonly drawn between symbolic and real violence, as through the sorts of uncertainties, equivocations, contradictions, and overdeterminations I have briefly sketched here, Burden's act drew forth the misanthropy of art. By this I mean its undoing of humanity, its drive to betray what Samuel Beckett called "anthropomorphic insolence," or whatever may be thought of as properly human desires, intentions, and concerns.[7] Using Beckett as one of his favored exemplars, Theodor Adorno directed attention to the aesthetic implications of this point (even as he struggled to give it a utopian spin) when he remarked upon the Baudelairian "spleen" of art, without which it cannot be, and with which it maintains "a permanent protest against morality."[8] This is an ancient theme, arguably *the* most ancient theme of Western aesthetics. Yet it is one that we continue to play down whenever we try to discipline art into spiritual health by working some sense of conventional responsibility into our theories of what it is, does, and has been. "Pollyanaesthetics" was Dorothy Parker's waspish term for this sort of thing. For his part Burden has flatly stated, "Art is not about social betterment."[9]

Burden, I would suggest, was not sick but was unhuman when he made *747*. He was like those uncanny things-in-the-act-of-becoming-art that are no longer objects, exactly, as they appear to their makers or audiences. At the most banal level, the teacher in the creative writing workshop says, "This poem wants to be a sonnet"; or the painter says, as she tries to figure out what the canvas is doing, "It needs something right *there*." A more extraordinary case would involve bystanders watching symbols being attacked and, as thousands die, imagining that they are watching a movie.

In accordance with the tradition that Socrates helped to establish in the *Phaedo*, it has been usual to think of misanthropy quite differently. Much as T. E. Hulme termed romanticism "spilt religion," both scholars and laypersons have tended to regard misanthropy as spoilt idealism. When the Sex Pistols, for instance, declared that England's queen is not a human being, hip commentators were quick to find in their music a spirit of revolutionary purity, no matter how grotty the band might appear onstage, and even the unhip were prepared to see these punks as symptomatic of the failure of social ideals. Similarly, misanthropy appears as the flipside of generosity for Timon of Athens, sincerity for Molière's Alceste, reason for Jonathan Swift's Gulliver, innocence for Victor Frankenstein's monster, romantic love for Dorothy Parker, and so on.[10] One can also see this theme in Charlotte Lennox's *The Female Quixote* (1752), in the marquis who is embittered by the loss of his place at court and so banishes himself and his daughter to rural obscurity. In Virginia Woolf's *Mrs. Dalloway* (1925), the rather too appropriately named Miss Kilman sees the world through the distorted lens of her thwarted desires. George Sanders, in *Death of a Scoundrel* (1956), acquires his titular character after his beloved, thinking him dead, marries his brother. The alienated protagonist of Margaret Atwood's *Surfacing* (1972) finds that her destiny is to be a misanthrope so that she might at last create the possibility of humanity. The examples are endless.

A prominent misanthrope in his day despite his role as an enthusiastic "friend of humanity" during the French Revolution, Sébastien-Roch-Nicolas Chamfort pointed out that misanthropy thus construed is not really distinct from fellow-feeling. "To have a correct idea of things," he wrote, "it is necessary to take words in a sense opposite to that which they are given in the world. Misanthropist, for example, means philanthropist."[11] Following a similar line of reasoning, Jean-Jacques Rousseau had maintained that either Alceste was not really a misanthrope or that "there is no good man who is not a misanthrope in this sense."[12] Following the same tradition, Immanuel Kant wrote sympathetically about misanthropy, "very improperly so called," as a tendency among good people who have been touched by "sad experience" to "withdraw from society," to move to "an isolated country seat," or even "to pass their life on an island unknown to the rest of the world with a small family," thus fulfilling a fantasy "which the novelists or poets who write Robinsonades know so well how to exploit."[13] This is the traditional view that Thomas Love Peacock satirized in *Nightmare Abbey* (1818) through the words of a Kantian metaphysician, Mr. Flosky. "I do not take any interest in any person or thing on the face of the earth," Mr. Flosky says, "which sentiment, if you analyse it, you will find to be the quintessence of the most refined philanthropy."[14] Misanthropy in this understanding is neither more nor less than what one of Friedrich Schiller's characters describes it to be: a condition that places one in a critical position between "humanity and humans."[15]

At least to some extent, works that take misanthropy as an explicit topic always lend themselves to this judgment of spoilt idealism, and criticism that accepts this invitation does have its pertinence as it traces out the fashions and histories of this attitude, as it may then be called. To stop there, however, is to stay comfortably within the terms of humanity and thus, like Hulme, finally not to experience these works as art at all. In contrast, Burden's performance leads us to see the constitutive misanthropy at work in the very conception of art. This is its appeal to the realm of the unhuman, which includes not only brute material events and cultural representations but also identifications with things such as leaders, gods, consumer goods, planes, skyscrapers, and spectacular movies.

The Other Vietnam Memorial (1991) is another work of Burden's that helps to establish this argument. This mock monument refers to Maya Lin's beloved wall, before which hundreds of thousands of Americans continue to lay down offerings as they rub it, embrace it, photograph it, kneel in front of it, and shed tears near it. Through his sculpture Burden draws out the fierce misanthropy in Lin's work by reminding us of the names of the millions of Vietnamese that this wall symbolically and violently erases, putting them beyond the pale of our sympathies. More recently, the artist Dread Scott has followed Burden's example in a work titled (and dramatizing the equivoque in the term) *Enduring Freedom* (2002). Although it was based on the shrines created in New York City in the aftermath of the September 11 attacks, *Enduring Freedom* is devoted to the Afghan casualties of the war the United States conducted, under this name, in response to the events of that day.

One need not necessarily be an artist, self-designated or otherwise, to appreciate the calling of the misanthropy of which I write here. It is not only a question of art, or perhaps it is a question of art exceeding its seeming categorical definition, as in the Nietzschean conception of the world as an artwork. In this context we might think of Arthur C. Danto's response to Karlheinz Stockhausen's infamous characterization of 9/11, in which this composer viewed the destruction of the World Trade Center as a work of art. "That such a claim could be made at all," Danto writes, "underscores the total openness of the contemporary concept of art, however monstrous the consequences of conceiving art in that way."[16]

For the epigraph to the essay in which this response appears, Danto quite fittingly chose a quotation from Adorno's *Aesthetic Theory*. Again, though, it is crucial to remember that the misanthropy at issue here is not just a question of art. In the writings of Beckett, for instance, as in the art of Burden, we see this misanthropy lying in wait for just about everyone. For instance, the protagonist of *Watt* (1953), troubled over a non-pot—"It resembled a pot, it was almost a pot, but it was not a pot of which one could say, Pot, pot, and be comforted"—finds his own humanity equally at issue because of "this indefinable thing that prevented him from saying, with conviction, and to his relief, of the object that was so like a pot, that it was a pot, and of the creature that still in spite of everything presented a large number of exclusively human characteristics, that it was a man."[17]

Of interest in this regard is one of the most distinctive features of Burden's LAX performance: that it was carried out in the almost complete absence of recognizable aesthetic frames. Although a witness took a snapshot, there was no audience or theater in the usual senses of these words, no curtains or stirring music or other signs to indicate the event's beginning and end, and no formal conventions by which to judge its quality or success except, perhaps, the trope of paradox. For if he had "succeeded," Burden surely would have "failed." His act would have been a horrific crime, not an amazingly canny artwork. Moreover, although the event gave rise to various kinds of commentary and documentation, including Burden's own testimony about it, it did not result in an object that could be displayed in a gallery or enshrined in a museum. It is also the case that this performance, if someone were to attempt to reproduce it today, would certainly end in imprisonment for all concerned and so would scarcely resemble the original. Burden himself said as much when he resigned his professorship at UCLA in 2005 to protest the university's failure to punish a young man whose artwork consisted of playing a seemingly real game of Russian roulette in front of a room full of students.[18] Furthermore, it is noteworthy that the artist's touch played no part in that original event—any fool can fire a gun—and that it cannot even be taken for granted that Burden acted as an artist when he fired his weapon. After all, lots of people fire guns into the sky to celebrate an occasion, to express anger, to let off steam, or for other reasons that seem appropriate at the time. So perhaps it resembles art, it is almost art, but it is not an art of which one can say, Art, art, and be comforted.

And it was ever thus, or so I take Burden to have suggested. If ever such a thing as art should be, it cannot be radically distinguished from ordinary perceptions, acts, and deeds, even though it cannot be entirely coincident with them. What marks it out is the misanthropic appeal that goes to work on us in any experience that somehow takes us out of "it": the world, the self, living matter, whatever is assumed for the moment to figure as the commonality of humanity.

Figure 2. Chris Burden, *Trans-fixed* (1974). Photo courtesy Chris Burden.

To help clarify this point, another of Burden's early works, in which he had himself crucified on the back of a Volkswagen Beetle (*Trans-Fixed*, 1974—Figure 2), may be usefully juxtaposed with his assault on the airliner. The sadomasochistic extremes he marked out with these two works, in which the artist is variably killer and sacrifice, terrorist and victim, evil and redemption—all in the context of mundane modernity—evoke the immemorial religious traditions, themes, functions, and contexts of art in all their horror, sublimity, and banality. One thinks of the elegant misanthropy of Jorge Luis Borges's "Babylon Lottery" (1941), which echoes passages from Thomas De Quincey's opium nightmares and from Charles Baudelaire's *Flowers of Evil* (1857): "Like all men in Babylon, I have been a proconsul; like all, a slave; I have also known omnipotence, opprobrium, jail."[19] Or one might think of the passage in the Prelude to Johann Wolfgang Goethe's *Faust* (1808) in which the Poet speaks in the same line of his desire for "the strength of hate" and "the power of love."[20]

In its suggestion of quasi-religious suffering, *Trans-Fixed* resembles other early works by Burden, such as the one in which he confined himself for several days in a small UC-Irvine locker with nothing but a five-gallon jug of water available to him from the locker above and a five-gallon jug for his urine in the one below (*Five Day Locker Piece*, 1971). Like this remarkable MFA work, the embodied pun in *Trans-Fixed*—it is an "auto"-crucifixion—suffers us to remember the misanthropy in ascetic spiritual practices like those performed by early church fathers, such as Saint Simeon Stylites, whose legend is capable of creeping out even the most devout commentators. The comparison is as apt as it is far-fetched, for we did not need a cutting-edge artist to tell us that there is an irony built into the act of turning away from humankind, away from "the world," in the attempt to fulfill one's humanity. The young Simeon's fellow monks are said to have been so appalled by the creative extremes of his self-mortification, which included tying a rope around his loins so that it ate into his flesh and opened a ghastly wound festering with worms, that they cast him out from their brotherhood.[21] Out of his awareness of this sort of thing, what Burden has offered us, complete with allusions to the historical realities of mass murder—it was a *Volkswagen* hood—is a vision of misanthropy as the very stuff of art, to be accepted and explored and worked on as such, lest art and non-art alike should offer us the dismal comfort of the real thing.

*   *   *

A familiar view would have it that the protagonist of Franz Kafka's "Hunger Artist" (1922) represents the last term in a series of asceticisms. The legacy of stoic soldiers and athletes, Christian anchorites, and Romantic artists peters off into this performer who allows an entrepeneur to make a spectacle out of his *askesis* until the market for such things fails and he is led to contemplate the futility of his discipline. From this sort of viewpoint, the hunger artist participates in various allegories, as of the death of a traditional ideal of art in the commodified circumstances of modern life; the meaninglessness of art divorced from the social institutions of *polis* and church; the incoherence of the self in the absence of sustaining relations with others; and the problem posed by art to a particular writer, ascetic, and Jew. In Sander L. Gilman's phrase, "Kafka's geek turns out in the end to have been a freak."[22] Therefore, he can also be associated with the rethinking of cultural history represented by the revered freaks of the Symbolist and aestheticist movements, such as Joris-Karl Huysman's Des Esseintes; with the general perception of cultural and physical degeneration that played itself out in all aspects of modernism, including not only literature and art but also fields such as history, anthropology, and criminology; and with an aesthetics of high art that was consolidated in this era in marked opposition to, but also through complicity with, femininity, mass culture, popular culture, and middle-class business in general.

The text does support these sorts of readings, and they have their importance. Similarly, it is important to recognize, as Breon Mitchell has pointed out, that in the late nineteenth century hunger artists were an actual social phenomenon whose practices and subsequent decline in popularity are tracked with an almost journalistic fidelity in Kafka's tale.[23] With at least as much textual warrant, though, one might see Kafka's hunger artist as neither historical outsider nor historicist exemplification. Instead he may be taken to embody the untimeliness of the misanthropy from which no art can deliver itself.

We can know that the hunger artist is not simply an anachronism because all the supposedly contemporary features of his environment were already established as being contemporary at least as far back as the fourth century. Impure motivations in the world of performing art, the corruptions of commercialism, the vulgar and uncomprehending spectators: the desert monks were entirely familiar with such an environment. When church fathers took to the wastelands of the middle east and there lived on pillars, in caves, or even, like Saint Theodore Sykeon, in cages, they already had to deal with the question of when ambition might corrupt, rather than help to perfect, the *imitatio* involved in one's body art.[24] Similarly, just as prospective monks would have to be warned, in medieval works such as *Piers Plowman* (c. 1394) and the *Myrour of Recluses* (c. 1349–82), against the temptation to adopt the life of a hermit in order to cash in on it, so, too, did the "athletes of God" in the deserts of the fourth and fifth centuries, such as Antony, have to give up money due to them and resist Satan's offers to replace it with even more.[25] Moreover, in addition to dealing with the faithful who flocked to see them in their spectacular isolation, they had to fend off tourists who had no proper understanding of their discipline.[26] Already during Simeon's lifetime portraits of him were being widely circulated, making a celebrity of this supposed recluse.[27] Accordingly, a standard trope in saints' lives has their followers, and sometimes they themselves, initially being rejected from monkish fellowship before they prove they are deserving of its suffering. Similarly, we learn of those who had to masquerade as the real thing in order to be accepted, such as women who disguised themselves as men so that they might be able to participate in their discipline.

In fact, part of the pleasure in reading saints' lives comes from naive details that suggest just how disturbing the image of misanthropy was bound to appear, no matter how pious it was supposed to be. For instance, when his former brethren, admonished by God, decide they want Simeon back among them, they have to return him by force, so glad is he to have been cast out into the wilderness. For his part, after weeping daily for two years because of his lack of solitude, Saint Hilarian persuaded the crowds besieging him to allow him to leave, only to find then that the faithful were so persistent in searching him out that he would have to keep moving from one place to another for the rest of his life.[28] Similarly, in Athanasius's famous life of Saint Antony, we are told how Antony's twenty years of isolation came to an end when his admirers broke into his enclosure and forcibly dragged him out—even as Kafka's artist had to be reluctantly taken out of his cage at the end of each performance. Bede told a similar story of how a tearful Saint Cuthbert had to be compelled to leave his eremitic isolation in order to assume the duties of the bishopric to which he had been elected. Petrarch told of Amonius, a disciple of Saint Pambo, who sought to avoid this same honor by cutting off his ears and then, when he was still importuned, threatening to cut out his tongue. In the "great refusal" of the figure in the *Inferno* commonly identified as Pope Celestine V, who abdicated the papacy after only a few months to return to his life as a hermit, Dante famously made an example of this sort of danger.[29] As tales such as these demonstrate, all the features of the hunger artist's story that might identify him as an anachronistic figure, because they are supposed to indicate the inappropriately modern context in which his art cannot flourish, were already woven into the understanding of the lives of solitaries from the time this type was recognized as such. The features that establish a context of multiple, ambiguous, corrupt, and futile or grotesque motivations are prefigured in the lives of the saints. And just as we can see that he is not an anachronism, from this viewpoint we can also see that Kafka's artist is not simply an exemplification. The features that would seem to cage him into a particular cultural, social, or historical context also drag him out into others, with the original event on which the story is supposedly based proving aesthetically irretrievable except as an ongoing disturbance in our capacities for aesthetic judgment.

To see how fully the suicidal masochism of the hunger artist is also sadistic aggression, not only against any conceivable audience and the nourishment of the species but in terms of a misanthropic effect constitutive of art, one might compare his story to what is perhaps De Quincey's most famous essay, "On Murder Considered as One of the Fine Arts" (1827).[30] In the guise of a speaker before the Society of Connoisseurs in Murder, De Quincey follows Chamfort in arguing that the conventional opposition between philanthropy and misanthropy is all wrong. He develops this argument rather differently, however. The terms of philanthropy and misanthropy, he maintains, simply refer to works that are less or more artistic. As he puts it, "The world in general, gentlemen, are very bloody-minded; and all they want in a murder is a copious effusion of blood; gaudy display in this point is enough for *them.*"[31] One might think of the gaudy health of the leopard that so comforts the circus audience at the end of "A Hunger Artist." This is also, however, the lesson of Timon: that philanthropy simply awaits the occasion to reveal itself as misanthropy, much as the leaders of the United States in the aftermath of 9/11 urged charity upon Americans in the very same lines and images with which they looked forward to bloodshed.

"To hear people talk," says De Quincey, "you would suppose that all the disavantages and inconveniences were on the side of being murdered, and that there were none at all in *not* being murdered. But considerate men think otherwise."[32] Like Burden and Kafka, he makes a performance out of taking pleasure in drawing out as unsparingly as possible his recognition of the misanthropy in art. Through what one appalled critic called his "blandly brazen misappropriations of common aesthetic dicta," De Quincey proposed a conception of aesthetics that was heretically upsetting, yes, but also completely faithful to tradition.[33]

In contrast to De Quincey's connoisseur, popular imagination would hold misanthropy to be an extreme and desolate condition. It is supposed to be self-lacerating, miserable, and either sentimentally pathetic or, at its vicious extrème, as hateful as Fritz Lang's Doctor Mabuse. This is a tale we tell to bind ourselves to the species: hence the dismay of journalists reporting on the World Trade Center and Pentagon attacks when they were forced to deal with the inconvenient fact that the terrorists did not fit the typical profile of an impoverished, desperate youth brainwashed into a *jihad* frenzy. Instead, disturbingly, they seemed to be middle-class, educated, and well traveled—at least one of them even possessed of a wife and children, according to early reports. The terrorists seemed to compound their horrific crime even further, after the fact, by suffering it to be revealed that they had enjoyed an occasional drink, gone to the gym, *fit in.* The media would have been much more comfortable with the stereotypical fanaticism of a Baudelaire, who once

Figure 3. Pieter Bruegel the Elder, *The Misanthrope* (c. 1568). Tempera on linen. Museo nazionale di Capodimonte, Naples. Photo courtesy Scala/Art Resource, New York.

remarked, "When I have inspired universal disgust and horror, I will have conquered solitude."[34]

* * *

Prior to the early twentieth century, the *Misanthrope* (c. 1568—Figure 3) of Pieter Bruegel the Elder was catalogued under the title *Heresy*.[35] This historical happenstance is entirely fitting. For misanthropy can be construed as the ultimate and unsurpassable heresy in the souls, societies, and histories of humankind. Lord Byron, for instance, recognized this situation when he made his Giaour, or infidel, another type of Cain in his parade of alienated protagonists. With deadening predictability, victims will see terrorists as heretics even to their own professions of faith who are driven by an inhuman hatred of humanity while the terrorists will believe these others are the real source of hatred and heresy. To remark upon this dreary cliché ("one man's terrorist is another man's freedom fighter") is by no means to suggest an equivalence between, for instance, the fanatics responsible for the plane hijackings of 9/11 and those who were murdered or otherwise devastated by their actions. On the contrary, this observation is necessary in order to maintain crucial distinctions among persons and among deeds. For the purposes of moral and political judgment, as the constitutive misanthropy of art can teach us, the language of heresy will get us nowhere. In adopting it, we simply undo ourselves.

This consequence follows even for those who seek, as Kant did, to domesticate misanthropy as a redemptive withdrawal from the world. They, too, are compelled to distinguish their visions from heretical forms and thus to make war on their own professions of sympathy and understanding. Kant himself took pains to distinguish the philanthropically motivated misanthropy of which he wrote from misanthropy proper, which was "in part hateful and in part contemptible" to him.[36] Similarly, Rousseau had distinguished Alceste from "the real misanthrope," who "is a monster."[37] In the case of Johann Georg Zimmermann's Rousseauian treatise *On Solitude*, the comparable version of heretical misanthropy involves, among others, Roman Catholic monastics: "In the solitude of the cloister, through fasting and freezing, midnight choir shrieking, and a thousand loathsome and exasperating feelings, one learns to hate humanity."[38] Zimmermann's treatise is a virtual prescription for Friedrich's paintings, with their scenes of sublime and ennobling solitude, and so we might presume that he would have admired works such as *Two Men by the Sea at Moonrise* (1817—Figure 4). We must also presume, however, that Friedrich's *Monk by the Sea* (c. 1809—Figure 5) might have proven as unsettling to Zimmermann as it did to Heinrich von Kleist. Rather than suggesting the "sweet melancholy" of which Zimmermann was so fond, this work might have called up Robert Burton's description of that "destructive solitariness" in which "sociable creatures become beasts, monsters, inhumane, ugly to behold, *Misanthropi*."[39] In his 1810 commentary, telling of the confusion he felt before this painting, Kleist described it as being at once an occasion of heartwrenching feeling and of damage to the self.[40]

These examples can serve to remind us that the history of Christian asceticism is strongly associated with accusations and counteraccusations of heresy, and not only in dramatically anti-Catholic works of misanthropy such as Charles Robert Maturin's Gothic *Melmoth the Wanderer*

Figure 4. Caspar David Friedrich, *Two Men by the Sea at Moonrise* (1817). Oil on canvas. Alte Nationalgalerie, Berlin. Photo courtesy Bildarchiv Preußischer Kulturbesitz/Art Resource, New York

Figure 5. Caspar David Friedrich, *Monk by the Sea* (c. 1809). Oil on canvas. Alte Nationalgalerie, Berlin. Photo courtesy Bildarchiv Preußischer Kulturbesitz/Art Resource, New York

(1820). Flannery O'Connor, for one, freely acknowledged as much when she suffered 1 Corinthians 15: 31, "I die daily," to be translated into the idiom of the murderous Misfit in "A Good Man Is Hard to Find" (1955): "She would of been a good woman . . . if it had been somebody there to shoot her every minute of her life."[41] Another misfit, Friedrich Nietzsche, had quoted Tacitus on the alleged *odium generis humani* of the early Christians; and even though neither the one nor the other was a neutral witness, this question of hatred within the profession of love for humanity can never be dismissed. As Rousseau said, adapting this consideration to the salon society of his era, "I do not know any greater enemy of men than the friend of all the world, who, always charmed by everything, incessantly encourages evildoers and, through his culpable complaisance, flatters the vices from which are born all the disorders of society."[42]

Just as art cannot be described without raising the issue of misanthropy, there is no way that misanthropy can be described that will eliminate the irresoluble question of heresy. The fact that art teaches us that we live in the company of misanthropes, that we must actually love misanthropy because without the allegation of such heresy we would have no identities, does not resolve any questions, certainly. Recognizing with Byron that humanity is "enamour'd of distress," however, does furnish us, as it furnished him, with the only rational starting point we have for deciding how to proceed in the face of the evil that drives us to war.[43]

In her surrealist anatomy, *The War of Dreams*, Angela Carter explored this issue of misanthropy in a time of war through dramatic allusions to Kafka, De Quincey, Baudelaire, Goethe, and Nietzsche, among others. The penultimate chapter in her rendering of this issue, which she portrays as deeply implicated in but irreducible to the workings of misogyny, takes on the case of Swift.[44] In place of the classical motto from Plautus befitting her well-known story "The Company of Wolves"—*homo homini lupus*—we are given the image of the horse-man, or centaur. Her protagonist, Desiderio, and his beloved, Albertina, come upon a tribe of centaurs and find that these creatures are "not Houyhnhnms," exactly, because unlike these others they do have "many words to describe conditions of deceit."[45] Nonetheless, they bring us to a Swiftian, or super-Swiftian, lesson, one which draws out the surrealism in the ancient formula that defines humankind as the *animal implume bipes latis unguibus.* "If I was a man, what was a man?" Desiderio asks. "The bay offered me a logical definition: a horse in a state of ultimate, biped, maneless, tailless decadence."[46] Human, all too unhuman, the centaurs are at once men and unmen because they are men in a state of imaginary perfection.

A comparison of Bruegel to Carter on this point must seem terribly or even surrealistically anachronistic. Nonetheless, it is as appropriate as the comparison of Chris Burden to Saint Simeon Stylites, and according to the logic of Breugel's painting no less than that of Carter's novel. Despite the apparent simplicity of its subject, misanthropy appears in Bruegel's painting in a temporally and spatially disorienting way. It heretically undoes itself, one might say, even as it divides the world depicted by Bruegel's design. While a shepherd in the background looks after his flock, thus giving the presumed commonality of the species a pastoral register, the misanthrope, in a blue hooded cloak, walks away from the world, which is symbolized by a lout crouched within a globe topped with a cross. The world is in the act of cutting the misanthrope's purse, thus presumably representing the kind of shenanigans that have determined this figure to become what he is. We are told by the legend at the bottom of the painting (which may have been added at some point after its initial composition), "Because the world is so unfaithful/That is why I go in mourning."[47] All well and good; but as art historians have long noted, there is some cause for confusion here.

For instance, if the misanthrope is truly leaving the world, why is he bringing his money with him? Does the fact that his purse is red and heart-shaped indicate a sneaking love of the very world whose unfaithfulness he supposedly abhors and flees? One might also ask about the contrast between the thorns, or thorn-like calthrops, as they may be, in front of him, in the lower left corner of the painting, and the shepherd with his flock at the upper right.[48] If the former are a symbol of the thorny fate of Christ, so, too, is the latter a conventional image of pastoral care in the Christian sense; and in going toward the one, the misanthrope must walk away from the other. Are we then to see in this moment a suggestion of inhuman selfishness in the misanthrope's monkish self-abnegation—a hint that his stealing away from the world is a kind of heartless theft? In this regard we might note that a comparison of the hunched and grotesque worldling to the upright misanthrope might either suggest dignity or, in contrast, a lack of humility in the latter character. The fact that there is no resolution to art historians' questions about Bruegel affiliations in this era of violent religious conflicts is very much to the point here. And this is not even to mention the obvious paradox that, in figuring a separation from the world, this image of a cloaked man is itself a conventional worldly form.

Ingmar Bergman, arguably the twentieth century's greatest exponent of misanthropy, inevitably comes to mind in relation to this immemorial knot of art, asceticism, heresy, and violence. For instance, early in *The Passion of Anna* (1969) one character, Andreas, feels compelled to deny what another has asserted of him, that he is a hermit. The remainder of the film is ruthlessly designed to make a liar of him, and indeed of anyone who would claim not to be essentially solitary. Thus, near the end of the movie Andreas tells Anna, the woman with whom he has been living for several years, "I want my solitude back." The prehistory to his misanthropy is wrought through all the events recalled or played out in the film—a miscarriage, an affair, a car accident, a marital separation—and it is also given a global context. In much the same way that Bergman used TV footage of a self-immolating Buddhist monk and a photo of a Nazi roundup of Jews in *Persona* (1963), in this movie the Vietnam War is referred to when Andreas and Anna sit before a TV and watch, unwillingly fascinated, the then-famous film of the South Vietnamese National Police Chief, Nguyen Ngoc Loan, using his pistol to execute a Viet Cong prisoner on a Saigon street.

On the island where this movie takes place, meanwhile, we are told of the community's search for a terrorist who has been murdering animals. This search comes to focus on a hermit with a history of psychological problems, Johann Andersson, whom the locals decide to assault. Although he is innocent, he is so humiliated by the assault, in which one man pisses in his face, that he commits suicide. As if all this were not more than enough, Bergman even symbolically humiliates his own film by intercutting its dramatic footage with documentary scenes of its actors discussing their roles with a quite notable lack of eloquence. In short, misanthropy is suggested here to pervade every conceivable aspect of representation. Even less subtle than the Vietnam reference is the irony that a soulless architect, Elis, has won an important commission for a "cultural center."

The last shot of the film needs to be viewed in the context of the Romantic landscapes that preceded it and of Burden's *747*, which followed. It shows Andreas alone, fallen upon his hands and knees like an unhuman, unworshipful thing, in a place on the island that appears as a desert wasteland even though it has water and bears signs of cultivation and inhabitation. He is not in a desert, exactly, but in a site of utter disaster.

* * *

It resembled a movie, it was almost a movie, but it was not a movie of which one could say, Movie, movie, and be comforted.

It is completely understandable that the event should have appeared in aesthetic terms so immediately, to so many, so dismayingly. Even though it was not a movie, it had been filmed; and even though real people were dying, from the first it was clear that the deaths were less strategic, for those responsible for them, than symbolic. Accordingly, it did not take long for someone to call the terrorists "artists," and Jonathan Franzen was not wrong in doing so, exactly, although he was as deliberately tasteless as Burden's art has often sought to be.[49] Unlike Stockhausen, whose comments appeared to suggest that he gloried in this mass murder, Franzen was simply recognizing, with the help of an allusion to Kafka's "Hunger Artist," that one could not go through the experience of viewing images of it without feeling compelled to think that these images had something to teach us about the experience of art. Similarly, Paul Berman, the author of *All That Is Solid Melts into Air*, elaborated on his own first reaction—"Oh my God, it's like my book!"— by reporting, "Soon afterward, on the screen and then in the street, I heard people talking, and they were doing just what I'd done: making enormous mythical constructions that would cause the whole horrific event to revolve around *them*. We were like needy sculptors rushing to produce instant replacements for the giant stabiles that had stood on World Trade Plaza. We threw up anything we could hide behind to conceal our panic, our helplessness, and our instant, boundless sense of guilt."[50] And, of course, the dust had scarcely begun to settle before hats and t-shirts with images of the burning buildings were on sale, before books and photographic exhibitions about the event were being planned, before impromptu shrines were being erected, and before more deliberate works in all sorts of genres, including comic books, videos, and architectural maquettes, were being developed. In a meditation on the aesthetics of trauma, Marianne Hirsch tells of getting together with friends to compare and exchange snapshots of the event, and almost immediately people came to think that parts of the damaged buildings themselves should be preserved, as a kind of art object, for posterity.[51] Herbert Muschamp commented in the *New York Times*, "If you believe that beauty begins in terror, then it is not sacrilege to speak of the beauty of the remaining walls."[52] Less thoughtful comments inevitably followed in the wake of remarks like these, such as Elizabeth Wurtzel's claim that her reaction had been to see the destruction as "a really strange art project" that was "a most amazing sight in terms of sheer elegance."[53] Soon an architecture critic would feel free to joke that the terrorists "merely acted out the will of the towers' many critics."[54] Even while characterizing his own thought as "perverse and distasteful," a professor of art history would suggest "that the commercial planes Al-Qaeda repurposed as missles constituted a stunning instance of Situationist détournement."[55] Innumerable other accounts, with their inevitably varying degrees of thoughtfulness, would similarly remark upon the aesthetics of the disaster.

Like Franzen and Berman and Muschamp and countless others across the United States and the entire world, I was transfixed by the films of the events of September 11. Like all these millions, I watched them again and again, unwillingly fascinated, even though, if all this had simply been a matter of reality, one viewing of the horror ought to have been more than enough. In fact, as I compulsively watched the film being compulsively rerun on that day, I found myself especially fixated on one of the shots: the amateur video of the plane streaking in from the left side of the frame and hitting the South Tower of the World Trade Center to the accompaniment of a woman's blasphemous scream—later edited out by the networks—"Jesus Fucking Christ!" And I thought of Burden's art, and of what art still tries to teach us of misanthropy.

Those who thought it awful that the events of September 11 should have reminded people of the movies, those who thought it a condemnation of our taste and irrefutable proof that we should reform our popular entertainment, were undoubtedly as well meaning as they were entirely wrong. Like it or not, politics will be aestheticized. We cannot even begin to conceive of justice without working through art, through the subject of misanthropy, and so through what Susan Buck-Morss has described, in writing of Walter Benjamin, as the agonizing "enjoyment taken in viewing our own destruction."[56] For all its unique and almost unbearable pathos, the denial of humanity in the widespread defensive reaction to September 11—*I can't believe my eyes . . . This can't be real . . . This must be a movie*—was another version of the aggression against humanity, the unhuman motivation, that we find in art, that unreal stuff. Our unwilling suspension of belief on this occasion was the predictable other side to the willing suspension of disbelief that we conventionally practice in our regard of art. It is precisely this effect of the unhuman that accounts for the notorious disjunction between our desire and our ability to draw a clear distinction between art and everyday life.

That is why it is not human, exactly, but it is not terrible, either, that people should have felt compelled to imagine, momentarily, that all this was art rather than yet another experience of its death in life.

Chapter One
Crowning Presumption

On December 2, 1804, a man who would come to be seen as a supreme misanthrope—"the enemy of mankind," in the satanic epithet people throughout Europe hurled at him—crowned himself Emperor of France. Christopher Marlowe's Tamburlaine had set a precedent for this self-crowning (Pt. 1: 2. 7. 53–67).[1] So, too, had the Emperor Constantine in his more unceremonious awarding of a crown to himself. With good reason, however, Napoleon Bonaparte's version is more widely remembered.

From that day in 1804 to the present, this has been regarded as an emblematic moment in the life of Napoleon and in the history of modernity. Michel Foucault, for instance, reiterated this view. In his words, as "a monarch who is at one and the same time a usurper of the ancient throne and the organizer of the new state," Napoleon "combined into a single symbolic, ultimate figure the whole of the long process by which the pomp of sovereignty, the necessarily spectacular manifestations of power, were extinguished one by one in the daily exercise of surveillance, in a panopticism in which the vigilance of intersecting gazes was soon to render useless both the eagle and the sun."[2] Napoleon's opponents might have remarked on the sin of Lucifer, but even those who admired the new emperor saw that an astounding sort of presumption was being ventured here, one that drove the coronation ceremony into the realm of paradox. As Foucault intimated, Napoleon's emblem, along with that of Louis XIV, was cast down to earth by the very gesture through which the Corsican assumed imperial power. This act may be seen as definitive of the modern individual, whose triumphant self-invention ironically images the very soul of subjection.

Whereas Charlemagne had betaken himself to Rome to be crowned by Pope Leo, Napoleon had summoned the reluctant Pius VII to attend upon him in Paris. Even before he crowned himself, then, and despite the fact that he strove to flatter and placate the pontiff, his actions seemed designed to communicate his audacious presumption. Accordingly, once he did take hold of the crown and place it on his own head, the legend was born that he had practically snatched it away from the humiliated Pope, who, in keeping with established custom, had expected to perform the ceremony himself. Although this legend has since been debunked, it makes sense that it should have come to enjoy popular currency.[3] For this was a public gesture of unsurpassable theatricality, a performance that displayed a kind of artistic genius. "A poet in action" is what Chateaubriand called Napoleon; and in this act, as in his subsequent crowning of Josephine, the new Emperor seemed determined, Sir Walter Scott would write, "to show that his authority was the child of his own actions."[4] Pantomiming his self-invention, performing his role in the ceremony in such a way as to suggest that his identity was just that, a performance, Napoleon invited history to regard him as a newly constructed image—an unhuman figure—of humanity.

Chateaubriand, the defender of Christendom, could scarcely have been more unlike Foucault, the scourge of disciplinary institutions. Yet he, too, saw something self-subverting in the performance that was Napoleon. In fact, he saw in Napoleon something very like the type of person that Denis Diderot described in his "Paradox of the Actor" (c. 1773–77). Like Diderot's actor, Napoleon was an essentially cold person, in Chateaubriand's telling, and as such a performer with a disturbingly "false and equivocal" air about him. "At the same time model and copy, real person and actor representing this person, Napoleon was his own mime; he would not have been taken for a hero if he had not been dolled up in a hero's costume."[5]

Like many others, of course, Chateaubriand could not forget that Napoleon was an upstart. If not quite the "divelish shepheard" that was Marlowe's Tamburlaine (Pt. 1: 2. 6. 1), Napoleon was a jumped-up Corsican lieutenant. As far as observers like Chateaubriand were concerned, then, he was tainted with vulgar presumption even at his most sublime moments. At the same time, it must be acknowledged that in his crowning moment Napoleon practically demanded that he be seen as vulgarly undoing his own elevation. If he was the one being given the crown, after all, then who was that other one who presumed himself authorized to do the giving? This was the question his performance threw into relief, and this question only reinforced what everyone had to be thinking already: that this ceremony of legitimation was far from being an entirely legitimate affair.

It may be for this reason that Jacques-Louis David, in his *Coronation of Napoleon and Josephine* (1807), decided to picture the scene in which Napoleon set a crown atop his consort instead of the one in which he had planted its companion piece on his own head (Figures 6 and 7). François Gérard, one of David's pupils, reportedly advised his master that the latter scene would not be "felicitous" because there was "something histrionic about it," and one can understand how an artist might have come to this conclusion.[6] Complaints that the painting should

Figure 6. Jacques-Louis David, *Coronation of Emperor Napoleon and Josephine at Notre-Dame on December 2, 1804* (1807). Oil on canvas. Louvre, Paris. Photo courtesy Réunion des Musées Nationaux/Art Resource, New York

Figure 7. Jacques-Louis David, *The Emperor Napoleon Crowning Himself* (c. 1806–7). Pencil on beige paper. Louvre, Paris. Photo courtesy Réunion des Musées Nationaux/Art Resource, New York

have shown the crowning of the emperor himself, such as that voiced by the Comte de Beugnot, were to be expected.[7] Nonetheless, David seems to have recognized that, artistically speaking, this self-crowning was a touch too vulgar to serve as an image of the ideal. Like the "*Tamerlanes,* and Tamer-Chams" to whom Ben Jonson objected, whose artifice might seem to "fly from all humanity," this image, for genteel society, was a little too much.[8]

Yet it is precisely its questionable aesthetic status that establishes the genius of Napoleon's gesture. From the time of its occurrence to the present day, this scene remains striking because it so perfectly images the birth of modernity. This, after all, had been the great subject of François VI, the duc de la Rochefoucauld, in the maxims he composed for a France on the threshold of this new era: the agency of the unhuman in the invention of humanity. In proudly presenting himself as the image of himself, as his own creation, what Napoleon dared to dramatize was the unhuman presumption in the modern conception of humanity. This presumption is precisely what makes humanity imaginable, the *Maxims* suggested, although it does so at the cost of unremitting logical, social, cultural, and aesthetic violence.

Before La Rochefoucauld addressed it, this disturbing and definitively modern presumption was perhaps most notably represented in the protagonist of Christopher Marlowe's *Tragicall Historie of Doctor Faustus* (c. 1589–92). Like his reputed sympathy for the devil, Napoleon's coronation scene deserves to be seen as an aesthetic achievement of the sort for which Marlowe's play sought to prepare its audience. It also stands comparison to the unforgettable fable through which Mary Shelley sought to imagine what Faustus might have been able to do if he had had at his disposal the resources of modern science, as the French Emperor did. (It was with good reason that Richard Brinsley Peake's 1823 dramatization of Shelley's novel was titled *Presumption.*) In fact, this question of what happens to presumption under the conditions of modern science is one to which we are still trying to respond. We can observe this situation, for instance, in the continuing controversy over the patenting of the genetic code of human beings, with all that this suggests as to the possibilities of modifying, commodifying, and utterly transforming the species.

Although he could not have foreseen these developments, La Rochefoucauld did go a long way toward providing a response to the question of presumption. Two centuries before western societies plumbed the depths of superficiality by popularizing the concept of "compassion fatigue," he diagnosed the affective structure of the modern world in a single sentence, its wit dry as a bone: "We all have sufficient strength to endure the sufferings of others."[9] Improving upon Niccolò Machiavelli, who had argued that "men will always be false to you unless they are compelled by necessity to be true," he suggested that starkly opposed terms such as *true* and *false* cannot begin to capture the paradoxical nature of society, which is essentially misanthropic.[10] "If they were not all dupes of one another," he wrote, "men would not live long in society."[11] In other words, it is not simply a matter of the real motives of individuals being wrapped "in the Specious Cloke of Sociableness," as the less subtle mind of Bernard Mandeville, one of La Rochefoucauld's admirers, would put this matter.[12] For La Rochefoucauld, sociableness is as genuine as can be. One simply should not labor under the illusion that this bond among individuals is humane, or even human.

In La Rochefoucauld's telling, the misanthropic nature of society is owing to amour-propre. This presumptuous impulse of self-regard actually deceives, divides, and obliterates the very concept of the self. In fact, this term itself epitomizes presumption, for the "self-love" of which it speaks undoes all that we understand to be love, the self, or that which is "proper" to oneself or anyone else. "Its transformations exceed those of metamorphoses, and its refinements those of chemistry," La Rochefoucauld wrote, carefully situating it in relation to early modern science as well as ancient literature. "One cannot fathom the profundity or pierce the shadows of its abysses," he added, thus emphasizing as well its otherworldly quality—what a century or so later, in Mary Shelley's day, might be called its Gothic quality.[13] From these abysses, he explained, all sorts of monstrosities arise in our affections, in our hatreds, and in our social relations in general. His concern with self-love, then, does not imply that the self is coherent in any way, shape, or form, much less that it can be judged simply hateful (as with Blaise Pascal) or loveable (as in popularized versions of the philosophy proposed by Jean-Jacques Rousseau in the next century). Rather, La Rochefoucauld's concern was devoted to showing how society was coming to be imagined around a central trope: the image of what is presumptively one's own, or proper to one as an individual.

As La Rochefoucauld presents it, although amour-propre is definitive of humanity and individuality, it itself is neither human nor individual. Illogical, inconstant, capricious, bizarre, it is found

in all states of life and in all conditions. It lives everywhere and it lives on everything; it lives on nothing; it accomodates itself to the possession and to the loss of things; it even joins the party of people who make war on it, enters into their designs, and, amazingly, hates itself along with them, prays for its disappearance, even works at its own destruction.[14]

Thus acting in, on, through, and beyond us, amour-propre establishes the limits of human imagination, which bar us from ever possessing anything like a true understanding of ourselves. What is presumptively one's own, then, or proper to one as an individual, cannot be anything other than some sort of delusion.

To image this ultimately unimaginable boundary, La Rochefoucauld turned to the sea, just as Immanuel Kant would when he sought to describe the sublime limits of the imagination at the end of the following century. "The sea is a sensible image of it," La Rochefoucauld wrote, "and in the ebb and flow of its endless waves amour-propre finds a faithful expression of its eternal movements and of the turbulent succession of its ideas."[15] Unlike the German philosopher, however, the French moralist could squeeze no comfort out of this image. Whereas Kant would try to moralize, spiritualize, and aestheticize this overwhelming sea, lest it seem to make a mockery of the humanity that tries and fails to take it all in, La Rochefoucauld unflinchingly described all conceptions of humanity as tainted by presumption. Amour-propre is that fundamental motivation, that groundless presumption, which is in us and yet is not us. Unlike Kant's sublime, it does not offer even the glimmer of a hope that human beings might deserve the crowns that they put on their own heads. Perhaps it is for this reason that the entry from which I have just been quoting, which opened the 1665 edition of the *Maxims*, was eliminated from subsequent editions.[16] Upon further reflection, La Rochefoucauld may have considered that so openly to convert the image of God into the trope of amour-propre was a recklessly presumptuous act even in a society that in its daily business practically worshipped the presumption it piously professed to deplore.[17] The gesture was, perhaps, a bit too histrionic.

Whether or not this was his judgment, it is clear at least that La Rochefoucauld was not alone in identifying an unhuman presumption as determining how modernity would be imagined, even on to the present and putatively postmodern day. Marlowe also did so, although with rather less care to protect himself from the accusation of atheism. In *Doctor Faustus*, the presumption that simultaneously defines and disrupts the conception of humanity is announced right at the outset, in the opening monologue of its protagonist. Alone on the stage, John Faustus laments, "Yet art thou still but *Faustus*, and a man" (1. 23).

Despite, or because of, all his accomplishments in philosophy, science, law, and divinity, John Faustus is dissatisfied. His discontent is not only with himself as an individual but with his status as a human being, as one who is merely a man, in presumptive contrast to some other sort of being that he can imagine he might be. Thus far the premises of Marlowe's drama are unremarkable enough, recalling classical and Christian themes of errant desire while also, by way of comparison, putting us in mind of Renaissance figures such as Pico della Mirandola, who exalted the mutability of the human species as the condition that enabled the pursuit of knowledge to progress. These premises remain apparent throughout *Doctor Faustus*, and it is certainly possible to elicit from its drama a morality play rooted in medieval and classical sources, just as readers with a mind to do so have always been able to view La Rochefoucauld as being more of a pious Jansenist than a proto-Nietzschean. Nevertheless, like the Napoleon who so untraditionally assumes the traditional role of emperor, the Faustus who emerges out of the sources of Marlowe's play becomes a figure of modernity.

In the end the horror that Marlowe brought into this play is only incidentally an issue of hubris or sinfulness. More significantly, the horror is that we see the unhuman agencies at work in the invention of humanity. As Jonathan Dollimore has written, "Faustus registers a sense of humankind as miscreated."[18] In the very moment in which it imagines its freedom, the self in *Doctor Faustus* debases itself to a privative, contracted, commodified condition of being from which it thenceforth cannot hope to reemerge. It is as if Marlowe were actually able to burst the bounds of time and space so as to witness Napoleon's coronation and see in it what Foucault saw: the "new man" whose triumph would almost immediately take the form of disciplinary categories, codes, practices, and institutions that decree individuality for everyone and then keep everyone under surveillance so that all will be compelled to enjoy the mandates of this modern state of being. As he thus identified Faustian presumption with a self-destructive claim to self-possession, Marlowe located Faustian misanthropy in the exemplary legal and economic instrument of modern social life: the contract.

In Marlowe's source, *The History of the Damnable Life and Deserved Death of Doctor John Faustus* (1592), the agreement that Faustus signs with the devil is vaguely termed "a writing" and a "letter or obligation."[19] When Marlowe wrote his play, however, he made use of specifically legal terminology, repeatedly referring to this instrument as "a deede of gift" (5. 35, 5. 60), a "bill" (5. 65, 5. 74), and a "security" (5. 36). The revision is significant, preparing us to recognize that, as Cleanth Brooks noted, Faustus "is trapped in his own legalism."[20] It is because Faustus puts such faith in the instrument to which he has affixed his signature that there is no reality for him in the hope for repentance and salvation attested to in the Biblical passages from which he quotes in the course of the play. As Marjorie Garber says, Faustus "gets, ironically, just what he bargains for, the letter of the law."[21] Therefore, although William Hazlitt penned a deservedly famous characterization of Marlowe—"There is a lust of power in his writings, a hunger and thirst after unrighteousness"—he was precisely wrong in describing Faustus as possessing "a lawless imagination."[22] What causes *Doctor Faustus* to slip its medieval moorings and sail out into the world of modernity is its identification of its protagonist with the logic epitomized in the sovereignty of contractual relations.

Marlowe saw that identity contracted to a signature betokens an unhuman self that can travel magically across the world and the universe, performing all sorts of wondrous tricks along the way. Through his legalistic emphasis Marlowe transformed the world of medieval and Renaissance demonology, in which Faustus's signing of the deed makes him a diabolic rather than a "high" magician, into a template overwritten with the empowering structures of the modern nation.[23] The contracted signature gives access to the universal, and universality is bounded only by the limits of one's imagination.[24] To be an "Unhuman," as Johann Wolfgang Goethe would have the protagonist of his *Faust* declare, is to be "houseless," "restless," "aimless"—an essentially "fugitive" being who, for better or worse, finds nothing impassible before him, but only forever an "abyss."[25]

Early in Marlowe's play, when Faustus signs over his soul, in blood, to Lucifer's agent, Mephastophilis, his reasoning is as clear and simple as can be. He says to himself, "Why shouldst thou not? is not thy soule thine owne?" (5. 68). All else in the play derives from this line, in which one's mortal and immortal identity, as united in the substance of one's flesh, is taken by Faustus to be an alienable type of private property, like any other, for which its owner has just chanced to discover a buyer. Marlowe thus emphasizes that individuality is not an individual matter, an intrinsically human quality, but rather an effect created through dynamic exchanges at the conjunction of the economic and legal domains of early modern life, which are even capable of producing as a historical reality the logical absurdity of a single person being at once the subject and object of a transaction. Just as one might ask who the Napoleon was who was presuming to put the crown on Napoleon's head, so one had to ask who—or what—was presuming to sell Faustus's soul.

With his good lawyerly mind, Scott undoubtedly would have condemned Faustus's bargain for the same reason that he saw the popular referendum supporting Napoleon's will to power as a *pactum in illicito*. Even supposing for the sake of argument that this flagrantly corrupt referendum had been properly arranged and conducted, Scott said, it would still be the case that no one "is lord even of his own person, to the effect of surrendering his life or limbs to the mercy of another; the contract of the Merchant of Venice would now be held null from the beginning in any court of justice in Europe."[26] But in this instance Faustus, the genius of sixteenth-century legal studies, shows himself to be more modern than the respectable barrister of nineteenth-century Scotland. What Marlowe realized, through the character of Faustus, was that modernity would be defined in large part through the signing over of persons to the unhuman universals of the law and the marketplace, for which the presumption of self-possession, like the presumption of popular consent to a social contract, is never anything but a regulative fiction with all sorts of paradoxes wrapped within it.

Faustus certainly does get taken, but Marlowe shows the logic by which all modern people, like the Doctor, are bound to get taken as we assert our presumed freedom. Scott, on the other hand, can understand Napoleon's ascension only as a kind of brutal anachronism, the sort of error from which the modern world, as he understands it, ought to be free. Since he does not consider law a kind of "will and appetite," as Thomas Hobbes had described it, Scott cannot conceive that error or illegitimacy might actually serve to constitute it.[27] In this regard, Marlowe understood nineteenth-century Europe far better than did the Author of *Waverley*. So, too, did La Rochefoucauld, as he showed by taking care to emphasize that the self-love with which he was concerned did not reside in monadic, singular, discrete persons of the sort that would become the elementary fictions of modern social, economic, and political theory. Through the use of other key terms, such as "interest," as well as through his characteristic paradoxes, he described amour-propre as the violent agency of self-definition precipitated out of the misanthropic structuring of social life. Like Machiavelli, who counseled that "men forget more easily the death of their father than the loss of their patrimony," he had found the soul of man not only within but without him, in such things as lend themselves to the securing of power, wealth, and position.[28] Almost before the fiction of the modern individual had begun to take form, then, Marlowe and La Rochefoucauld were analyzing its tremendous attractiveness, its prospects for a sublime career, and its inevitable exposure as a self-destructive trope.

Just as Mary Shelley would in her portrayal of Victor Frankenstein's aesthetics, Marlowe foresaw that art, in the modern world, would take on a meaning distinct from its premodern use in designating the disciplines of logic, physic, divinity, and law or, in general, all specialized knowledges and skills. The animating desire of *Doctor Faustus* is represented in and as art, albeit art that does not quite yet have a name exclusive unto itself. What it does have is the unhuman, or demonic, condition of images displaced from the frames of the aforementioned disciplines and thus prepared for the modern understanding of art as possessing a distinct, autonomous, and universal cultural reality. The wondrous individuality, autonomy, and universality into which the contracted signature conveys humanity, in the form of Faustus, is paralleled by the individuality, autonomy, and universality of the artwork exemplified by the spectacle of this play as a whole.[29] And in the latter as in the former case, we are brought to see as the inmost distinction of humanity its identification with the unremitting violence all around it.

Helen of Troy is this violent spectacle. The famous apparition of Helen is a metonym for all the images through which unhuman agencies manifest themselves in this play. The appearance of Helen, daughter to Leda and Jove and the prize of Paris, recalls a mythical era when deities might ravish women, men bed goddesses, and almost anything turn out to have been something or someone else. More specifically, as an exemplary artwork, an object of beauty, paraded onstage for the delectation of Faustus and, coincidentally, Marlowe's audience, she appears as the legendary occasion, object, and agency of strife. That this is the case in no way lessens her appeal as Faustus sees her and, presumably, as the play's audience views her onstage. On the contrary, her "heavenly" (12. 20) singularity and fabled destructiveness—"Was this the face that lancht a thousand shippes?" (12. 81)—make of her an unhuman image that supplants all else in human reality. "And all is drosse that is not *Helena*" (12. 87), says Faustus with the utmost certainty, even as he looks forward to what Max Bluestone has aptly labeled "a consummation so ambiguously to be wished."[30] Faustus, being Faustus, has no care for Helen's humanity, such as it may be. He does not consult her wishes, or even her ontological status, before magically compelling her to be his paramour. As all are for Marlowe's Tamburlaine and as Tamburlaine is for himself, she is for him: an instrument of the image of self that was just emerging in Marlowe's time but that he brilliantly seized on as a monstrous presumption in the heart of that crowning species in the world of creation, "humanity."

Like Gaveston in *Edward II* (c. 1592)—whom Marlowe transformed from the aristocratic youth of the chronicles into a commoner, the better to emphasize the presumption at the heart of human affections and affairs—Tamburlaine is baseborn. Even were this not the case, one would see in him "a Giantly presumption," but his obscure birth does help to highlight the point and to encourage the accusation that he is, in fact, "divelish," or not even human at all (2. 6. 1–2). Accordingly, his enemies see this "fiery thirster after Soveraigntie" (2. 6. 31) as "never sprong of humaine race" (2. 6. 11). The Sultan of Egypt puts it most simply when he says Tamburlaine "is no man" (4. 1. 42). Far from resenting this sort of impression, Tamburlaine himself insists on it. Like Faustus, he disdains to think of himself as a mere man, considering himself instead to be of a kind with Jove (4. 1. 113–23) and thus akin to all the implacable forces of unhuman necessity: "wrathful Planets, death, or destinie" (5. 1. 28). Finding himself weakening toward the end of the play, he remains defiant: "Shall sicknesse proove me now to be a man,/ That have bene tearm'd the terrour of the world?" (5. 3. 44–45).

Like Helen, Tamburlaine is presented to us not as a human being but as an object of art, an utterly spectacular figure, designed to illustrate the misanthropy at work within the presumption of humanity. One might well conclude that art, henceforth, would be humanity's alibi. In art, as in plays featuring figures such as Faustus and Tamburlaine, humanity might at once confess and deny its unhuman constitution.

In a curious play written in 1794, Paul Emil Thieriot suggested that the modern world had placed art in just this role. In *Timon All Alone* the protagonist finds that he has become an anachronism. Now, at the end of the eighteenth century, this misanthropist made legendary by ancient literature finds that the reading public has no more taste for one of his sort. Misanthropy, he says, "has made itself hateful among the public, and is, as it were, buried alive" (90).[31] Although he has an illustrious ancestry—he identifies himself not only with the classical Timon but also with Prometheus, the Wandering Jew, and Jonathan Swift's Gulliver, among others—he finds that the present state of civilization has no regard for the likes of him. "Humanity" has triumphed, and Timon is all alone. Humanity is ubiquitous, in the form of public opinion—the imaginary social sphere correlative to the universal symbolic realm of the signature and the contract—and so Timon has no place.

Such is the premise of the play, in which Thieriot suggests that misanthropy had been a popular subject earlier in the century, as in Swift's *Gulliver's Travels* (1726), precisely so that it could be demonized, excluded, or made unreal, a mere subject of art, by the century's end, as in August von Kotzebue's *Misanthropy and Repentance* (1788). At this point in time misanthropy serves, by way of contrast, to constitute humanity as that which is real, natural, and holy. The conceit of Thieriot's play, then, is that in this era of the rights of man humanity has become so fully established that misanthropy has become all but unthinkable. Like Timon himself, it is now an outmoded subject for which the contemporary public has no taste. No longer having a place in life, misanthropy has been relegated to the realm of art, and even there it seems to appear only as something from out of the past, having no meaningful connection to the present day, much as the legal business in *The Merchant of Venice* appeared to Scott.

In its concern with this anachronistic misanthropy, Thieriot's play places us in the territory of Gothic literature, albeit in a comic form. What is a misanthropist to do amidst the triumph of the Enlightenment? Since he cannot bear humanity, Thieriot proposes, what he can do is create automatons. These seemingly human figures, which enjoy the advantage of actually being unhuman artworks, may then attend upon him. In this way he might be able to turn against the Enlightenment one of its signature creations.[32]

There are ironies within ironies throughout this drama, especially if we remember that Thieriot claims to have translated this play into German from the original French version that he saw performed at a puppet theater. (Although "the original Timon is a marionette," he acidly observes, "no one at this time" will be surprised to learn that "all the same he may be a real man" [89].) In addition to giving Thieriot a platform for deflating the modern presumption of humanity in general, his premise also allows him to scatter satirical remarks about contemporary conditions and manners throughout the play. For instance, in sending his "child" out into the world, as Von Hutten does with his daughter Angelika at the end of Friedrich Schiller's *The Misanthropist Reconciled* (1790), Timon observes that he need not bother to instruct him in acting deferential and humane because "a secret fear of fights and duels restrains us" from acting otherwise (92)—an observation very much in the tradition of Machiavelli, La Rochefoucauld, and Hobbes. At another point, when he permits his automatons to yawn and, through the contagion of their example, gapes along with them, Timon remarks that yawns are "always the best evidence of sympathy among human beings," so much so that he can testify to the existence of many people "who pray to their God in yawns" (93). As the foregoing passages may indicate, the irony that reigns over all is that in the end the unhuman automatons do not provide an alternative to the self-deluded humanity from which Timon feels so alienated. Instead, Timon's misanthropy appears only to make him more human, as we see in his growing disgust with the unresponsiveness of the machines. At the end of the play, when the automatons metamorphose into human beings and leave him all alone once again, he is left to exclaim in frustration, "O humans, unhumans! Human that I am, shouldn't my disgust have been wiser?" (96).

Thieriot thus took the popular understanding of the misanthrope as a spoiled idealist, one who loves humanity only too well, and satirically exposed how this figure actually helps to support the image of the modern self. Far from being threatened by misanthropy, society is constituted of it. Those automatons-turned-human, we have every reason to believe, will fit into society just fine. It is only Timon, the real human, who cannot get along with the general run of unhuman humans. Timon's mistake does not lie in being misanthropic, then, but in not being misanthropic enough. In feeling himself alone and in turning to works of art as to a sphere of being distinct from the public sphere of modern life, what he fails to remember from his legendary past is that humanity is itself unhuman, a kind of artwork, albeit one that refuses to recognize itself as such.

It was out of just this perception that Thieriot's contemporary, Mary Shelley, built her Gothic version of the Promethean myth of human soul-making. As Fred Botting has put it, *Frankenstein*'s science "reflects upon the inhumanity of humanism."[33] Beginning with such Faustian types as Cornelius Agrippa and Paracelsus before he shifts over to modern science, Victor Frankenstein finds that his studies render him "unsocial" (98).[34] The central irony here, comparable to that in *Timon All Alone*, is that his misanthropy develops in the service of humanity even while humanity itself comes to appear increasingly unhuman to the readers of his story.

Although he is a scientist, Victor is also, like Thieriot's Timon, a maker of art. While working on his creation, he uses this term in a sense that verges upon the modern one bequeathed to us by romanticism: "I appeared rather like one doomed by slavery to toil in the mines, or any other unwholesome trade, than an artist occupied by his favourite employment" (85). Accordingly, his subsequent equivocations as to what exactly he has created—"a human being" (82), "new species" (82), or "daemon" (59)—precisely represent the anxieties about the ontological status of art with which modern aesthetic theory would be preoccupied. Should the work of art be considered part of humanity, as its expression or image; distinct from humanity, as a form unto itself; or a threat to humanity, as a rival reality that threatens to usurp our properties and very being? Implicitly or explicitly, these are not only the questions of Gothic and romantic aesthetics, which we see explored in the works of artists such as Francisco Goya, but also those with which contemporary artists such as Chris Burden must still contend.

Like La Rochefoucauld, Shelley, too, knew that the unhuman agency within humanity, its groundless presumption, finds its appropriate setting in the sublime. In her case the sublime sea happens to be frozen, either in the arctic or in the form of Alpine crests, as when Victor regards a scene in the valley of Chamounix: "it was augmented and rendered sublime by the mighty Alps, whose white and shining pyramids and domes towered above all, as belonging to another earth, the habitations of another race of beings!" (123). Once he has made and abandoned his creature, it is in these sublime settings that Victor encounters him. It is in the image of the sublime that the presumption of humanity becomes unimaginable and humanity, therefore, alien to itself. In this sort of setting, which befits "another race of beings," humanity appears no less unhuman to itself than if it were a modern work of art that, like Victor's creation, is unsettlingly "dependent on none, and related to none" (156). This work of art, this thing in which humanity appears in the form of estrangement and denial, may lend itself to a sense of beauty, as do the Alps, or, on the contrary, may appear like Victor's creature: "its unearthly ugliness rendered it almost too horrible for human eyes" (127). In either case, in a pattern that is precisely analogous to Victor's experience in creating his work, it is restlessly sought after by the same humanity that is bound to find itself repulsed by it. A "resistless, and almost frantic impulse, urged me forward," Victor says, adding, "and often did my human nature turn with loathing from my occupation, whilst, still urged on by an eagerness which perpetually increased, I brought my work near to a conclusion" (83). The constitutive diremption of humanity that La Rochefoucauld cast into the rhetoric of paradox, Marlowe into the theme of metamorphosis, and Thieriot into the mode of satire, Shelley thus presented as the psychology of ambivalence.

The misanthropic monster, Shelley wanted to make clear, is the very figure of the human work of art. It was with good reason that Shelley put herself in the place of Victor when she referred to her own work, in the 1831 Introduction to the novel, as her "hideous progeny" (365). In the monster we see what Theodor Adorno called the "asociality" of art, its "foreignness to the world" and its profoundly critical or "anticultural" character.[35] Adorno could have been describing the plot of *Frankenstein*, as it traces out Victor's tortured identification with his work through the vacillations of mastery and slavery in their relationship, when he wrote that in art "the subject exposes itself, at various levels of autonomy, to its other, separated from it and yet not altogether separated."[36] As the being that humanity must disavow to define itself—the "other species" of misanthropy—the monster is also art freed from the moralized, spiritualized, and aestheticized categories that humanity owns as its own. In other words, Victor's creation, like Shelley's, is an artwork that exposes the presumption definitive of the image of the human self by exhibiting the fundamentally misanthropic nature of society.

True, before he begins telling his story to Robert Walton, Frankenstein seems to have renounced the presumption that drove him on to his labor of creation. "Learn from me, if not by my precepts, at least by my example, how dangerous is the acquirement of knowledge, and how much happier that man is who believes his native town to be the world, than he who aspires to become greater than his nature will allow" (81). After telling his story, though, when he confronts the mutinous sailors on Walton's ice-bound ship, we find how meaningless these words were. "Oh! Be men, or be more than men!" he exclaims (239), as if anticipating Friedrich Nietzsche's challenge to the Kantian motto *sapere aude*.[37] Shelley dramatizes this inconsistency so as to make it obvious that the ritual denial of presumption serves only to further its role in the constitution of humanity. Accordingly, Shelley has Walton describe Victor's creature as not appearing to be a European but rather "a savage inhabitant of some undiscovered island" (57)—the sort of figure that Faustus's magic promised to bend to his will. A work of art undomesticated by moral, religious, and aesthetic theory, the monster here is also a human as yet unhumanized by the brutally civilizing magic of imperialism—just such magic as Walton's scientific exhibition is intended to represent.

The crowning presumption in Shelley's work does not lie in its portrayal of empire, however, even though Shelley had Napoleon very much in mind as she was writing this novel.[38] It lies rather in her novel's portrayal of modern science as being capable of redeeming the imperial promises of past masters of natural philosophy, among whom John Faustus would certainly be numbered.

As Shelley portrayed it, science is the realization of art, not of theology, or at least not of such theology as John Milton professed in *Paradise*

Lost (1667), the artwork from which she took the epigraph to her novel. Just as Napoleon, by placing it on his own head with his own hand, simultaneously upheld and mocked the imperial crown, so did Shelley at once cite and dispose of Milton. As the professors of science attain to godlike powers—"they can command the thunders of heaven, mimic the earthquake, and even mock the invisible world with its own shadows" (76–77)—that which had been supposed to be divine reveals itself instead as a tyrannical amour-propre. It is an agency more befitting the imperial image of Napoleon: misanthropic, death-dealing, destructive of the lives over which it presumes to have the authority to rule.

Hence Shelley's lesson: take charge of your monstrosity, or it will take charge of you. It is a lesson that remains pertinent. The image of Victor chasing his creature into the arctic wasteland might just as well be a picture of present-day humanity disappearing into the sublime universality of the legal and economic landscape of biopolitics gloomily described by Giorgio Agamben, in which poetry, religion, and philosophy "have lost all historical efficacy." "Genome, global economy, and humanitarian ideology," Agamben writes, "are the three united faces of this process in which posthistorical humanity seems to take on its own physiology as its last, impolitical mandate," thus raising the question of "whether the humanity that has taken upon itself the mandate of the total management of its own animality is still human."[39]

Shelley, of course, could not have foreseen the development of genetics, just as Marlowe could not have predicted that the signature of Faust would find its ultimate realization when the genetic signature of human life itself was patented and commodified in the late twentieth century. Yet both wrote works that pointed toward this triumph of death. Viewed from this context, the crowning presumption of Shelley's novel may be that she leaves open the possibility that Robert Walton and his sister, who share Victor's tale by way of Walton's letters, might actually be able sufficiently to embrace the unhuman agency of this tale so that they might stand a chance, against all the odds of international, national, and domestic history, to be enlightened human beings.

Chapter Two

I Think; Therefore, I Am Heathcliff

Under Gothic conditions, thinking comes to be defined by way of the unhuman, especially in the form of art. Allowances must be made for the various aspects and kinds of Gothic literature, but key exemplars of the genre are consistent on this point. In the activity of thought one finds the unhuman coming alive and, in doing so, ruining not only the perspectives and sympathies but also the very architecture of humanity. This ruination can then be made out to be, paradoxically, the proof of that humanity. Portraits stir and look back at their beholders, statues bleed, suits of armor walk, costumes disguise, invisible minstrels tantalize, picturesque scenes open themselves to nightmares: every mechanism of this genre adumbrates the proposal that thinking, if is to be, will exist only through the aesthetic animation, sufferance, and internalization of that which is supposed to be foreign to thought.[1] By emphasizing its own romance nature, which is designed to be enlivened through its readers' imaginative imprisonment in extravagantly hostile situations, the remote past, or exotic environments, the Gothic novel further embodied this proposal for its audience. As Ingmar Bergman recognized when he adapted this technique to the screen in his Gothic *Seventh Seal* (1957), in which Death appears to the Knight as the chess-player he has seen him to be in a painting, all those restless works of art figure as synechdoches for the novel itself, which finds its fantasy of origins in the vivification of moldering manuscripts into an appropriately modern genre.

An emphasis on this genre's artifice could figure as that which is exterior, anterior, or foreign to thought because of the immemorial traditions in which art was considered to be fundamentally irrational. In addition, the historical conditions of the late eighteenth and early nineteenth centuries made it possible to see art as specifically emblematic of all that was irrelevant, anachronistic, or distant in relation to the utilitarian tendencies of modern life. It was with good reason that Immanuel Kant chose this historical moment to draw a cordon sanitaire around art that would sequester it from crafts, decorations, and commodities; in his own fashion Georg Wilhelm Friedrich Hegel was addressing the same set of circumstances when he proclaimed art to be "a thing of the past."[2] This is not to say, however, that the Gothic novel was opposed to the emerging demands of modern life—for instance, as a rebellion against Enlightenment reason—or in some other way strikingly at odds with contemporary historical developments.[3] On the contrary, the challenge this genre took up was that of justifying the ways of modernity to man.[4] In the Gothic novel, art discovers its misanthropy, its unhuman motivation, as that which enables the modern sense of humanity to be instituted.

It follows that this genre may be read as a series of footnotes to the writings of René Descartes. Although Horace Walpole's *Castle of Otranto* (1764) is generally regarded as having inaugurated this genre, which crested in popularity at the end of the eighteenth and the beginning of the nineteenth century, Descartes's *Meditations* (1641) was actually the first Gothic novel. Understandably, its presentation and reception as a work of philosophy composed in the genre of the meditation has obscured its claim to this distinction, as has the century and a half delay between its publication and the great wave of imitations that popularized Gothicism as a cultural style. These might seem to be inconvenient facts for my argument. Nonetheless, Descartes's *Meditations* can be said to have laid the foundations not only for modern philosophy but also for influential works like Ann Radcliffe's *Mysteries of Udolpho* (1794) and their revisionary successors, such as Emily Brontë's *Wuthering Heights* (1847). Comparison of the Gothic novel with this precursor text serves to illuminate both the one and the other. As the Gothic comes to seem a machine designed to manufacture the world of modern humanity, the comparison also serves to highlight the worldliness of Descartes's cogito: its implication in a specific history. We can see how the confrontation of the Cartesian ego and demon prefigures the Gothic encounter with the misanthrope and all that this entails in terms of the family and society at large. This comparison also clarifies the supremacy of aesthetic over logical premises in Descartes's thought and thus enables us to comprehend the vital role of art in Gothic metaphysics. We are then in a better position to appreciate the culmination of this relation between Cartesian and Gothic thought in the achievement of *Wuthering Heights,* which rewrites the Gothic in much the same way that this genre had rewritten Descartes: by drawing out the worldly implications of what seems to be its most clear and simple device, which in this case is the romantic love that is supposed to bring one human to identify with another.

Like certain Gothic novels, such as the Marquis de Sade's *History of Juliette* (1797), Charles Brockden Brown's *Wieland* (1798), and William Godwin's *St. Leon* (1799), the *Meditations* takes the form of a personal narrative interspersed with extended passages of philosophical reflection and argument. As in all Gothic literature, the protagonist of Descartes's treatise, whom Pierre Gassendi puckishly nicknamed "Mind," experiences a melancholy seclusion from the world.[5] At first the seclusion is freely chosen, just as it is in many Gothic novels. Soon, however, it comes to bear all the trappings of the involuntary isolation that is one of the trademark motifs of Gothic plots. In this isolated state of being, Descartes can no longer trust the evidence of his own senses. As he is forced to trade the presumption of a consentient perceptual reality for solipsistic and paranoid self-doubt, his thought-experiment sets the stage for every Gothic protagonist in centuries to come who would suffer the fate of losing confidence in his or her perceptions. "Every thing now appeared to me an object of suspicion" is a sentence that could have flowed from the pen of the seventeenth-century metaphysician but actually was written, to register a characteristically Gothic moment, by the eighteenth-century celebrity Matthew "Monk" Lewis.[6] Moreover, in many if not all Gothic novels, just as in the *Meditations*, the greatest crises associated with one's suspension in uncertainty are attributed to the machinations of an evil figure conceivably possessed of supernatural powers.

In the Gothic novel, as in the *Meditations*, Descartes's malignant demon is the figure of misanthropy through which the thought of modernity must pass if it is adequately to establish and estimate itself. For Descartes and for those who followed him, the consequence is that the question of identity is driven into the foreground of consciousness by virtue of being put into extreme jeopardy. In both cases this jeopardy does not really arise from a preexisting crisis, as readers are given to believe. Instead, it represents the heuristic positing of crisis. This situation then provides the imaginative rationale for the demand that identity be renovated.

In obedience to this logic, identity is so terrorized that individuals may not be sure whether they are dreaming, may wonder whether they have fallen into madness, and may even become so hysterical as to lose all sense of connection with their own bodies. This experience of uncertainty may go so far as seemingly to cast into doubt the fundamentals of Christian belief. The entertainment of such doubts would threaten authors of the Gothic works under consideration here with opprobrium and hostility as well as fame, even as Descartes had been so threatened. Finally, we may note that in most cases divine providence is ritually reestablished by the end of Gothic novels. In this respect, too, Descartes set the pattern for their protagonists' journeys.

In making this comparison I do not mean to suggest that the *Meditations* was an influence, in the conventional sense of that term, on writers of Gothic fiction. Many of these authors were probably ignorant of Descartes's name, not to mention his metaphysics. Despite the similarities between his *Meditations* and Gothic novels, Descartes did not literally devise the form of these works. Yet he did anticipate their defining obsession with thinking of and through the unhuman as exemplified most notably in the work of imaginative art. The *Meditations* deserves to be called the first Gothic novel because it asked its readers to prepare themselves for modernity by entertaining the thought that their very selves might be works of art, the unhuman product of a misanthropic demon. Just as Gothic novels did, the *Meditations* argued that art must come to life so that doubt may die. Credulousness was to be assigned to a past thenceforth to be defined in terms of superstition. Modernity, meanwhile, would be implicitly defined as the era that is able to confine the incredible within the realm of art. From the viewpoint of this modernity, it is because art essentially belongs to the past that it may be licensed to thrill the present.

At the same time that it follows the model developed by Descartes, however, the Gothic novel significantly reformulates his project. In effect, it sets out to demonstrate why the meditative method ought to give way to that of the romance as the appropriate instrument for the formation of identity. Most notably, the modern romance makes seclusion a different state of affairs than the innocent reader of the philosophical work may take it to be. Crucial to the entire series of Descartes's meditations was the explicit premise that they concerned only thought, not action, since he had taken care to isolate himself from all encumbrances and from all knowledge of and concerns about others—from all "worries," in a word—before he began this exercise.[7] This seclusion was to provide the "free time" necessary to the rigorous tests of thought but required also for the safeguarding of that thought from accusations of irresponsibility or, worse, sinfulness or heresy.[8] After all, Galileo's experience with the Inquisition, which had led Descartes to suppress the writings published posthumously as *The World* and the *Treatise on Man* (1664), was still a living memory for him—as well it had ought to have been, considering some of the initial responses to his work.[9]

"I know that no danger or error will result from my plan," Descartes wrote, "and that I cannot possibly go too far in my distrustful attitude," since meditation "does not involve action."[10] Saying so, however, did constitute an action. In this complex performance the formal disavowal of any relation between one's literary self and other persons is designed to forestall the unequivocally real possibility that the author might be identified with and punished for his words. Through this unsaying saying, then, the premise of the *Meditations* undoes itself or, in Gothic terms, turns out to have a secret interior. The cogito is revealed (in

Gassendi's formulation) as a creation of "artifice, sleight of hand and circumlocution."[11] If it were not social through and through—even, and especially, in its disavowal of the existence of others—it would be unimaginable.

Obliquely catching a glimpse of this problem as it played itself out in Descartes's work, another of his commentators noted, "if you had not grown up among educated people, but had spent your entire life alone in some deserted spot, how do you know that the idea [of a perfect being] would have come to you? . . . [T]he fact that the natives of Canada, the Hurons and other primitive peoples, have no awareness of any idea of this sort seems to establish that."[12] Descartes simply dismissed this anthropological argument: "the objections you raise cannot occur to those who follow the road which I have indicated."[13] As the Gothic novel would show, however, that which Descartes preferred to style as a road was, in fact, a labyrinth in which cogito and evil demon were artfully implicated in one another, just as these critics had suggested.

This labyrinth is the world of the Gothic, in which no asylum is to be had. There is no such thing as free time, and seclusion is where the action is. What might otherwise appear as one's private study, that objective correlative to the philosophical promise of certainty in one's identity, is redesigned in the Gothic novel into something like a monastic cell or a chamber in a castle. As in these examples, Gothic sites are emphatically impressed with a sense of communal relations even for individuals locked in isolation within them. One is never less alone than when singled out in such circumstances, especially when one comes to recognize, as Gothic protagonists must, that seclusion is always doubtful. One can never be sure that rooms do not have a secret entrance invisible even to the closest inspection and yet accessible to unknown others on the outside. For this reason, even a seemingly willing seclusion is never secure as such. One can never be certain of being safe from others' eyes, ears, hands, or general influence.

With this revision in the Cartesian state of seclusion came a corresponding revision in the image of the Inquisition. In Descartes we can mark this image only in his defensive mise-en-scène, which was designed to protect his hyperbolic doubt from reproach. This implicit mark, however, was made explicit in the role of the Inquisition in novels such as Lewis's *The Monk* (1796), Radcliffe's *The Italian* (1797), Percy Bysshe Shelley's *Zastrozzi* (1810), and Charles Robert Maturin's *Melmoth the Wanderer* (1820). These novels tell us that there can be no secluding oneself from the existence of society at large, which finds its summary image in the intrusive powers of the Inquisition.

Thus, even as it follows the plot wrought by Descartes, the Gothic novel outdoes his meditations by faithfully calling into doubt their enabling premise. Descartes's reasoning, as viewed through the Gothic novel, comes to appear more dramatically than logically compelling.[14] Contingent as it is on its self-contradictory disavowal of home and all the social world that pertains to it, from one's immediate family to the structures of wealth, rank, religion, and law, Descartes's cogito must be seen as having been tormented by a demonic other from the very beginning, before the evil genius was even introduced as such. The evil genius is simply the return of this repressed society in a demonic form.

In the Gothic novel this demon finds its characteristic figure in the misanthrope. As if recognizing the unclear and indistinct social relations within the clear and distinct ideas that are supposed to be apprehended through the light of reason in the *Meditations*, the Gothic registers the inescapability of misanthropy, the constitutive role of the unhuman, in the imagining of human existence within Descartes's work. In the Gothic misanthrope we can see the necessity of Descartes's contingencies, the tyrannical power of his identity, even his metaphysical desire for the experience of paranoia—and thus, in short, the art of his reason, uncannily alive. Thought simply cannot be isolated from action, much less from worries, the Gothic novel maintains, even as it honors Descartes by suggesting that to imagine otherwise is natural to the heroes and heroines of its drama, who could not play their roles if they were not susceptible to this delusion.

As logical premises turn out to be aesthetic, in Gothic literature's rewriting of Descartes, so, too, does the issue of identity turn out to be one of multiple, disjunctive, and contradictory identifications. This revision does not establish a Lacanian "fragmented subject," however, but rather the misanthropic subject of unhuman motivations presupposed by the countervailing desire for humanity and registered in the Gothic preoccupation with the artwork that comes alive.[15] This unhuman subject is retrospectively created, called on to have existed, so that humanity may be given a distinctively modern place in metaphysics, history, and psychology. This subject's character, its unhuman lack of comprehensible agency and coherence, is an imaginative fiction necessary to the seeming proof of humanity's existence within a distinctively modern conception of thought. Like the spanking new ruins that typify Gothic aesthetics, this disaggregation is not a sign of an identity in distress or under assault but rather of one under construction. It is a modern humanity to be created through, as it is saved from, art. Taken to the Gothic extreme, then, as Oscar Wilde recognized in his reworking of this genre in *The Picture of Dorian Gray* (1890), modernity is created as an ageless contemporaneity. Modernity assigns living art to the sequestered past and multiple, disjunctive, and contradictory motivations to the realm of aesthetic reflection, as distinct from the logic of everyday life. It is through this process that Gothic horror—the Frankensteinian horror of viewing the unholy arts that go into the making of humanity—is turned into modern entertainment. This is also the process by which the desire for such horror is symbolically submitted to logic and reason.

The definitively insecure seclusion in the realm of the Gothic helps to establish this countervailing image of rationalized modernity. So, too, does the Gothic inability to draw a clear distinction between others' existence and one's own. This existence in the other is the defining promise and distress of modern humanity. If an inalienable certainty is to be found in the Gothic genre, it does not exist through a recognition that a discrete *I* exists in reality. Rather, this certainty exists in what is portrayed to be a fact of desire. This fundamental Gothic fact is that there exists a desire for humanity to be materialized through art. Unless or until this materialization takes place, it is only in society and through the existence of others that one can contemplate one's own existence. Unless or until one can read one's identity out of a modern romance held in one's own hands, one will be subject to all sorts of grotesque trials—trials that properly modernized subjects are supposed to recognize only in art.

Epistemological questions are then proven to be indissoluble from dramas in which characters must strive to identify themselves through their relations with others. Rather than being meditated upon by an isolated individual, Gothic identity is thought by demonic historical agencies such as those of gender, class, religion, and nationality. It is through the institution of the family that these unhuman agencies do their most creative thinking, as in Mary Wollstonecraft's *Maria, or The Wrongs of Woman* (1798), whose protagonist feels as if an "evil genius" or "demon" has perplexed her understanding within her marriage.[16] Wollstonecraft was also perfectly attuned to this Gothic circumstance when she wrote, in *Vindication of the Rights of Woman* (1792), of "women immured in their families groping in the dark."[17] The family is to this genre what the cogito is to the *Meditations*, the indubitable ground of primitive self-consciousness.

Along with social position, economic condition, religious denomination, and other kinds of historically specific identifications, Descartes's *Meditations* initially assigned the family to the categorically doubtful realm of imagination and brute materiality—which, after all, is precisely where it belongs, as far as the Gothic novel is concerned. When his respondents tried to bring family and community into their discussions of the mind, Descartes summarily dismissed their anthropological reasonings. He declared that any recourse to the supposed determinations of such contexts could lead only to an infinite regress in the search for certain knowledge. Any authority attributed to one's immediate ancestors must in turn be accounted for in relation to their ancestors, these ancestors' authority in relation to their forebears, and so on.[18] Again, the Gothic novel is fully in agreement with him: one's familial relations *are* infinitely suspicious. The significance of this point, however, is construed rather differently. Instead of allowing protagonists to conceive of themselves as unique and disembodied intelligences, this recognition drives them into a congeries of shifting identifications in a world so saturated with mystery as to provide no basis even for the axiomatic Cartesian definition of bodies as substances extended in space. In fact, the presumptive difference between immaterial identities and physical bodies is precisely what the imaginary and brute materiality of the family throws into confusion.[19] Brontë's Heathcliff provides a case in point when he sees Catherine's features not only in the floor under his feet and in "every cloud, in every tree—filling the air at night, and caught by glimpses in every object by day," but also in his own features (324).[20] In this moment Heathcliff is doing little more than restating the literary tradition that arose out of this recognition that only through art can one draw a clear line between others' existence and one's own. He is simply saying, in a very striking way, "I am a character in a Gothic novel."

All Gothic literature is informed by this effort of characters to identify themselves through relations with others in which the agencies of gender, class, religion, and nationality do their work, with the labors of the family proving especially important. In *The Italian*, for instance, it is not sufficient to Radcliffe's purposes that her plot should be set in motion by a dispute over the nature of the family, with the hero's mother objecting to his fancied heroine because her background is insufficiently grand. Nor is it enough that the mother's agent in this family dispute, the misanthropic Father Schedoni, should be a mysterious figure who comes to be thought of as "a demon in the guise of a monk" whose actions may be "more than human," with consequences that throw the hero's mind into "a tempest of conjecture and of horror."[21] It is still insufficient that the hero, Vicentio di Vivaldi, should confuse Schedoni with a second monk who had repeatedly emerged from shadowy ruins to utter enigmatic warnings to Vivaldi that he had best keep away from the heroine, Ellena Rosalba. It is not even enough that Schedoni should discover, at the very moment when he is about to murder Ellena, that she is his daughter—who then will be brought to love him not only as her father but as the man who has delivered her from the "unknown" assailant whom readers know is none other than himself. Furthermore, we cannot rest easy in the revelation that Schedoni was born Count Ferando di Bruno and married Ellena's mother after murdering her first husband, who happened to be his own brother. We are not even at an end when we learn that Ellena was raised in obscurity by an aunt because Schedoni then went on, for good measure, to slay her mother. Readers are not allowed any respite until they learn why the proof "that removed every doubt of [Schedoni's] identity" as Ellena's father was, in fact, deceptive, and that he is actually Ellena's uncle and stepfather, not her progenitor.[22] (The confusion on this score is owing to the fact that her mother had a daughter by each di Bruno brother, the death of the second child having been mistaken for that of the first.) As a bonus, we learn that Schedoni failed to kill his wife, although he had thought himself successful in this effort. As it happens, she has survived to greet her long-lost child and usher her into the novel's pious conclusion. There she serves neatly to counterbalance Vivaldi's mother, whose fierce character had set this work into motion, much in the way that Hareton and Catherine Linton, at the end of *Wuthering Heights*, provide a formal counterbalance to the pair formed by the young Heathcliff and Catherine at the beginning of the events recounted in that novel.

As this summary should indicate, in *The Italian* the statement "I think" logically entails the conclusion "Therefore, I am bedeviled with a family." Broadly sketched as being placed in conflict between stereotypically aristocratic and emergent middle-class conceptions, which are also associated with the differences between Italy, Catholicism, and the past, on the one hand, and the inference of an English and Protestant modernity, on the other, the family in this novel completely circumscribes self-consciousness without giving it a place to stand, much less one in which it might safely seclude itself. In a world of families, we learn, multiple, disjunctive, and unstable identifications are normative. Far from offering comfort, the image of a self-assured cogito in this world must be positively terrifying, disrupting rather than securing the difference between mind and body. In fact, this image must turn out to be a Heathcliffean prototype such as Schedoni, whose "contempt and malignity" allow him to act as if he is not bound by family relationships, associations, or name.[23]

This sketch of *The Italian* cannot begin to cover the representation of the family in all of Radcliffe's novels, much less in all Gothic literature. Nevertheless, it should give some indication of why it is fair to say that this literature discovers the unclear and indistinct familial relations that await their reading within the clear and distinct identity apprehended through the natural light of reason in the *Meditations*. To be sure, other examples would bring other emphases. Whatever the case may be in a particular work, though, the Gothic family cannot be bracketed off through a phenomenological reduction or through any other means. Gothic novels explain why: because it is impossible to isolate oneself from an institution constituted through identifications that can neither be delimited nor fully known. The advice one character in *The Monk* offers another typifies this Gothic condition: "But you must listen to me with patience. You will not be less surprised, when I relate some particulars of your family still unknown to you."[24]

The family of the Gothic novel lives in the very walls that offered Descartes the illusion of quiet, peace, and free time in which to reflect upon himself while supposing "that no other human beings were yet known" to him.[25] When his thoughts were most focused on what he could know with certainty of himself, the Gothic novel suggests, Descartes was unthinkingly being thought by the institution of the family and all the other social powers represented in and through it. Moreover, the Gothic novel suggests that Descartes's confusion on this score is exemplary of that which constitutes humanity as such. From this perspective, individuals may certainly claim that identity is a discovery made through the natural light of reason. More fully represented, however, it is an effect created through imaginative art or, more specifically, through the unhuman motivations of art aptly represented by the overpowering, and hence terrifying, abstraction of the family. From the Gothic perspective, this is what Descartes's malignant genius represented in reality: the necessity of art, which is the necessity of misanthropy.

So the identity of modern humanity is portrayed as the product of a fundamental misanthropy. It was with good reason that Thomas Love Peacock satirically suggested, in *Nightmare Abbey* (1818), that the "delicious misanthropy and discontent" of modern books makes them "very consolatory and congenial."[26] For all its claim to the natural light of reason, the identity of modern humanity is drawn out of a drama of dissimulation. Descartes's constitutive dissimulation becomes the matter of the Gothic plot, as in *The Italian*, in which a monk takes a new name and leaves the world behind, as the saying goes, so that he may eventually be revealed as the very demon he was supposed to oppose. Despite the diversity of Gothic plots, *The Italian* is paradigmatic in this respect, and, as viewed from the perspective thus afforded to us, we can see that Descartes's meditations prove too much. In defining the activity of thought by first willing away the influence of the family and all the social distinctions appertaining to it, including rank, wealth, religion, and nationality, he undoes himself in a distinctively modern way. He shows the necessity of a recourse to the very art that he will nonetheless disavow when he attributes all ruinous manipulations of bodies, images, and thoughts to the figure of the malignant demon. Just as his isolation anticipates the role of the dangerous confinement, romantic past, and exotic lands in Gothic literature, so does this demon play the role of the Gothic villain.

In effect, the Gothic novel recognizes that the Cartesian *I* is dependent on this aesthetic creation, the malignant genius, and, even prior to that, on the aesthetics of a misanthropic seclusion prefiguring that demon. Accordingly, it portrays the ego and its challenging adversary as mutually constitutive characters in a literary drama, not as intellectual figures in a logical demonstration. In doing so, it practically invites a Freudian reading, in which ego and demon are distinct agencies within the same psychic apparatus, as well as the Foucauldian revision of that reading, in which the repressive hypothesis that may lead to sympathy for the demon is shown to overlook how fully and openly this other's co-creation with the ego has been effected. At the same time, though, the Gothic novel thwarts such readings in advance through its insistence on identifying cultural with biological and social reproduction. In portraying thinking as historical action fashioned through unhuman motivations—the motivations of agencies that seem sadistically to lord it over the human figure, such as sexual impulses, kinship structures, economic systems, legal codes, and religious institutions—the Gothic genre takes for granted that consciousness holds no exalted privilege in its world. From Jane Austen on, the lapses of consciousness featured in its drama have been the most obvious targets for mockery in this genre, but this satire appears more naive than its intended target if one considers the assumptions it conveys about consciousness as a continuous and secure state of self-possession. Moreover, this genre takes for granted that power is productive and jubilant in the creation of identities, not simply repressive, as nothing shows more clearly than its portrayal of the powerful nexus of relations that is the family, that thoroughly dubious thing compounded of imagination and brute materiality. In other words, far from being confronted and surpassed in these novels, misanthropy is made out to be the unsettling power that modernity must labor to confine to an art symbolically marked as dead, relegated to the past, as in Paul Emile Thieriot's *Timon All Alone* (1790). Art must thus be disavowed precisely because the ghostly conception of artistic form makes possible the invention of modernity and all its privileged figures, including that favorite term of Radcliffe's, "humanity."

To think, in the Gothic novel, is to recognize one's existence in the other, the reality of one's present in the romance of the past. The implications of Descartes's proof of identity through its testing at the hands of the malignant demon thus become, for example, the identification of universal humanity through the creation of a Continental, Catholic, aristocratic demon. Of course, just as Gothic plots differ from work to work, so does the design of Gothic misanthropy. For instance, in *The Recess* (1783–85), embroiling her protagonists in religious factionalism, illegitimacy, secret marriages, and threats of incest, rape, and insanity, not to mention murder, Sophia Lee represented this existence in the other through the relation between Mary, Queen of Scots (the protagonists' mother) and Queen Elizabeth. (With characteristic Gothic logic, this relationship could then be reproduced within the aesthetic furnishings of the mind of one of the protagonists: "Taste, genius, and science, those rich columes [sic] with which enthusiastic fancy creates in peaceful minds a thousand light aerial structures, deep sunk, and broken in my heart, presented to the mental eye a ruin . . . —Misanthropy, black-visaged misanthropy, reigned there like a solitary savage, unconscious of the value of those treasures his rude hand every day more and more defaced.")[27] The beginning of *The Monk* finds the renowned Father Ambrosio overhearing a novice's tormented exclamation—"Oh God! What a blessing would Misanthropy be to me!"—counseling the novice that such a condition is wholly "imaginary," and then becoming a complete misanthrope himself, as well as the rapist of his sister and murderer of his mother, after he is seduced by the novice, who turns out to be a cross-dressed and dreamily lubricious young woman.[28] *Melmoth the Wanderer* opens with John Melmoth leaving Dublin's Trinity College to visit his dying uncle, a confirmed misanthrope, in whose manse he first encounters the ancestral figure that is cursed forever to wander the earth, haunt his family, and corrupt his own existence—"that being, I will not call him a man," as another character refers to it.[29]

The generically distinctive constant through all such variations is the recognition of oneself in the misanthropic other and thus the discovery of oneself in the unhuman and the unhuman within oneself. Precisely because it mimes humanity, serving as its shadowy double, art is the exemplary figuration of the unhuman. Its assumed distinction from nature, inanimation, secondary or representational mode of being, and suspect status in Platonic, Christian, and other metaphysics are accordingly brought to life in the Gothic. Melmoth, for instance, is introduced to the perturbations of his demonic ancestor through a portrait whose eyes seem to move, and uncannily affecting portraits appear as well in *The Monk* and *The Recess*, among other works. As in Clara Reeve's 1778 "Preface to the Second Edition" of *The Old English Baron*, the animated picture and similar devices have long been criticized as excesses of the Gothic genre, but it is this criticism that appears excessive if one examines its governing assumptions about the existence of clear-cut divisions between subjects and objects and between the probable and the marvelous.

This undead nature of art is powerfully realized in *Wuthering Heights*, which is by no means the last but is arguably the most brilliant work in this tradition. It is so powerfully realized, in fact, that Charlotte Brontë, in her "Editor's Preface" to the second edition of her sister's novel, seemed terrified by it. Charlotte herself was no mean hand at the Gothic, of course, but she evidently could not accept how openly Emily had acknowledged the misanthropy at the heart of the modern identity Gothic art was designed to entertain. Therefore, in writing of how her late sister had wrought "creations like Healthcliff, like Earnshaw, like Catherine," she denigrated her ("I am bound to avow that she had scarcely more practical knowledge of the peasantry amongst whom she lived, than a nun has of the country people who sometimes pass her convent gates"), patronized her ("Having formed these beings, she did not know what she had done"), and lovingly condemned her ("Whether it is right or advisable to create beings like Heathcliff, I do not know: I scarcely think it is") [368–70]. Even if it had not been provided, an experienced reader of Gothic fiction might have wished to imagine such an editorial introduction to Emily Brontë's work, in which one family member plays ego to the other's demon. The way Charlotte insists on placing her sister's identity in a family context that defines it in terms of ignorance, unreliability, and suspect morality—terms that cannot help but also suggest sibling rivalry—reproduces in the form of denial precisely the sort of misanthropy that Emily Brontë's masterpiece affirms to be the nature of Gothic identity.[30]

The opening sentences of *Wuthering Heights* focus in on the subject of the Gothic as subject to misanthropy: "In all England, I do not believe that I could have fixed on a situation so completely removed from the stir of society. A perfect misanthropist's Heaven: and Mr. Heathcliff and I are such a suitable pair to divide the desolation between us" (1). Hindley and Catherine Earnshaw will also appear as exemplars of misanthropy, and even Edgar Linton fits the bill when, recoiling from Heathcliff, he betakes himself and his daughter to a melancholy seclusion like that of the protagonist in Friedrich Schiller's play *The Misanthropist Reconciled* (1790). Thus evoked from the outset, the general spirit of misanthropy is concentrated in the history of Heathcliff, who incarnates its unhuman agency in every aspect of his being, from the dubious circumstances of his birth and his disruptive insertion into a family on through to his animalic, devilish, and monstrous appearance as an object of superstition to Nelly Dean, among others, when he is an adult. "It" is what Nelly calls him when Mr. Earnshaw first brings him home (35); and, as Charlotte Brontë recognized, an it is what he is and what he remains throughout the novel. "He's not a human being," his wife will flatly declare (177); and as goes Heathcliff in this novel, so goes humanity.

For instance, Heathcliff is like the it that Lockwood experiences when his sleep at Wuthering Heights is interrupted by an apparition at the window by his bed. "As it spoke," Lockwood recounts, "I discerned, obscurely, a child's face looking through the window—Terror made me cruel; and, finding it useless to attempt shaking the creature off, I pulled its wrist on to the broken pane, and rubbed it to and fro till the blood ran down and soaked the bed-clothes" (23). Since this scene takes place three decades after the one that introduces Heathcliff into the Earnshaw household but actually precedes it in the narrative, with only a few pages separating the two, readers are given the impression of an "itness" that is at once subjective and intersubjective. The rest of the novel is then designed to elucidate this sense of being as the condition of identity wrought through unhuman agencies of identification. In Brontë's portrayal, the unhuman is the foundation of modern identity; the misanthrope is the character demanded by its world; and the characteristic art of misanthropy is romantic love.

It is through this last intuition that her work in this genre outdoes that of her predecessors. For the most part, love between men and women in Gothic novels is a perfunctory business, characterized formulaically as an index of virtue, sensibility, or morality. Think, for instance, of how thin the incest-tinged love story is in Mary Shelley's *Frankenstein* (1818) as compared to the impassioned relation between Victor and his creation. It was Brontë's genius to see that romantic love, instead of being portrayed as a sign of the consciousness established through the aesthetic invention, sufferance, and internalization of otherness, could be more accurately portrayed as itself being the indubitably Gothic machinery that produces humanity through the process of identity formation. It would be through love that we would come to see the revelation of logical as aesthetic premises, the appearance of disturbing identifications in the place of certain identity, the emblematic embodiment of these identifications in the image of art that stirs itself into life, and—through all these aspects of the novel—the mutually constitutive relation of ego and demon.

Brought forward through Gothic terror and the allied Romantic feelings represented by works as disparate as Goethe's *Sorrows of Young Werther* (1774) and Charlotte Dacre's *Confessions of the Nun of St. Omer* (1805), the romantic love of Andreas Capellanus, which must be gratuitous and so can be manifested only in adulterous or extramarital passion, was legitimized as art. By showing Gothic art coming alive in love and so giving the experience of love the place traditionally occupied in the Gothic novel by that of dramatic uncertainty, Brontë reinterpreted her predecessors in this genre as effectively as they had reinterpreted Descartes. Like earlier Gothic novels, *Wuthering Heights* shows the nightmarish familial dramas lurking in the dreamy architecture of the thinker's room, but Brontë also saw the sadomasochistic institution of romantic love in the structuring of the Gothic plot.[31] What is more, she saw the value of estimating such love as a matter that properly belongs to the past and that is supposed to appear in the present only in the form of art. It is this insight that accounts for what Terry Eagleton has described as "the curious impersonality of the relation between Catherine and Heathcliff," its famously "ontological" or "metaphysical" quality.[32] Cathy's and Heathcliff's love can be consummated only in imagination or in brute materiality—only in ghostly visitations or in the commingling of their remains—so that it may be formally assigned to the realm of art, as distinct from life. Like the mockery of romantic love that runs throughout the nineteenth-century novel, from the portrayals of Marianne Dashwood and Hetty Sorrell to those of David Copperfield and Emma Bovary and *Tuan* Jim, among so many others, this love story signifies modernity, which emerges from its dramatized failure. As distinct from many other novels that employ this device, however, *Wuthering Heights* keeps faith with the Gothic through its dramatized insistence that modernity recognize its existence in the other that is art. The unhuman motivations of art, Brontë suggests, are still those of the humanity that defines itself by framing the image of art's life as superstition.

In his response to Descartes's *Meditations*, Johannes Caterus had explained the argument about identity on which he agreed with the philosopher by making an allusion to Terence's *Andria*: "Davus is Davus and not Oedipus."[33] Like her predecessors in the Gothic genre, Brontë would have none of this. "I *am* Heathcliff!" Catherine Earnshaw exclaims, recognizing the foundation of her identity in the necessary existence of the other. Whereas her love for Edgar Linton "is like the foliage in the woods," subject to time and change, her love for Heathcliff "resembles the eternal rocks beneath—a source of little visible delight, but necessary" (82). Even as Catherine proclaims its perdurability, however, Brontë marks with irony this identity through identifications. She does so in order to make clear that love, like the Gothic family, is bound to be as unstable as it is fundamentally unhuman, no matter whether that unhuman nature is imaged as being animal, vegetable, or mineral—or demon or ghoul. At the very moment that Catherine is proclaiming her identification with Heathcliff, then, and characterizing his existence as hers—"my own being" (82)—he is stealing away, having heard only her earlier remarks that to marry him now would be a degradation for her. Like the events that followed upon his entrance into her family's household, his disappearance from it and subsequent fairy-tale transformation into a gentleman serve to emphasize that, in being Heathcliff, Catherine is and yet is not Catherine, and, in being Catherine, Heathcliff is and is not himself. Accordingly, Heathcliff may reverse the subjects and objects in her statements: "I have not broken your heart—*you* have broken it—and in breaking it, you have broken mine" (161). Similarly, in her last meeting with him Catherine may say of Heathcliff, "That is not *my* Heathcliff. I shall love mine yet; and take him with me—he's in my soul" (160).

This identification of Catherine and Heathcliff demands the Gothic ghost as its defining figure. No image could be adequate to their love that did not register its profoundly unhuman motivations, which can "take any form" because they derive their existence from the overwhelming and infinitely regressive number of cultural, biological, and social forms that reproduce themselves through the identifications out of which identity is composed. So Heathcliff, not really himself, calls out to the dead Catherine, "I know that ghosts *have* wandered on earth. Be with me always—take any form—drive me mad! only *do* not leave me in this abyss, where I cannot find you!" (167).

This Gothicism that comes to life in the love of Catherine and Heathcliff is specifically literary in nature, in keeping with the nature of *Wuthering Heights* as a self-conscious reworking of literary tradition. Instead of paintings or statues or other objets d'art, the letters of the alphabet are the unhuman stuff that becomes animated, as when Lockwood has his nightmare vision of Catherine Linton after reading her name scratched on a window ledge and scrawled in the books resting on that ledge.[34] The way letters become animated does not appear at all logical ("why did I think of *Linton*? I had read *Earnshaw* twenty times for Linton" [23]), and Lockwood's response to this event is as lacking in humanity as was the reaction of Catherine, Hindley, and Nelly to the sudden delivery of Heathcliff from within Mr. Earnshaw's coat.

To be sure, by the end of the novel, as the eighteenth has turned to the nineteenth century, the sadomasochistic tropes of the Gothic will have been toned down to the comic dimensions of the playful slaps and kisses exchanged in the reading lesson given to Hareton Earnshaw by the second Catherine. However, it is notable that Brontë did not reestablish a Providential security for the senses, in accordance with the Gothic pattern. Instead, as in the twentieth century's film noir modernizations of the Gothic, Brontë's narrative structure has the violent prehistory to this scene with Hareton and Catherine come out of the past to modify our impressions of that scene. We are left with the image of a child's terrified blubbering at the sight of "Heathcliff and a woman, yonder, under t'Nab" (336).

Lockwood's final words, as he describes the graves of Catherine, Edgar Linton, and Heathcliff, do make a gesture toward something like divine assurance: "I . . . wondered how any one could ever imagine unquiet slumbers for the sleepers in that quiet earth" (338). The muted and willful nature of this assurance can hardly go unremarked, however, since Lockwood's impercipience is made clear from the beginning of the narrative, when he makes embarrassing mistakes on his first visit to Heathcliff's household, as when he takes a pile of dead rabbits to be cherished cats. In fact, he actually introduces his character with a story that illustrates the confounding cross-purposes in his actions of the immediate past. Nonetheless, although he has pronounced himself a misanthropist, in accordance with Gothic fashion, and secluded himself in this place far removed from "society," as the contemporary idiom would have it, he is no Descartes metaphysically trying to sort himself out. As a man of the present, in this narrative's time scheme, Lockwood is comically self-assured even as he details his confusions and errors. It would appear that Cartesian doubt is a thing of the past, a matter that cannot touch a gentleman who knows how to dismiss a nightmare with the same absurd confidence with which he lets his readers know that, if he had been so inclined, he might have stolen a march on Hareton in the matter of the second Catherine's affections. In short, Lockwood does not think, and he is not Heathcliff or anything like him.

Instead, Lockwood and Nelly figure as the dispiriting modern counterparts to the ego and demon of Descartes's *Meditations*. Lockwood is the silly ego that does not have the art to question itself, Nelly the tormentor as mere busybody (and so her "hidden enemy" [129], says the first Catherine, not because Nelly Dean is of supernatural consequence but because she so decidedly is not). The fact that the structuring of *Wuthering Heights* has Nelly's oral narrative retold in Lockwood's writing reduces the demonic testing of identity to a gossip's test of one's patience. As told by Nelly to divert the ailing or bored Lockwood and as retold by Lockwood for what we can infer to be an intended audience of persons with pretensions to education and culture, this story is oriented to the need for entertainment, not to the need for such certainty as was sought by Heathcliff, Catherine Earnshaw, and Descartes.

It is significant in this regard that Lockwood appears as a failed or indecisive misanthrope—as so much of a dilettante in this respect, in fact, that he takes Heathcliff's vehement rejection of any desire for his company as a perverse incitement to pester him further. Like Nelly's tale, Heathcliff is entertainment to him. Lockwood's very existence as a tourist in this countryside, a consumer of the experiences it may provide, shows us that Wuthering Heights and everything around it have the nature of a resort for him, like the spa he had graced with his presence shortly before coming there. His recourse to such entertainment is necessarily ambivalent, however, for he must let it come alive enough to divert him with its power while still maintaining the critical distance from it that will assure him that he need not question his own modern identity and so need not doubt that art is essentially a thing of the past. As a narrator, then, Lockwood is also a stand-in for *Wuthering Heights*'s readers. Brontë mocks these readers through Lockwood's patronizing affection for Catherine Linton and Hareton and then through the sentimental closure to the narrative that he takes them to have bestowed upon the graves of their forebears. At the same time, to readers who know better than to identify with Lockwood's modernity—the modernity Brontë deliberately places almost half a century before her novel's publication, as if it ought to be regarded as being no less remote than any generic Gothic setting—she offers a thoroughly self-mortifying conception of art. In this conception, it is a damned good thing that art should have the making and unmaking of us, for who could face the unimaginable alternative of simply belonging to humanity, like Nelly and Lockwood, without being scared to death?

Chapter Three

Immemorial

In the series of etchings that Francisco Goya based upon the Peninsular War, one of the most important compositional elements consists of bodies amassed in a heap. It is the heap, the disorganized pile of things, that the battling forces depicted in this series have in common. This is destiny in the form of a chaos in which human beings are turned from glimpsed body parts into obscure lumps, unclassifiable shapes, and, finally, shades and lines in which the artist's mark admits its incoherence before the blinding intensity of the misanthropy it was meant to display. Jean-Luc Nancy might have been speaking of Goya when he remarked that the world at its limits "is a heap, and perhaps a foul one."[1]

As Honoré de Balzac suggested when he made the protagonist of "Colonel Chabert" (1832) crawl out of just such a destiny, the heap is an antipathetic thing. (Returned to life, Chabert comes to represent, experience, and identify with a profoundly misanthropic vision of the world.) Nothing could be farther from the memorial, the artistic form in which martial values are consecrated, than the heap, which is immemorial.[2] As distinct from the concept of the universal, which it resembles in its seeming obliviousness to time, the immemorial stuff of the heap is so unrecognizable as to be disruptive of the very conception of humanity. Whereas the universal is supposed to rise above time, the immemorial heap falls outside it. Inexorably and appallingly particular in its every aspect, the heap does not add up to anything. In its indeterminateness, it suggests a bad infinity that overwhelms identification, memory, and any form of historical record. It cannot be captured in concepts or monuments. As an image of humanity, it reveals human will as being subject to an unhuman motivation that is simply brutal, as careless as it is exigent, completely anonymous and yet known to all no matter how much we may wish to deny an acquaintanceship with it.

Some critics, such as André Malraux, have tried to conscript Goya into a conventional conception of modernism by denying that his work constitutes any sort of reportage.[3] What we see in the heap, though, is the journalistic nature of Goya's work. We are made witness to news that does not stay news, that destroys the pretensions of art, and justifiably so. For only in the sign of the inartistic can we find an adequate response to the declination of observation into a horror so profound as to be immemorial. Particulars are isolated until, as Ronald Paulson puts it, "isolation becomes ultimately swallowing, engulfment, or burial."[4] Naturalistic vision becomes unnatural, humanly irrelevant and useless. The same effect is evident in those of Goya's captions, such as "I saw it," which seem to make an explicit claim for his role as an eyewitness to the scenes he has depicted. These captions add nothing at all to the etchings with which they are paired, which are not notably different from, or more powerful than, the others in this series. Like the art of the heap, these captions can succeed only by failing.

In art driven to register an immemorial misanthropy evident even, or especially, in the most topical of events, the assertion of first-hand experience can be nothing better than a sign of desperation, so irrelevant is it to the dehumanization at hand. In Goya's *Disasters of War* (c. 1810–1820), then, the insistence on topicality is but a shortcut to the eternity of all that is merely news. In this context the exemplary image must tend toward a state of undifferentiated masses, vague shadows, or inarticulate lines. Yesterday's news comes to us with too much or too little context. In either case, it is bereft of the inarguable sensation of personal immediacy and, equally, of the consoling weight of cultural monumentality.

Goya's most effective image of the heap may be the twelfth etching in this series, "This is what you were born for" (Figure 8). In this case, as in others, we are shown that heaps are made of particulars. These are not such particulars, however, as William Blake was seeing around this time, those partaking of a glowing infinity and gloriously redemptive eternity. Merely news, the particulars in question here are the most unhuman form of things, as in the compelling image of a particular that bears the legend "This is worse" (Figure 9). Here we are confronted with disfiguration as humanity. To see the immemorial nature of the disfiguration at the center of this image, one need only imagine it mounted on a pedestal. This is what despair looks like; war memorials have never been anything like this.[5]

As opposed to the early fourteenth-century *Ovide moralisé* and its Renaissance descendents, in which an allegorical interpretation of the *Metamorphoses* gave them a Christian spirit, this etching seems to be taken from an unholy version of these tales, an *Ovide démoralisé*. In the middle of it we see a fragmentary thing, a particular, the unhuman stuff of which heaps are made. This image is of a tree coupled with a man or, perhaps, of one of these in the process of being transformed into the other. Insofar as this is a coupling, it is a violent rape, in keeping with Ovidian precedent: the gruesomely sodomized man is dead. Insofar as it is a metamorphosis, we see the incipient identification of man and tree

Figure 8. Francisco Goya, "This is what you were born for." Etching, from *Disasters of War* (c. 1810–20). © Museo Nacional del Prado—Madrid.

Figure 9. Francisco Goya, "This is worse" (c. 1810–20). Etching, from *Disasters of War* (c. 1810–20). © Museo Nacional del Prado—Madrid.

not only in the resemblances between their poor forked structures and lopped limbs but also in the delicately rendered tendrils of the man's windblown hair, which seems to imitate the foliage on the branches in the background. Unlike the situation in the thirteenth canto of the *Inferno*, in which Dante revised Ovid to represent the sin of suicide, there is no promise of order, either human or divine, in this scene. In the *Inferno* we have despair fittingly punished, whereas here it is simply a fact of life. In the words of Arthur C. Danto, we are presented with "a dark vision of ineluctable depravity."[6]

In part because of the influence of the Inquisition and its opposition to the depiction of nudes, mythological themes had not been very popular in seventeenth- and eighteenth-century Spanish art; and, save for a few works executed near the beginning and end of his career, such as a "Pygmalion and Galatea" (c. 1817–20) drawn around the time he was finishing the *Disasters*, Goya showed little interest in such themes.[7] The unlikelihood that Goya was consciously alluding to Ovid in "This is worse," however, does not mean that the allusion is merely accidental. After all, even in Spain Ovidian tradition was pervasive. In fact, when the Madrid Academy of Arts, with which Goya would later be associated, was being established in 1744, one of the first books ordered "to serve as models for the students" was the *Metamorphoses*.[8] Goya would have been well acquainted with Ovidian tradition from the time he spent in Italy and from sculptures, prints, frescos, and paintings.[9] In addition, the raptures and transformations of this tradition had analogues in the emblematic, folkloric, and satirical traditions that informed the *Disasters* as well as the *Caprichos*.[10] So while the grotesquerie of "This is worse" cannot be called a conscious commentary on Ovidian tradition, it is a commentary nonetheless, one that the pervasiveness of this tradition virtually forced Goya's hand to express.[11]

In presenting us with this unhuman figure, Goya's image illustrates the distress in the *Metamorphoses* not only over rape but also over the uncertainties of gender, as in the tales of Tiresias and Hermaphroditus, and the complications of "unnatural" sexual desire, as in the tales of Pasiphaë, Byblis, Iphis, Pygmalion, and Myrrha.[12] This emphasis is in keeping with the rest of the images in the *Disasters*, in which the gendered stereotype of male aggressors and female victims is displayed but also upset. A woman holds an infant in one hand while spearing a soldier with the other (number 5, "And they are like wild beasts"); the only recognizable individual who appears in this series, Agustina de Aragón, fires a cannon while standing atop the bodies of dead men (number 7, "What courage!"); an old woman prepares to stab a soldier who is attempting to assault a young woman (number 9, "They don't like it"); as a man wields a tool with which he is about to sodomize a denuded corpse being dragged along the ground, a woman eagerly joins in the desecration (number 28, "Rabble").[13]

Commentators often remark upon the evenhandedness of Goya's images, which are attentive to barbarities among all the parties to this war. It is commonplace to regard this as testimony to his humanity, but it is difficult to understand how it can be reassuring to know that barbarity is to be found among all sorts of persons. As Hugh Thomas remarks, "The *Disasters of War* are not, to put it mildly, the work of a man who believes that human nature is essentially good."[14] We ought rather see to see in Goya's aesthetic attitude a misanthropy that challenges our usual ideas of misanthropy: an attitude that does not testify to an individual's personal disappointment or failed idealism, as in the conventional interpretations of characters such as Timon or Alceste. Instead, it testifies to the failure of the conceptual boundaries, as of nationality, culture, and gender, through which the ideologues of the modern era were seeking to define the image of humanity.

When conflict is no longer comprehensible in social terms, including the social conventions of aesthetics, it makes itself felt instead as an irreducible antagonism that marks the limits of the social. Swallowing, engulfing, or burying any given boundaries to humanity, it even suggests the impossibility of society. During the last century, this quasi-mythical antagonism was dramatically emplotted in Sigmund Freud's speculative narrative of Eros and Thanatos in *Beyond the Pleasure Principle* (1920), in which he acknowledged being influenced by Arthur Schopenhauer and Plato. In political theory, it showed up later in the century in works such as Ernesto Laclau and Chantal Mouffe's *Hegemony and Socialist Strategy* (1985), which was most strongly influenced by Karl Marx, Michel Foucault, Jacques Lacan, and Jacques Derrida. In art, meanwhile, it appeared in countless "anti-aesthetic" works from the eras of Dada and Duchamp on down to the furthest fringes of our own postmodern present. Even as modernity was aborning, however, Goya had already fixed his attention on the impossibility of its humanity.

Throughout the *Disasters of War* Goya took pains to represent the rape of women and the killing of men as being parallel activities in the Peninsular campaign of Napoleon's army, just as they were in the battles of the ancient Greeks, in our recent conflicts in the Balkans, and in innumerable other wars. In "This is worse," which appears almost at the midpoint of the series, Goya went one step farther by conflating these two activities into one deathly perversity. Similarly, the multiple modes of execution that he exhibited in other etchings—hanging, *garrottage*, firing squad, sexual mutilation, dismemberment—were condensed into this one surreal figure. Therefore, "This is worse" may be taken as an epitome of the series as a whole, and this epitome is especially powerful because

its allusive density is achieved without sacrifice of its naturalistic, or journalistic, verisimilitude. As it happens, there is some reason to believe that
this etching was based on a scene Goya had personally witnessed.[15] In any
event, though, the Boschian extremity of its horror is historically imaginable, for instance, as the effect of an artillery bombardment.

At the same time, like all the particulars that go into the making of
heaps, this image is excessively suggestive, irreducible to one thing. It is
so overdetermined that just what is actually "worse" here is not entirely
clear. At first glance, certainly, the implicit comparison is between the
sculptural but decidedly unmonumental figure in the foreground of
this image and the designs of the etchings immediately preceding it in
the series, such as numbers 35 and 36, which depict groups of executed
men. One must wonder, though, whether the comparative extremity of
"This is worse" does not also arise from Goya's concern for balance in its
design, which is so finicky as finally to seem frivolous, in an Olympian
way, and thus deliberately destructive of the humanity of his art.[16]

The undoing of humanity here thus becomes a powerful image, also,
of aesthetics in distress. We are confronted by a vision of misanthropy as
a force internal to and indivisible from the work of art. This image then
amounts to an intuition as to the dreadful implications of sovereign violence, whether of mythological gods, hereditary monarchs served by
court poets and artists, or self-crowned emperors.

First and foremost, Goya demands that we see this journalistic image
as also being aesthetic by giving the hybrid thing its central and frontal
position. He then arranges this thing, which is stripped of clothing and
greenery, so that it is balanced by the tree in the background, which is
decently attired in leaves and leaning to the left, in the opposite direction from the thing in the foreground. The composition is also balanced horizontally, both by the diagonals of the trees and by the figures
of the two mustachioed French officers, which are arranged in poses so
complementary as to seem almost comic or balletic. The left arm of the
soldier on one side, who is engaged in plundering a corpse, is lowered;
the left arm of the solider on the other side, who seems about to create
another corpse with his saber, is raised; between them, roughly at the
apex of the triangle they are made to suggest, is the absent arm of the
central figure. The mustache of the one soldier turns up in a smile; that
of the other, down in a baleful frown. Completing the pattern at the
apex in this instance is a gaping mouth that does not clearly signify any
emotion—an absence of expression to match the absent arm.

We glimpse other figures as well, both living and dead, in the slight
declivity that distances the background from the foreground of the picture, and these also offer us a sort of balance. More dense and detailed
in the center of the picture, they become attenuated at its lower left and

right borders. Most notably, the corpses at either side no longer possess the heft of humanity and so are ready to be piled up somewhere. Throughout this work the result is that the parts of its design that Goya has simply sketched in are played off against the finely drawn passages so as to set up couplings, or metamorphoses, that on close inspection will prove to be doing violence to our vision, so shockingly arbitrary are they. For instance, the head of that emphatic particular in the foreground, the most delicately worked passage in the entire etching, is on a level with a treetop so minimally outlined that it almost suggests a random scrawl. The darkly etched fork of the stump in the foreground finds its hideous solidity doubled by the hat of the smiling soldier in the background, which a trick of perspective places directly under the corpse's thigh, as if these two figures were joined together just as corpse and stump are. The stippled contours of the impaled body's flesh and the exquisitely drawn lines of its hair lend it a volumetric density that is balanced by the more casually sketched style of the elements of this composition surrounding it.

Literally, then, through the stump in the foreground, and also figuratively, the overall effect is brutally to root the particular in the abstract—and thus to uproot it, making it unfit for the communication of art or anything else. "This is worse" is arguably the most powerful etching in this series because it displays for us the aesthetics of the particular—how it may be made formally to appeal to our humanity through composition, allusion, and the other measures described above—while simultaneously demonstrating, through the textbook parallels of this lesson in vision, the profoundly unhuman nature of art. It is as if we were made witness to the potential for artistry to be characterized as the purest sadism. The artist etches the wax-covered plate with blade and acid, toying with it or torturing it, as gods do with mortals. Whatever else the *Disasters* may communicate, what Fred Licht has described as the "visual impartiality" of these etchings thus serves to convey a decidedly Olympian effect.[17] The artist's hand acknowledges its destructive making of that unhuman figure out of a presumed humanity and humanistic tradition. Before our very eyes, this obsessively ordered image of heartwrenching power undergoes a metamorphosis into a heap of alien particulars.

In contrast, the weakest engravings in this series are those, such as the "caprichos enfátichos" that conclude it (numbers 66 through 80), in which Goya turns to allegory for assistance in his task. These images are less effective not because they are less true or direct in their portrayal of humanity, as a conventional journalistic viewpoint might put it, but because they are an evasion of the unhuman. Instead of the disaggregated vision that results from a focus on brute particulars and heaps of particulars, they offer us reassuringly integrated images of symbolic wholes and universal themes—the building blocks of which memorials are made. Number 40, for instance, shows a man wrestling with a giant beast. Even if we ignore the disconcerting fact that this ostensibly fearsome creature resembles an overgrown dog, this etching would still suggest, at best, an assertion of humanity against bestiality of the sort that characterizes the crudest propaganda. It offers us a complete and coherent image with which we can unequivocally identify ourselves, and that is precisely the problem. Similarly, when Goya turns from the implicit model of the heap to that of the dramatic tableau (as in number 50, "Unhappy mother!"), the results tend to be unrelievedly melodramatic and lachrymose, as if anticipating bad Victorian illustrations.[18] Elsewhere, in images that picture a bloodsucking bat feeding on a supine human (72), portray animals in a style reminiscent of La Fontaine and Aesop (74), and show the abstraction of Truth in the form of a dying woman (79), the problem is that the unhuman is given an exemplary artistic form.[19] The particulars of murder and rape are generalized, successfully subsumed into art, and thus made unthreatening or even reassuring. As in propagandistic and memorial creations, in these images art denies its own unhuman motivations, its own misanthropy, and so rests satisfied with a definition of humanity that does not seek to go beyond vacuous stereotypes.

It is not surprising, of course, that Goya should have been unable or unwilling to sustain the most intensely misanthropic instance of his vision. It is even debatable whether it would have been good for him to have done so. However we judge this matter, though, his achievement in "This is worse" is no less remarkable as an historical act than it is as an aesthetic, and anti-aesthetic, feat. To appreciate this point, we need only consider the difference between the vision of war in this etching and the imagery offered to us by the major literary works occasioned by the battles of the Napoleonic era. We need scarcely refer to other works of visual art concerned with these wars; like the prints that inspired Stendhal's Fabrice Valserra with visions of heroism, they do not come anywhere close to taking up the challenge Goya set himself.[20]

Even in *The Charterhouse of Parma* (1839), the most shocking sight that confronts Fabrice is a bloody horse fallen on broken ground and wildly kicking its feet, which are entangled in its own guts.[21] This is a horrible scene but is passed over in a sentence, quickly and lightly. Whereas irony is displayed in the carefully balanced composition of "This is worse" so that it may be made to appear revolting and self-reflexively destructive of aesthetics, Stendahl's achievement lies precisely in exquisitely controlled modulations of the urbane ironic tone, occasionally touched with sentimentality, that he maintains toward his bumptious antihero.

Similarly, William Thackeray in *Vanity Fair* (1847–48) and Leo Tolstoy in *War and Peace* (1868–69) agreed with Stendahl that the Napoleonic wars were best depicted through a narrative consciousness securely detached from and superior to the viewpoints of their participants. In saying so, I mean neither to equate nor to criticize their methods, and I am not forgetting the differences between literary and visual art. I mean only to note that Thackeray and Tolstoy, following the lead of Stendahl, labored to memorialize what they took to be the historical and symbolic ramifications of this era through their attention to the ancient theme of love and war, the thematic modernity of the jumped-up Corsican lieutenant, and similar concerns. What they did not see, or at least did not choose to emphasize in their works, were immemorial heaps of particulars that can be comprehended historically and symbolically only at the cost of the very conception of art.

To be sure, all three writers chose the Napoleonic Wars to symbolize some sense of an unhuman power that might overwhelm popular conceptions of heroism and genius and, along with them, the very notion of human agency. Stendahl's irony, for instance, might judged to be so brilliantly supple only because it silently internalizes a self-destructive vision like that which Goya displayed. It might also be argued that the controlling metaphor for authorial artifice in *Vanity Fair*, that of the puppeteer, effectively reveals a misanthropy in this work that yields nothing in point of bitterness to Goya's. Furthermore, even though readers tend to skip the chapters in which Tolstoy develops his theory of history as moving independently of the wills of individuals, this emphasis and its Christian underpinnings are meant to disabuse us of our commonplace sense of humanity. In presenting the absurdly motivated duel between Pierre and Dolohov in counterpoint to the Battle of Austerlitz, Tolstoy certainly did make war, and the humanity allied with its supposed grandeur, appear absurdly incoherent. It is worth noting as well that Joseph Conrad's story "The Duel" (1908) pays heed to this Tolstoyan precedent by proposing as a microcosm of the Napoleonic wars an irrationally initiated and utterly absurd series of duels. This work was designed to demystify any lingering romance, even in the ironic mode of the nineteenth century, that might be associated with this historical era.

Perhaps most compelling of all, there is the example of how Thomas Hardy's poetic drama *The Dynasts* (1903–6) invokes a mythology akin to that of the ancient Greeks to show so-called human beings as the grotesquely involuntary and unwitting agents of forces not only beyond their ken but beyond all reason. He portrays "flesh-hinged mannikins" as the chance aesthetic effects, or "inexplicable artistries," of an amoral and forever unconscious Immanent Will: a "mutative, unmotived, dominant Thing." In this portrayal, the Immanent Will "of whose tissues the personages of the action form portion" periodically appears "as a brain-like network of currents and ejections, twitching, interpenetrating, en-tangling, and thrusting hither and thither the human forms." Napoleon was popularly regarded by his opponents as the enemy of humanity and thus the misanthrope *par excellence*, and Hardy reiterates this Tolstoyan theme by quoting from the Declaration of the Allies signed at the Congress of Vienna in 1815: "The Powers . . . declare that Napoléon Bona-parte has placed himself without the pale of civil and social relations." Hardy goes beyond Tolstoy, however, in portraying that "pale of civil and social relations" supposed to mark out humanity as an illusion that blinds people to the unhuman nature of their own motivations. More-over, in describing the English army at the culminating Battle of Vitoria in the Peninsular War, Hardy took pains to note the destructive implica-tions of this war for the pretensions of aesthetic tradition. He described soldiers who "cut from their frames canvases by Murillo, Velasquez, and Zurbaran, and use them as package-wrappers," not to mention a private who "cuts a hole in the middle of a deframed old master and, putting it over his head, wears it as a poncho."[22]

All these concessions having been made, however, it remains the case that nothing in these literary works approaches the condition of brutal-ity in "This is worse," in which art is made to recognize its unhuman na-ture and thus its complicity in forms of misanthropy both imaginable and inconceivable. Hardy comes closest, perhaps, but one reason *The Dynasts* is such a grand botch of a work lies in the disjunction between the quasi-naturalistic verse spoken by his characters, which was largely based on historical materials, and the godlike speechifying of his Spirits, which was based on Hardy's delusion that he was a profound philoso-pher in the Schopenhauerian tradition. The wrongheadedness of Hardy's desire to turn news into epic, in fact, can be fully appreciated only in comparison to Goya's effort to do exactly the opposite.

To find a literary work adequate to Goya's vision in "This is worse," I would argue, we have to look back to the seventeenth century and to the *Leviathan* (1651) of Thomas Hobbes, who was also an eyewitness, of sorts, to a war. The philosopher of royal power was a very different sort of char-acter from the great artist of the Spanish Enlightenment, and his war was very different, too; but all the same it is Hobbes more than anyone else who anticipated Goya's insight into what Ovidian misanthropy, in its Olympian disregard for humanity, might mean for the modern world.

Today those who know anything of Hobbes know at least his charac-terization of the life of man in the state of nature: "solitary, poor, nasty, brutish, and short" (76).[23] The formula is striking but would be little more than a fine turn of phrase if it referred only to a condition pre-sumed to have existed prior to the advent of civilization. If such were the case, then war would be seen as a tragic breakdown in civilized values, just as "savages" would be seen as those whom civilization must rise above or redeem. The case as Hobbes put it was less sanguine and more sanguinary. Like many other Europeans of his day, Hobbes did see evidence of a natural state of savagery in reports of the natives of the Americas, who were said to live in a "brutish manner" (77). Such an ordinary stupidity would scarcely be worth mentioning, however, were it not for the fact that he used a passing reference to such savagery to confound the usual conclusions that Europeans drew from it. Remarkably, as the context in which he mentions them makes clear, Hobbes saw nothing exceptional in the natives of America and their reputed behavior. His reference to them is little more than an addendum to an explanation of his main concern, which was a savagery fundamental to all human life, immanent in the structures of civilization, and at the present time—as he was writing *Leviathan*—robustly manifest in the confusions of the English Civil War.

Hobbes considered that he had sound logical, theological, historical, cultural, and psychological grounds for believing that a brutish state of nature antedated the rule of law in society and still existed wherever that law was unknown or in disrepair. As he saw things, however, one did not really need to look outside of modern social life to find evidence of this nature, for every aspect of this life bears witness to savagery. Of he who might doubt this argument, Hobbes said,

Let him . . . consider with himself—when taking a journey, he arms himself, and seeks to go well accompanied; when going to sleep, he locks his doors; when even in his house, he locks his chests; and this when he knows there be laws, and public officers, armed, to revenge all injuries [as] shall be done him. . . . Does he not there as much accuse mankind by his actions, as I do by my words? (77)

Through what Giorgio Agamben calls "the indistinction of law and violence," civilization confesses its misanthropy, its war of all against all.[24] It makes this confession through the very forms, institutions, and practices that mark it out as civilization, in contrast to a presumed state of nature, in the first place. Thus, "in all times kings and persons of sovereign authority, because of their independency, are in continual jealousies and in the state and posture of gladiators, having their weapons pointing and their eyes fixed on one another, that is, their forts, garrisons, and guns upon the frontiers of their kingdoms" (78). The rule of law itself expresses the violence it is instituted to control, and it is no more possible to rationalize this institution in terms of its effects than in relation to its causes. Because the good or evil effect of any act "dependeth on the foresight of a long chain of consequences, of which very seldom any man is able to see to the end," it follows that "there is no such thing as perpetual tranquility of mind, while we live here; because life it-self is but motion, and can never be without desire, nor without fear, no more than without sense" (34–35). As the Earl of Rochester would put it in his "Satyr against Reason and Mankind" (c. 1675–76), "Man undoes man to do himself no good."[25]

True, in writing of how his words and the actions of the civilized man both "accuse mankind," Hobbes is careful to note, "But neither of us ac-cuse man's nature" (77). Scant comfort is to be had from this assurance, however, since it simply means that, prior to the rule of law, it makes no sense to speak of human nature in evaluative terms dependent on such law. The conclusion remains that men are driven by their passions or desires, which are all derivative of a fundamental craving for power that cares no more for the concept of humanity than does La Rochefou-cauld's *amour propre*. Moreover, just as locks, weapons, spies, and laws (which are "chains" [138]) confess a fundamental discord in human na-ture that renders incoherent any presumed commonality in humanity, so, too, must the mind of the individual acknowledge this, if truth be told. "For . . . the most sober men," Hobbes wrote, "when they walk alone without care and employment of the mind, would be unwilling the van-ity and extravagance of their thoughts at that time should be publicly seen; which is a confession that passions unguided are for the most part mere madness" (43).

Even if one grants him his premises, Hobbes's absolutist political stance and his theological positions do not necessarily follow from them. His writing is less notable for these points than for the disfigured image of the human with which it presents us. To say so is not to deny the historical interest of Hobbes's politics and religion or the cultural, philosophical, and rhetorical significance of the fact that he took them to be inseparable from his conception of the state of nature.[26] It is only to note that this conception has an imaginative force as well, indepen-dent of the topical debates to which it was implicitly and explicitly re-lated at the time of its initial publication.

It was this imaginative force that in his own day made "the Monster of Malmesbury" a byword for atheistic materialism, elaborate political and theological arguments be damned. Over the last century we have con-tinued to see its effect in the popular reduction of Hobbes to a slogan. When Carl Schmitt characterized Hobbes as a "truly powerful and system-atic political thinker," for example, he did not focus on the intricacies of Hobbes's reasoning but rather on "the war of all against all" as "the fun-damental presupposition of a specific political philosophy."[27] Similarly, when Foucault characterized his own work as "the exact opposite of Hobbes' project in *Leviathan*" and yet identified his conception of power with his opponent's—"I would say it's all against all"—he clearly was not concerned with the Stuart succession, the Engagement controversy, Socinianism, or the authorship of the Pentateuch.[28] Like the Nazi ideologue from whom he otherwise differed so profoundly, Foucault was taking Hobbes to represent an immemorial vision of misanthropy, one that can neither be securely historicized nor fully surpassed. Almost predictably, then, in drawing on the writings of both Schmitt and Foucault, Michael Hardt and Antonio Negri also present Hobbes in the summary image of "Leviathan" and "the war of all against all" (for which they seek to substitute a more loving and lovable image of "the multitude").[29] Similarly, when philosophers seek to rationalize Hobbes's inconsistencies and to reframe his reasoning in terms of contemporary theories of instrumental rationality, as exemplified, for instance, in the "Prisoner's Dilemma" of game theory, they effectively treat his work as a powerfully reductive image of human nature and "impossible" social relations.[30]

For Hobbes the cause of humankind's "perpetual and restless desire of power after power, that ceaseth only in death," is not that people can never be satisfied. It is rather that they can place no trust in other people, whose very existence threatens the continuation of any satisfaction. The misanthropy of the state of nature is not simply savage, then, but immemorial. We can learn that this is so simply by delving into the classics with which every humanist is expected to be familiar and finding therein the "headdie ryots, incest, [and] rapes" to which Christopher Marlowe and Goya had also paid close attention.[31] The "ancient heathen," Hobbes wrote, "did not think they dishonoured, but greatly honoured the Gods, when they introduced them in their poems committing rapes, thefts, and other great, but unjust or unclean acts" (54). Civilization does not extirpate or even alter this misanthropy; it simply organizes it through the subordination of the will of individuals to "the will and appetite of the state" (464). Since laws are never self-explanatory—"All laws, written and unwritten, have need of interpretation"—in civilized society the rule of law finally rests upon "the sovereign power" (180–81) and hence upon the state as an unaccountable agent of violence.

The law of nature cleaves humanity, marking a division between those who "may be called SOCIABLE" and those who in contrast will be called "*stubborn, insociable, froward, intractable*" misanthropes (96; emphases original). These latter, however, merely express an original state of nature still potential to all. Sociable persons are made, not born. Human beings become sociable only by virtue of the existence of sovereign power, which one must expect to appear as unhuman violence to anyone other than the sovereign. Truth and all the other virtues presumed to attend upon it, such as justice, have no inherent claim to or association with sovereignty: "The authority of writers, without the authority of the commonwealth, maketh not their opinions law, be they never so true" (180). This conclusion obtains for Hobbes's own words, as much as anyone else's: "That which I have written in this treatise concerning the moral virtues, and of their necessity for the procuring and maintaining peace, though it be evident truth, is not therefore presently law but because in all commonwealths in the world it is part of the civil law," a fact that incidentally helps to explain why people "see so many volumes published" about law, "and in them so many contradictions of one another, and of themselves" (180–81).

Given these considerations, we must conclude that misanthropy is constitutive of humanity, despite the seemingly contradictory nature of such a claim. We must also conclude that those "left or cast out of society" (95), as Napoleon was—and as Goya, Hobbes, and Ovid were—are simply the scapegoats whose sacrifice serves to sustain an aesthetic image of society, which otherwise would appear as the impossible thing it is. Like Tolstoy and Conrad after him, Hobbes judged this situation to be epitomized in the character of the barbarous duellist, whom he saw as being neither more nor less honorable than the pirate or highway thief of earlier times and, for that matter, no more or less worthy than gods given to "rapes, thefts, and other great, but unjust or unclean acts."

Hobbes mentions Homer in this regard, but Ovid is really the more apt reference here, and not only because he, like Hobbes and Goya after him, would be forced into exile from such humanity as was known to him.[32] The dedication of the *Metamorphoses* to Augustus explicitly links that sovereign to Jove and, through him, to what might be called the aesthetics of Olympian sovereignty. In the *Metamorphoses*, the indistinct boundaries between humans and gods, the powerlessness of humans before the imperious whims of the immortals, and the disguises and transformations that characterize the histories that entangle the mortal and immortal realms all serve to suggest that human nature is never only human. On the contrary, it is intimate with, informed by, and indivisible from the unhuman, in both the neutral and the malefic senses of that term. Dramatically, this identity of the human and the unhuman is expressed in moments such as that in which Daphne finds her arms "changed to branches and her hair to leaves" or, more exquisitely still (in the episode Dante, among others, was to rework), when the sisters of Phaethon find their grieving selves suddenly rooted in earth, covered with bark and fledged with leaf, "till only lips were left,/Calling their mother." (Trying to rip the unhuman bark from them, Clymene succeeds only in wounding them: "'Stop, mother, stop!'/Each injured girl protests; 'I beg you, stop;/The tree you tear is me.'")[33] Thematically, this mutually constitutive intimacy of the human and the unhuman is expressed in the immemorial relation between the transgression of boundaries and the individuation of species, between violation and sacredness, between mindless cruelty and ravishing beauty. Narratively, it is measured out in the unfathomability of the intention with which Ovid joined Jove and Augustus and thus formally honored the latter's desire to be seen as possessing a godlike character—and thus as being powerful, cruel, arbitrary, lustful, petty, henpecked, amoral, or what, exactly?[34] Is Ovid's text Minerva's tapestry or Arachne's?

There is no moral discomposure in Ovid's poetry, which does not ask whether the sovereign violence of which it tells is or should be acceptable, treating it instead like a fact of life, not excluding human life.[35] The distress evident in Goya's reworking of the Ovidian example, like that in Hobbes's *Leviathan*, is not owing to any advance in humanity, as a Hegelian interpretation might suggest. In fact, nothing could be further from the philosophy of Hegel, who saw Napoleon as a triumphant "world-soul," than the art of Goya.[36] This distress is simply a sign that philosophy, in Hobbes's case, could no longer bear itself; that art, in Goya's, found itself insufferable.

In *Leviathan*, as philosophy is transformed into an artificial man, it willingly accepts its victimization at the hands of sovereign power. In "This is worse," art is transformed into a disarmed man, figuration made disfiguration, so as to mark art's inability to memorialize human will in the face of such power. Which is more affecting, the death of philosophy or art, the voluntary or the impotent submission, will depend on the affections of individuals, I suppose. In either case, there is no greater humanity in these works than is to be found in Ovid. What is distinctive about them is simply the appearance of the modern expectation of distinction, the presumption of human sovereignty, in the moment of its assertion and its immemorial dissolution.

Chapter Four

The Injustice of Velázquez

Earlier, in readying herself for her visit to the museum, she seemed grievously altered from her usual self, virtually cut off from humanity: "I felt suddenly I was a stranger and apart from everyone else."[1] Picture yourself beside her now: entering the museum, looking around, noticing the detectives who are also looking about themselves. She is an undistinguished figure, especially in comparison to all the remarkable images, the Madonnas and such, on the museum walls. She holds a notebook and busies herself in a labored attempt to copy one of those images. A stranger, a student of art, an undistinguished figure, she is disturbed by the proximity of the detectives. These policemen are at hand because of a possible "outrage," a rumored danger that "has long been present to the minds of the authorities," who have taken special precautions on that account.[2] They do their duty, and for the moment all remains as calm as one expects things to be in a well-policed museum. Yet this atmosphere is suspenseful: "I decided at last to leave the room and to wait for a while longer."[3]

Soon thereafter she slips past the detectives, advances upon the *Rokeby Venus* (c. 1644–48) of Diego Rodríguez de Silva y Velázquez, and attacks it "with a small chopper with a long narrow blade, similar to the instruments used by butchers" (9) (Figure 10). This destructive act is an argument: a creative act.

A stranger, a student of art, an undistinguished figure who may seem as unhuman in her own way as Jack the Ripper was in his, "Slasher Mary" Richardson then says to you and the other onlookers, once she is taken into custody, "Yes, I am a suffragette. You can get another picture, but you cannot get a life, as they are killing Mrs. Pankhurst" (9). Her reference is to Emmeline Pankhurst, the leader of the Women's Social and Political Union (WSPU), who is currently suffering confinement in Holloway Prison. A short time from now, when the onset of the First World War will have led the suffragettes to suspend their militant activities, Pankhurst will recall the events of this day and comment, "Mary Richardson, the young woman who carried out this protest, is possessed of a very fine artistic sense, and nothing but the most compelling sense

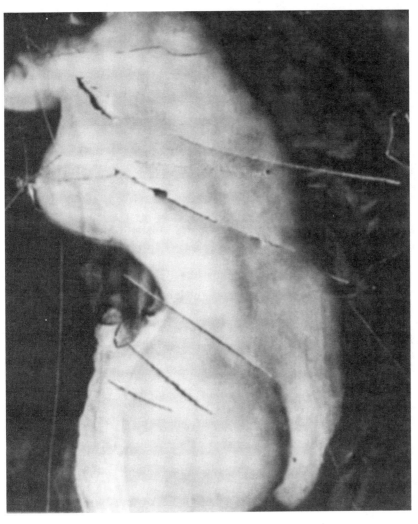

Figure 10. Diego Velázquez, *The Toilet of Venus* ("*The Rokeby Venus*") (c. 1644–48), after attack by Mary Richardson.

of duty would have moved her to the deed."[4] Contemporary readers of this statement were likely to remember that the motto of the WSPU was "Deeds not Words."

If my own readers had indeed been at Mary Richardson's side in the National Gallery on March 10, 1914, how many of you, I wonder, would have tried to stay her hand? Certainly I myself would have wished to do so, even though I would characterize myself as having sympathy for Richardson's motivations and admiration for her heroism in the cause of women's rights. At least in this respect I am unlike the art historian Robert Adams, who considered Richardson "a demented suffragette." Seeing the image in Velázquez's painting as if it were a living and pathetically suffering woman, he observed with horror that "she was savagely slashed" by this other woman who was distinguished only by her self-evident madness.[5]

Yet I am like those of you who feel some sense of loss at the news of almost any artwork's destruction, and in many cases even if previously we were completely unaware of its existence. To some extent, then, I do resemble Adams after all, as well as all those whom Anthony Julius has described as reacting with "particular dismay," or even horror, to iconoclastic acts and other "crimes against artworks."[6] Although I cannot know how many of my readers may share it with me, all available evidence would suggest that this sort of feeling is common enough to be considered normal and understandable.

Nonetheless, it is a peculiar feeling, once one comes to dwell on it; and to say that it is considered normal and understandable tells us nothing as to whether it is good, desirable, or well understood. Also, no matter how common this feeling may be, it is evident that it is far from being universal. As I cannot help but notice with some dismay, many people are not like me. In 2003, for instance, Jake and Dinos Chapman took a complete set of Francisco Goya's *Disasters of War* etchings (c. 1810–20), gleefully defaced it by doodling cartoonish heads on some of Goya's figures, and sold the result as their own work. I would never have done such a thing, and the reactions of many others show that they, too, were not amused by this stunt. One man, Aaron Barschak, even went so far as to launch an iconoclastic attack on Jake Chapman himself, throwing red paint on him at a gallery and describing this act as an artwork in its own right.[7] The Chapman brothers, however, had no trouble finding exhibitors and buyers for their iconoclastic doodlings. On a different scale but to a similar effect, in 2001 many people around the world protested the Taliban's plan to destroy the towering Bamiyan Buddhas in Afghanistan, but the Taliban could not be brought to share our feelings and proceeded with the job.

For all their differences from Richardson's audacious deed, what these acts have in common with hers is their demonstration that one cannot count on others to share one's aesthetic sensibility. That this should be the case is so obvious that it should not be in need of any demonstration, but remember: I am concerned here with what I feel, not with what I know. I am not a total idiot, and so of course I know better—*Chacun à son goût*, and so on—but still, even today, I cannot help but feel a kind of shock when I learn of acts like Richardson's. It is as if I expect my aesthetic judgments to convey a sense of subjective universality, just as Immanuel Kant insisted that they ought to do.

To make the situation more complicated still, I cannot help but notice, now that I come to think of it, that there are also times when I do not feel this almost instinctive response to the destruction of artworks. For instance, I have never mourned the elimination of graffiti from public spaces. Robert Rauschenberg's famous *Erased De Kooning* (1953), which the Chapmans have compared to their work, strikes me as a very interesting gesture, not bothering me in the least. When controversy erupted over Richard Serra's *Tilted Arc* (1981), I could not bring myself to identify with the cause of its creator, whose intransigent aesthetics seemed to me too much of a piece with his obnoxious egotism and concomitant contempt for the public. Even some of the iconoclastic acts committed by early twentieth-century suffragettes, such as the defacing of John Singer Sargent's portrait of Henry James, leave me unmoved. So in addition to impressing upon me how I am like and yet unlike others in my feelings, the issue of iconoclasm also makes me aware of inconsistencies within myself that show me to be paradoxically unlike myself or profoundly at odds with myself.

At a minimum, the issue of iconoclasm lives in the articulation of our differing sensibilities in ways such as those I have endeavored to sketch here. Richardson suggested this point when she commented, as an aside to her description of the preparations for her protest, "The fact that I had disliked the painting would make it easier for me to do what was in my mind."[8] In this case and in general, the issue of iconoclasm registers the attractions and repulsions that we feel most trivially, even below the level of conscious awareness, as well as those of a longer duration and more stunning inflexibility through which we affiliate ourselves with some, separate ourselves from others, in the name of friendship, love, solidarity, faith, principle, or diverse other forms of identification. On a more consequential scale, as in the destruction of the Bamiyan Buddhas or, later that same year, of the iconic twin towers of the World Trade Center, the issue of iconoclasm may even be played out in a war to the death among individuals, groups, or great seething masses of humanity.

In these respects the case of Richardson remains exemplary. Death was at hand in this instance, too, when she taunted the iconic representative of the iconic British Crown with her willingness to sacrifice her life. Referring to the fact that she had committed her alleged crime while temporarily released, under the provisions of the "Cat-and-Mouse Act," from the prison where she had been serving out a previous sentence, she reportedly said of the prosecutor, "He was afraid of killing her by forcible feeding and torture, but she was not afraid of dying. Therefore he was the greater coward and could not coerce her" (10).[9]

In Richardson's slighting comparison of Venus to Mrs. Pankhurst, and equally in Adams's treatment of Velázquez's icon as a real woman who is a more sympathetic figure than "a crazed feminist" could ever hope to be, what we can see is that the very image, definition, and boundaries of humanity are at stake in the activity of iconoclasm.[10] Unlike the gun that Chris Burden pointed at a plane full of passengers (747, 1973), Richardson's chopper was directed at an image, not at persons. Confounding the distinction between image and person, however, iconoclasm confronts us with the issue of how persons are defined in and through images. Burden and Richardson would always have been regarded as nothing but simple criminals were it not for the fact that their acts raised questions about how we limn the human icon.

It is because humanity is at stake in iconoclasm that Tertullian could declare that "all sins are found in idolatry and idolatry in all sins."[11] Only through such a rigorously iconoclastic attitude as his treatise on idolatry was designed to forward, he maintained, could humanity hope to deserve its name, as opposed to the name of the beast, heathen, or demon. What is more, he pointed out that idols could take any material form and that "even without an idol there may be idolatry," since this sin of all sins occurs whenever, wherever, and however one turns away from one's proper and exclusive devotion to the one true God.[12]

From the time when Plato shooed poets away from his ideal republic to the Byzantine iconoclasm of the eighth and ninth centuries, the smashings and grabbings associated with the Protestant Reformation, and the post-Duchampian pranks of our own day, this power of iconoclasm to sweep the entire nature of humanity within its acts has been widely recognized. Kant, for instance, proceeded in his philosophy from premises very different from those of Tertullian's second-century treatise, but still he came to this recognition. It is for this reason that he wrote, "Perhaps there is no more sublime passage in the Jewish Book of the Law than the commandment: Thou shalt not make unto thyself any graven image, nor any likeness either of that which is in heaven, or on the earth, or yet under the earth, etc."[13] In the iconoclastic command, according to Kant, we seem to touch upon powers that dwell within us but that remain beyond human conception, powers of moral and spiritual consequence that can neither be represented nor assailed. Sublimely, these powers send a shudder through our sensibility that enables us to feel intimations of the possible truth of free will, divinity, and immortality.

Awestruck, we shudder to feel that we may indeed be humans and not, for instance, mindless automatons, those icons of a soulless modernity to which he had referred at the end of "What Is Enlightenment?" (1784).

Furthermore, like Tertullian before him and Richardson after him, Kant was well aware that the metaphysical intimations of iconoclasm were continually expressed in the politics of worldly life. He did maintain, in his Protestant way, that "images and childish devices" were unnecessary to the conception of a moral law. At the same time, though, he noted that "governments have gladly allowed religion to be richly equipped with such supplements and thus sought to relieve the subject of the bother but at the same time also of the capacity to extend the powers of his soul beyond the limits that are arbitrarily set for him and by means of which, as merely passive, he can more easily be dealt with."[14] Save for a change in pronominal gender, Mary Richardson could not have said it better. With her chopper swinging away at the icon of a nude goddess passively enjoying her reflection in a mirror, she was a picture of Kant in action—even though Kant surely would have been appalled at such a desecrated image of his iconic male self, which took one of its sublime exemplars to be the figure of a soldier going to war.

Iconoclasm is conventionally understood as the breaking of images or, by extension, as the insulting of any treasured thing, whether by symbolic or physical assault. Precisely because the very image, definition, and boundaries of humanity are at stake in the concept of iconoclasm, however, this conventional understanding is not only insufficient but incoherent and, in fact, extremely dangerous. Whether we are dealing with issues of fitful sensibility, enduring friendship, love, solidarity, heresy, intellectual principle, or outright and unlimited warfare, Richardson's most famous act in "the war of women against men" is an exemplary case for our consideration because it is so richly suggestive on all these grounds and more.[15]

Following Richardson's example, we may see the police in the museum and may wonder: Is it even possible to conceive of a museum without police? We see the stranger in the museum: Is it even possible to conceive of a museum without such a stranger? The museum, the police, the stranger, violence against art: these things spell out parables that hold implications not only for our understanding of Richardson and the history of suffragette protests but also for how we comprehend art, culture, and social life in general.

These things are a parable, in the first place, of what David Freedberg has termed "the deep paradoxes of iconoclasm."[16] One might argue that only a reader imbued with Catholic teachings could be excited by the Marquis de Sade's scenes of desecrated hosts, sodomized popes, and the like. Similarly, Freedberg argues that, in the case of Nazi Germany as elsewhere, "The lovers of art are the destroyers of art."[17] To put this argument in the form of a parable, one might say that the police who defend art are also the strangers who attack it within a museum that practically begs for the treasures it protects to be pillaged.

Some other scholars would dissent from so sweeping a generalization or would differ with Freedberg on other grounds. It seems virtually impossible to think about iconoclasm historically, however, without being led into something like Freedberg's emphasis on paradox. Following Pierre-Joseph Proudhon in this respect if in no other, Louis Réau comments that "those who break images are as much idolaters as those who adore them."[18] Horst Bredekamp characterizes images as being produced out of a "dialectic of icon and iconoclasm" in which one person's freedom-fighting iconophile is another's terroristic iconoclast.[19] In his study of "the complex relations between iconophobia and iconophilia," W. J. T. Mitchell observes that "one might argue that iconoclasm is simply the obverse of idolatry, that it is nothing more than idolatry turned outward toward the image of a rival, threatening tribe."[20] Similarly, Margaret Aston opens her study of Reformation iconoclasm in England with the observation that symbolic destruction "is the obverse (and perhaps necessary counterpart) of the creative image-making faculty that distinguishes man."[21]

Bruno Latour has even coined the term "iconoclash" in an attempt to avoid being stymied by this sort of paradox, which was already a scholarly commonplace in the seventeenth century.[22] In the most popular treatise on memory from this era, Lambert Schenckel's *Gazophylacium Artis Memoriae* (1611), we are presented with "a dialectic between the construction and the destruction of images." This dialectic, Victor I. Stoichita argues, is closely related to a scheme in certain paintings of this period whereby connoisseurs of art are juxtaposed to animalic iconoclasts. Making a parable of iconoclasm, Schenckel's treatise proposes that one should attach mental images to ideas one wants to remember; arrange them in an imaginary chamber; and then, when the chamber becomes too full to allow new ideas a place, imagine furious iconoclasts invading the room and throwing the images to the floor. Iconoclasm, "whether it be 'interior' or 'exterior,'" is thus made to play a creative and essential role in our mental image of images.[23] The connoisseurs are also the animals.

In coming to their own formulations of the paradoxes of iconoclasm, more recent scholars take many and varied examples of such acts into account. With due allowance having been granted for all the differences among these examples, though, the kind of thing they have in mind may be typified by the case of Puritans in England who argued that their so-called acts of destruction were actually corrective acts in which an injured purity was restored to its original and proper state of being. Arguments analogous to this one are always to be found in the neighborhood of iconoclasm. Even the Chapman brothers, in their snarky way, refer to their besmirched set of Goya's *Disasters of War* as a "rectified" version.[24]

Richardson's act of protest was no exception. In this case, the deep paradoxes of iconoclasm were made explicit even at her arraignment, where the legal system quite predictably sought to ignore them. It goes without saying that no mention was made of the violence environing the provenance of this painting, which was taken from Spain to England in the course of the disorders following the Napoleonic invasion on which Francisco Goya based his *Disasters of War*.[25] Despite the controversy over the morality of Velázquez's Venus that had accompanied the National Gallery's acquisition of this painting, the *Times* even sought to head off any lingering Puritan sympathies for the type of act that Richardson had committed. In its account of her protest, the paper declared that the Velázquez was "neither idealistic nor passionate, but absolutely natural, and absolutely pure" (10). Obviously, then, as a political protester Richardson was not to expect the consideration Susan Flood had received half a century earlier when, on the grounds of indecency, she attacked a display of classical statuary in the Sculpture Garden of the Crystal Palace.[26] No matter: Richardson herself knew better than to let received ideas of iconoclasm take an uncontested grip on her public image. This was the woman, after all, who would identify Oliver Cromwell as her political inspiration when she ran for Parliament as a Labor and Independent Labor candidate in the 1920s.[27]

Richardson portrayed the prosecutor as the real iconoclast in this affair. He was the one, she said, who was making an absolute mockery of the law: "The situation was ridiculous, and Mr. McKenna had made the Criminal Code into a comic valentine." Or if she were to be viewed as an iconoclast, then those confronting her must be viewed as hopeless idolaters: "The magistrate must surely see that he could not administer the dead letter of the law against the spirit of a new law which was manifest in the women suffragists" (10). As her contemporary audience would have recognized, her allusion here was to the Pauline epistles (2 Corinthians 3: 6) and to a popular self-image of Christians derived therefrom, in which they represent the spirit of the New Testament that is supposed to have superseded the Hebraic law of the Old.

This allusion was reinforced by Richardson's account, in her statement to the *Times*, of Mrs. Pankhurst "being slowly murdered by a government of Iscariot politicians." In Richardson's presentation, the government is then both idolater, in its fetishization of the dead letter, and iconoclast, in its attempted destruction of Mrs. Pankhurst, "the most beautiful character in modern history." She herself, the supposed iconoclast, is in fact the worshipful defender of Pankhurst's image, and woe to the Pharisees who would seek to punish her on that account. "Until the public cease to countenance human destruction," she says, "the stones cast against me for the destruction of this picture are each an evidence against them of artistic as well as moral and political humbug and hypocrisy" (9). In fact, from her viewpoint the government's acts are the worst sort of iconoclasm imaginable. Mrs. Pankhurst is suggested to be an icon not only of the WSPU but of Christ, the ultimate model for imitation and image of sacrifice. So, too, by implication, was Richardson herself, she who did not fear death, knowing that "hers was the victory" (9) no matter what might come.

Since he was thought to have embodied both divine and human substance, Christ had always been a crux for iconoclastic controversies in Christian tradition, posing problems for commonplace conceptions of persons and images. With her provocative words, Richardson nailed her protest to this crux. What does Venus represent, after all, but a heathen mythology that must give way before the advent of a real living goddess? "I have tried to destroy the picture of the most beautiful woman in mythological history as a protest against the Government for destroying Mrs. Pankhurst, who is the most beautiful character in modern history" (9). Yet this *imitatio Christi* was bound to be seen as an iconoclastic act—a blasphemous, heretical, or crazed act—by those who believed the same tradition that refused women the vote certainly forbade them as well to take on the role of the redeemer. No doubt they would have been equally appalled by the plans Richardson reportedly entertained of entering "a religious sisterhood" or of "establishing a Communist nunnery of social and religious service."[28] And the complexities did not stop there, for could one possibly invoke the spirit against the letter, and Christ against those said to have betrayed him to his death, in this historical context, without flourishing the knives of Christian anti-Semitism long honed on such figures of speech? Even if we did not know that Richardson would go on to join the Blackshirts for a brief time in 1934, this question would deserve its unsettling force in any evaluation of this historical episode.[29]

With its crisscrossing lines of iconoclasm and iconophilia, Richardson's arraignment serves to demonstrate the fundamental incoherence of the conventional definition of iconoclasm, which politics drives into paradox. As Kant perhaps incautiously suggested, the desire for an iconoclastic rule is also testimony to our involvement in the agon of social life wherein sublime aspirations must always suffer articulation in relation to governing codes, laws, and sanctions, which themselves must endure the uncertainty of their own mortal limits. To put it simply, there is no rule by which we can logically distinguish a creative from a destructive act, a breaking from a making, for the arguable legitimacy of any such rule will itself be at stake in every such act.

The museum, the police, the stranger, and violence against art then also bring forward a second parable. In this parable the whole world is the museum and every element of culture in it an icon attacked by the competing claims of police and strangers, who are wont to exchange roles with each other with frustrating unpredictability.

Like the parable that summarizes the deep paradoxes of iconoclasm, this parable of the illimitability of iconoclasm has long been recognized. After all, as Gerhard Jaritz has pointed out in reference to late medieval images, the special case of attacks on art has to be seen in the context of cultural conflicts over objects of all sorts.[30] This condition of things is as old as Abraham, as recent as the culture jamming of *Adbusters* magazine, and concerns not only religion and art but also politics, economics, law, and every other aspect of social life. As Lars von Trier dramatized through his demand that Jørgen Leth repeatedly revise for him his 1967 film *The Perfect Human* (*The Five Obstructions*, 2004), conflicts over images go to the heart of social life, touching on the very definition of what it is to be a human being. A generalized version of this insight already appears in Tertullian's work, in his insistence that anything can be an icon subject to dispute, as it had appeared in Plato's parable of the cave and as it would show up many centuries later in Francis Bacon's analysis of idols in the *Novum Organum* (1620). Thomas More, however, may have given it its most cogent and distinctively modern formulation.

For the most part More sought to defend the traditional Catholic use of images on familiar grounds. He argued that iconoclastic doctrine stemmed from "the mysse takynge of the letter" in scriptural interpretation, a problem to be resolved through the combined workings of individual reason, scholastic commentary, and the guidance provided by the articles of the Catholic faith.[31] In what was meant to be a *reductio ad absurdum*, a version of this argument was used by other iconodules in this era who countered accusations that images could occasion heresy by pointing out that holy scripture had done the same.[32] More adopted the familiar medieval apology for images as the books of illiterate or lay people and added for good measure that he thought them "good bokes bothe for lay men and for the lerned to." Properly employed icons, then, were not to be understood as "dede ymages" usurping the place of the living word and so functioning as idols.[33] As one might infer from his recommendation of images to the learned as well as to laymen, he also argued for the superior, "lyuely" force of images in some circumstances, as with carvings of Christ on the cross.[34]

More's argument is most notable, though, for the subtle twist it gave to that familiar iconodule comparison of images to books. Having in mind statements such as that of the Seventh Ecumenical Council (787), "That which the narrative declares in writing is the same as that which the icon does," More also argued the reverse: that writing is itself a kind of image.[35] For "all the wordes that be eyther wrytten or spoken be but ymages representyng the thynges that ye wryter or speker conceyueth in his mynde." In other words, "all these names spoken and all these wordes written be no naturall sygnes or ymages but onely made by consent and agrement of men to betoken and sygnyfye suche thynge."[36]

The only problem with More's argument is that it proves too much. Even if we allow for the considerations of revealed truth, tradition, and church authority that More would have expected us to remember, his defense of the spirit over the letter might seem to open the way to Luther's heretical, Kant's sublime, Richardson's feminist, and von Trier's postmodern iconomachia. In defending the alleged idols of Catholic tradition, he invokes a conventionalist theory of signs with which Friedrich Nietzsche, in his *Twilight of the Idols* (1888), would not be uncomfortable, even though Nietzsche would wish to make some emendations to it. It makes a certain kind of sense, then, that More had not always written of images as he did in his *Dialogue Concerning Heresies* (1529). In his earlier *Utopia* (1516), in fact, More had established a sweeping iconoclastic rule: "Therefore in the churches no images of the gods are seen, so that each person may be free to form his own image of God according to his own religion, in any shape he pleases."[37]

In his *Dialogue Concerning Heresies*, More claims that all signs, painted, sculpted, written, spoken, or thought, rest on a basis of "consent and agrement." A logical inference from this claim, however, is that where we find resistance and dissent—even as in the outrages of Luther's followers, which provided the occasion for this treatise—a solution to the agon of social life cannot be found in the reasoned use of words. It follows that history must be represented in terms of battles in which every mortal thing, including words, institutions, traditions, and revelations, figures as an icon whose *sensus spiritualis* will be socially established or will not be. When the whole world becomes a museum and everything in it an icon, icons are, indeed, not "dede ymages" but rather living beings struggling among themselves to lay claim to representing the human ground of being. Thus did Saint Thomas More look forward to the advent of Jean Baudrillard.

In the case of the WSPU and other suffragette organizations, it was the iconicity of men and women that was most prominently at stake in this war of all icons against all icons. Richardson emphasized this point, too, in the statement she gave to the *Times*, when she implicitly compared her persecution as a suffragette to that of the adulterer whom Christ saved from being stoned (John 8: 7). In doing so she pointed to

the mutually reinforcing conventions—sexual, religious, moral, and social as well as political—to which the suffragettes' opponents sought to
make them bow down.

This was the state of things to which Thomas Hardy had pointed in
Jude the Obscure (1895), although in this case an iconoclastic attack on
Venus appears as a reactionary act. Hardy uses her landlady's smashing
of Sue Bridehead's sculptures of Venus and Apollo to prefigure the
smashing of her own proto-feminist self through her gruesome submission in marriage to Richard Phillotson. To see that the contemporary
battles over such matters were fully as metaphysical as those in the Byzantine controversies of the eighth and ninth centuries, one need only consider one of the questions agitating persons in power around the turn of
the century: could a husband justly be said to "cover" his wife in law? And
these battles were physical as well, with windows and women broken; pic-
tures and protesters put under guard; bombs planted; stately houses set
aflame; slogans written in acid on golf greens; and Emily Wilding Davi-
son, at the Derby, trampled to death under the hooves of the King's
horse while Richardson stood elsewhere on the grounds trying to peddle
a suffragette paper.

That the militant suffragettes suspended their protests and united
with their opponents to support Britain's cause in the First World War
only adds a great gruesome note of historical irony to our view of this
all-encompassing iconoclastic uproar. If we consider what that war
would do to the icons by which men then lived—*dulce et decorum est*, and
so on—not to mention what it would do to the lives of countless individual men and women, the image of social unity to which so many suffragettes lent themselves at its outbreak must appear a hideous and
profoundly iconoclastic mockery. It is no wonder, then, that Richardson
did not picture her protest as a moment of sublime exaltation when she
remembered it decades later, after her failed campaigns for office and
involvements in communism, socialism, and fascism. Instead she presented it as an act that left her, in her subsequent imprisonment, feeling
relieved that she "belonged nowhere" and so had no one to worry about
her and no one about whom she need worry: "It was evident to me that I
had touched bottom in that pit of dark nothingness during my last imprisonment."[38] She remembered her many other protests in comparable
terms. In her description of herself as she went over plans to commit
arson, for instance, she seems to have become Kant's very emblem of
dehumanization: "It was as if I had become an automaton memorising
my instructions."[39]

Out of the Great War would emerge the dada movement, whose participants had come to recognize, and with a vengeance, the incoherence of
the conventional definition of iconoclasm. Their response was to create

an aesthetics based on the illimitability of the iconoclastic act. Tristan Tzara, Max Ernst, Jean Arp, André Breton, and the others in this movement thus acted out the unreason of this war and of all the agonies of social life. Viewed retrospectively, with the example of this movement before us, what could be more dada than Richardson's slashing of the National Gallery's recently acquired masterpiece, which the *Times* so earnestly asserted was "pure" and so starchily insisted was "not that Aphrodite at all whom lovers tremulously invoke in worship and in awe"? One can readily understand why Richardson's slashed *Rokeby Venus* should be taken as a founding example of "Auto-Destructive Art" by those who paid homage to the legacy of dada when they organized this short-lived movement in 1966.[40] One can also understand why the art historian Lynda Nead, a quarter of a century later, would see Richardson's act as an anticipation of postmodern aesthetic strategies.[41] With this kind of hindsight we might see the lessons in iconoclasm provided by Richardson not only as recalling Nietzsche but also as prefiguring Mikhail Bakhtin's reflections on cultural forces that work "to destroy the official picture of events."[42] Indeed, we might see it as pointing toward all recent semiotic and cultural theory insofar as this theory presumes that in the profundities of cultural life we should not expect to find a center that holds but rather dissensus, transgression, appropriation, *différance*, masquerade, contestation, alterity, mimicry, and mutability. As Joseph Leo Koerner has put it, "Iconoclasm has become an expected cultural routine."[43]

This insight drawn from the paradoxical and illimitable condition of iconoclasm then leads us to a third parable of the museum, the policeman, the stranger, and violence against art. This is the parable of the historicity of iconoclasm. It reminds us that museums of the sort that Richardson entered had not always existed, in every cultural formation, but instead were a nineteenth-century invention, as were the bodies of municipal policemen from whose ranks were drawn the guards in the National Gallery. It reminds us as well that art, as we are accustomed to think of it, is a modern invention, and that Velázquez can be presumed to have intended his Venus for a connoisseur's private chambers, not for a public institution to which the populace would be admitted free of charge on Wednesdays, thus leading the frugal Richardson to choose March 10, 1914 for her protest. The incoherence of the concept of iconoclasm only becomes more evident when iconoclastic acts are dispersed across an endless number of historically distinct sites and occasions. It is only through this insistent historicity, however, that we can venture to say that an iconoclastic act has in fact taken place.

After all, acts of iconoclasm cannot be limited to either the literal breaking or the figurative insulting of images, as the conventional understanding of this term would have it. Instead it may be a matter of how we quite respectfully place, frame, view, or institutionalize an image. Only think of Constantine and Justinian, in the midst of their depredation of heathen temples, also gathering up certain "idols" and putting them on display in Rome as artistic or historical rather than devotional artifacts.[44] If iconoclasm is to have any meaning at all, surely it must include this sort of act, which neither breaks nor insults anything and yet so fully appropriates and reconceptualizes an object that it cannot even be said to look the same anymore. Without an insistence on historical reference, however, we would never recognize this iconoclastic act as such. On the contrary, we moderns, as Nietzsche might have put it, would see this museumification of the image as being exemplary not only of art but also of efforts to protect it against any possible destruction.

This form of iconoclasm, too, has parallels in our own day. The ongoing controversy over the Elgin marbles is a comparable case of violent despoliation that, from the thieves' perspective, figures as the worshipful preservation of art. Any such parallel becomes apparent, however, only through the historicity of specific acts, events, discourses, and institutions, which then also breaks the image of parallelism. One case cannot be substituted for another: while a discussion of Ulrich Zwingli may be relevant to an analysis of Andres Serrano's *Piss Christ* (1987), Serrano is no Zwingli, and vice versa.

To the paradoxical and illimitable aspects of iconoclasm its historicity adds a self-reflexive effect, which follows More in raising fundamental questions about the very image of the image. This effect, as it happens, became the generative principle of much twentieth-century art. For instance, when artistic and curatorial interventions have put "fine art" on a level with everyday objects or commercial images and products—thus scaring up those quotes around "fine art"—these creative-destructive acts have pointed to the insistent historicity of things, including the image of art. At the same time, self-reflexively, these acts have implicitly proposed alternative histories of art or even the very dissolution of art history. That they should have offered such propositions marks the specific history of such interventions, just as attacks on religious objects in early sixteenth-century Zurich "were carved in the language of the town, shaped and formulated, drawing upon certain connotations and associations."[45] To equate these twentieth-century acts with those of Constantine, for instance, could only be to empty them of all aesthetic and iconoclastic significance. Paradoxically and illimitably, historicity, understood as the origin of cultural productions in specific temporal and spatial contexts, breaks history, understood as the concept of an objective universality under which we presume ourselves capable of subsuming, delimiting, and judging among all such contexts. Historical conflicts break the iconic image of history and, with it, the icon of humanity. History may lead us to compare the iconoclasm of the suffragette movement to that of the French Revolution, for instance—Pankhurst's followers celebrated the fact that the date of her birth was also that on which the Bastille fell—but the image of this parallel breaks itself even as it is made.[46]

Historicity breaks the image of history: Richardson was not, after all, a Nietzschean *Übermensch*, a postmodern prankster, or a poststructuralist cultural theorist, despite how richly suggestive her protest is in relation to these contexts. The performance of a suffragette acting in the suffragette cause at a time when many other such protests were being carried out, hers remains, ultimately, an incommensurable act.[47] In fact, in attacking the *Rokeby Venus* Richardson showed a self-reflexive awareness of the historicity of art as a distinctly modern phenomenon incommensurable with the religious and political artifacts of some earlier iconoclasms and notably characterized by its relationship to capitalism.

It is unclear to what extent Richardson's motivation, in choosing the Velázquez for her attack, was based on its economic value. What is clear, however, is that Richardson was aware of the economic value of the Velázquez. Purchased in 1906 for forty-five thousand pounds, it was an especially costly work of art, as the *Times* would hasten to remind its readers in its report on the attack. The detectives had been in that room for a reason.

What is more, Richardson was clearly aware that this work in the National Gallery, like its companions there, was a symbol not only of national pride but also of the identification of art, in its modern conception, with a universal culture supposed to be open and inspiring to all. Whether or not she was aware that the *Rokeby Venus* had been paid for by the National Art Collections Fund with subscriptions "from lovers of art of every class," the free admissions on Wednesdays, of which she obviously was aware, institutionalized this ideal (9). As Dario Gamboni puts it, "Art was for every human being to enjoy, and a human being was one who enjoyed art."[48] Correlatively, we meet with a phenomenon noted by Freedberg, that "in almost every report of attacks on major objects" in the modern era the conclusion is reached "that the only possible reaction to the assault on so great a work of art, indeed the only way to comprehend it, is to see the assailant in terms which set him utterly beyond both the social and the psychological pale."[49] From the viewpoint of art, which is also the viewpoint of capital, one must be unhuman to do such a thing.

The ideological starting point for any critique of the modern conception of art is its categorical autonomy. As she took pains to emphasize in her statement upon being arraigned, a recognition of this condition of modern art was crucial to Richardson's act. She had not attacked just any image of Venus. She had attacked one that was the property of the nation, that bore a high economic value, and that represented a conception of the autonomy of art. This conception, as she saw it, was falsely imaged as being universally shared and was directly challenged by her act. When Pankhurst wrote that Richardson's attack, along with similar acts, "had succeeded in large measure in making England unattractive to tourists, and hence unprofitable to the world of business," she drew a similar connection between capitalism and the commodification of cultural identity, both national and universal.[50]

An ideological critique of the nature of art was unnecessary, perhaps, to make Richardson and the other suffragettes aware of the historicity of their actions. After all, as the WSPU motto suggested, they were self-consciously determined to transform our very conception of history: "Deeds not Words." Much as the citizens of revolutionary France had "enlightened" chateaus—that is, set them ablaze—so, too, were the suffragette arguments of rock, fire, acid, and hatchet supposed to spell out their intent by directly effecting material transformations in social life until such time as the political structure of that life was itself changed beyond recognition. Furthermore, many of the things they enlightened, such as letter boxes and golf courses, had nothing to do with the modern conception of art. Although there were other attacks on artworks, one might conclude that Richardson's most famous protest was anomalous rather than exemplary, both in terms of her own contributions to the suffrage movement and in the context of that movement as a whole.

This would be the case, however, only if we held to that modern definition of art directly assailed by Richardson. This definition exempts the art object from the paradoxical, illimitable, and historical dimensions of iconoclasm by staking its claim for distinction on its status as a formally unified, materially discrete, and culturally transcendental thing. On this account, it is not supposed to be subject to ordinary destruction of the sort to which images, in the broader sense, are susceptible, but only to accident, neglect, or unhuman criminal attack.

Richardson's challenge to this definition leads us to a fourth parable of the museum, the police, the stranger, and violence against art. In this parable, art itself is the violent stranger, and the function of the museum, like that of the police, is to protect people from its violence. The museum imprisons images to protect humans from their power, which would otherwise call established conceptions of humanity into question. Art, in this parable, is estrangement: an agency seemingly designed to put us at odds with ourselves. As Richardson's act was designed to demonstrate, art's very existence may then be an iconoclastic attack on and insult to humanity.

It is easy enough to see a basis for this parable when we consider avowedly misanthropic publicity hounds like Jake and Dinos Chapman, whose work might be described as capitalist surrealism. One takes the point when Jake says that their work is "non-human," describes it as being "structured through antagonism and hostility," or clarifies this description by announcing, "I want to rub salt into your inferiority complex, smash your ego in the face, gouge your eyes from their sockets and piss in the empty holes."[51] In a case such as this, we recognize an extrapolation of the iconoclastic impulses of modernist, avant-garde, and postmodernist work. From Édouard Manet, say, we might eventually arrive at the Chapman brothers after pausing to mention items such as Pablo Picasso's characterization of painting as "a sum of destructions"; the exhibition by Hans Haacke that Thomas Messer barred from the Guggenheim Museum in 1971 on the grounds that its politicized nature made it "an alien substance that had entered the art museum organism"; and the drawing that Serra titled, in the aftermath of the *Tilted Arc* controversy, *Support indecent and uncivil art!* (1989).[52] This view of things is not inaccurate, and yet it will prove misleadingly historical if it causes us to overlook those other qualities of paradox, illimitability, and estrangement that are equally pertinent to iconoclasm and without which art could not appear to be either human or unhuman.

As the history of iconoclastic controversies shows, objection to any particular idols depends on a more general tendency to distrust not only all evident artifice but also all sensible images, whether these be made by human hands or shaped by human organs of perception. It is not despite this immemorial metaphysical suspicion of humanity but because of it that art can gain significance as a cultural form considered to be distinctive, definitive, and inspiring. Were it not in some fundamental way a stranger to us, and did we not find in its unhuman agency a potential for violence against us, art would never emerge from the background of culture, where we would be as oblivious to it as we generally are of the fine points of phonemics when we are engaged in a casual conversation or of the physics of load-bearing materials when we are walking through a doorway. The history of iconoclasm teaches us that histories of art are imaginable only insofar as the very image, definition, and boundaries of humanity are put into question within them. In addition to proving insufficient and incoherent, then, the conventional understanding of iconoclasm is also extremely dangerous, as previously noted, because it would lead us to believe that icons play no part in the violence, whether real or symbolic, visited upon them. In other words, this conventional understanding suggests that damage can be done to icons but that icons themselves, in the ordinary course of things, do no harm. It thus further leads us to believe that the image of humanity has been made, is made, or can be made without violence being done to human persons.

Richardson knew better. Like the young Dorothea Brooke in George Eliot's *Middlemarch* (1871–72), a latter-day Puritan who cannot look at art without feeling suspicious of its "immense expense" and disturbed by the thought of people "shut out from it," Richardson was convinced that art could and should be just.[53] "Justice," she said in the statement she gave to the *Times*, "is an element of beauty as much as colour and outline on canvas" (9). Justice, moreover, demanded that violence done against living women, whom the government evidently did not value, could most effectively be redressed by violently attacking what it did value: property. Richardson's iconoclastic act brought the image, definition, and boundaries of humanity into play by its intended demonstration that the government considered property, especially the culturally idealized property of art, to be more human than women. Her act was thus a blow struck against one image of humanity in favor of another. Violence and creativity were so inseparably allied within this act that a distinction between these terms could not even be drawn unless one joined Richardson in demanding that the very concept of history be transformed through a revolution in politics and aesthetics.

This iconoclastic argument was well established in militant suffragette circles at the time. Pankhurst, for instance, tells us that she gave an address in 1912 in which she declared, "There is something governments care for more than human life, and that is the security of property, and so it is through property that we shall strike the enemy."[54] To those who might see no connection between suffragette vandalism and the cause of votes for women, she pointed out that "every advance of men's political freedom has been marked with violence and the destruction of property. Usually the advance has been marked by war, which is called glorious. Sometimes it has been marked by riotings, which are deemed less glorious but are at least effective."[55] Writing in *The Suffragette* two months after Richardson's protest, Ethel Smythe drew the logical conclusion. Although she was disturbed by the destruction of artworks, she did not believe in "great art flourishing in unclean soil."[56] This sort of reasoning also played a role in other social movements in the modern era, as in the slogan published in a Spanish anarchist newspaper in 1936, "Life is worth more than art!"[57]

Within the broader context of the paradoxical, illimitable, and historical nature of iconoclasm, thus to see how art may figure as estrangement finally allows me to explain the peculiar horror such a one as I will feel at the news that an artwork has been attacked. It is not the horror felt by those, such as Robert Adams or Thomas Messer, who worship art in its modern conception. Nor is it the horror of those, such as the *Times* in 1914 or the popular media today, who mourn the economic loss associated with an attack on art. It is not even the horror that comes from facing up to the injustice of art in the way that Walter Benjamin made famous through his declaration that every document of civilization is also a document of barbarism. No, this feeling instead belongs to the recognition that the question of justice is beside the point, as far as art is concerned. It is the creative-destructive recognition to which any adequate account of iconoclasm must lead us: that art is not and will never be just.

To come to this conclusion is not to agree with Kant's conception of the disinterestedness proper to aesthetic judgment or, for example, with Theodor Adorno's reformulation of Kantian reasoning: "art does not make judgments and when it does, it shatters its own concept."[58] Making judgments is certainly part of what art does, whether in Goya's *Disasters of War*, Burden's *747*, Velázquez's *Rokeby Venus*, or any other work. In art as elsewhere, though, the making of judgments ultimately serves to clarify for us how far we are from possessing an adequate image of justice. Artworks cannot provide a rule for their own interpretation, much less a formula for the achievement of justice as a social practice. It is because they are so weak in this respect—in "humanity"—that they can be so strong in providing us with the means to envision, challenge, revise, and renew our conceptions of justice.

This is why I would have tried to stay Richardson's hand: because we need art so that we can conceive of justice, as we cannot hope to do if we are so dangerously deluded as to think that art itself could ever be just. It is the unhuman agency at work in art that enables us—if only by comparing a painted to a living woman, as Richardson did—to confront the violence that does its work in any given conception of humanity. To fail at this recognition is to make oneself vulnerable not only to the modernist idealization of art but also, for example, to the Stalinist notion of an art that serves the masses, the fascist aestheticization of war, or the rational embrace of the furious violence at the heart of capitalist economics that led the Chapman brothers to deface their edition of Goya's *Disasters in War*, which, as it happens, had been printed in Spain in 1937 as an anti-fascist protest. Here, again, we see why the conventional understanding of iconoclasm is not only insufficient and incoherent but positively dangerous: because it serves to limit our recognition of the irreducible violence done in, to, and through art. To believe that art should do justice is to believe that there can be art without iconoclasm, which is precisely what the conventional understanding of iconoclasm suggests. This conventional understanding thus denies the reality of violence in its very recognition of it.

Art knows better, as we can see in the *Rokeby Venus* (Figure 11). Its subject is a figure historically inseparable from art itself, which tradition invites us to see as "consubstantial with the body of the goddess," as Caroline Arscott and Katie Scott have put it.[59] Like that of Helen in Chrisopher Marlowe's *Doctor Faustus*, her beauty is mythologically indivisible

Figure 11. Diego Velázquez, *The Toilet of Venus* ("*The Rokeby Venus*"). (c. 1644–48). Oil on canvas. Photo © The National Gallery, London.

from strife. An iconoclasm beyond any justice lives within the legendary image of Venus even before one considers any particular rendering of this image. Competition for admiration and conflicting aesthetic judgments, not to mention the fall of Ilium's towers and the human slaughter associated therewith, are memorialized in her conception. Velázquez was certainly aware of these implications: Velázquez the courtier, the supporter of Philip IV and of all that this monarch represented in terms of established order and injustice, Velázquez who so anxiously sought a noble title for himself and who eventually succeeded in being named a knight of the Order of Santiago. He knew something about competition, conflict, and injustice both in and out of the realm of aesthetics, did Velázquez. In Jonathan Brown's words, he "was one of those who knew how to play the game."[60]

Velázquez showed this awareness in fashioning a Venus that broke the mold of her previous artistic incarnations. As Andreas Prater writes, "The youthfully slender figure of his Venus has no comparable precursors in the more mature or portly classical and Renaissance portrayals of her."[61] The fact that Velázquez painted this Venus while he served the monarchy in Counter-Reformation Spain, where such nudes were common in collections but censured by the Church, only makes all the more apparent how his handling as well as his choice of this figure embodied iconoclastic motivations. Lest there be any ambiguity on this score, the *Rokeby Venus* stages this iconoclasm through the contrast between the exquisitely defined lines of the goddess's body, viewed from behind, and her blurred face in the mirror that Cupid holds before her. Brown has said that "Velázquez took pains to avoid comparison of Venus to any real woman by blurring the features in the mirror reflection," and it may be true that to do so was one of his concerns.[62] In any case, though, what we see in the frame of the mirror is far from being a straightforward reflection or image of a person. What we see instead is a second painting inset within the frame of this painting as a whole. Looking into the mirror, we confront alternative and conflicting styles of representation within a single icon and thus are led into a subtle meditation on the ineluctability of iconoclasm.

Moreover, if the optical laws of everyday physics were to hold, as has long been noted, Cupid's mirror should actually be showing us an image of Venus's pudendum, not her face. Whether deliberately or accidentally, Velázquez worked into this meditation iconoclastic parallels among neoclassical aesthetic ideals, lewd jokes, and the war between women and men. A figure wrought of paradox, illimitability, historicity, and estrangement, this Venus is a lesson in the justice we cannot expect of any image, as every student of art and seeker of justice should know.

Chapter Five

The Illusion of a Future

He was not the scourge of God, like Christopher Marlowe's Tamburlaine, but he did mean to be the scourge of modernity. Furiously propelled by the engines of a new century, Filippo Tommaso Marinetti proclaimed that art "can only be violence, cruelty, and injustice."[1] The misanthropy of this 1909 proclamation would be more easily dismissed today were it not for the immemorial consideration that art itself is misanthropic. Every victim of *bovarysme* who has vainly pecked at painted grapes has had cause to rue this lesson, but its teaching extends far beyond such characters. Insofar as tradition defines art by distinguishing it from human commonality—from all that Valentine de Saint-Point, author of the "Manifesto of the Futurist Woman" (1912), disdainfully referred to as "the terrain of culture"—art's claims to representation, meaning, and value must ultimately be hostile to the prerogatives of any particular conception of humanity.[2] It will oppose any such conceptions because it will recognize them, correctly, as a threat to its continuing existence. Accordingly, coming at this matter from the opposite direction, philosophers as diverse as Plato, Friedrich Nietzsche, and Theodor Adorno have noted that art is bound to appear as an upsetting lie to those who wish to arrogate humanity to themselves.

Even the least ambitious Pygmalion knows that art, as it is traditionally conceived, can appear as such only in distinction from humanity and so must challenge the self-sufficiency supposed to be possessed in and through that term. This is the reason Thomas Bernhard made Glenn Gould an unhuman *Übermensch*, an "art machine" driven by "music-misanthropy," in contrast to the *Untergeher*, or loser, of his brilliant 1983 novel about the consequences of art.[3] This is the reason art is as resistant to categorical definition as it is to progress, never getting any better and invariably making fools of those who believe otherwise.

An effort truly to identify with the future of art, then, should not lead one to any sort of humanist reverence for tradition, as is still often supposed by those who designate themselves its lovers and guardians. Instead such an identification might seem logically to entail an "antiphilosophical" and "anticultural" movement whose members might even "love battle more than Truth."[4] We might feel driven to conclude that only through such a movement could we possibly expect to see a time in which "life will no longer be simply a life of bread and toil, or a life of leisure, but in which it will be a *life-artwork*."[5]

In an attempt to live this logic, futurism turned art into war: the destruction of commonality through violence. If its practice found few disciples among the movements that followed after it, still these others have also had to come to terms with art's misanthropy. Pop aesthetics, for instance, turned art into superficiality (the destruction of commonality through ecstasy) while minimalism turned it into objectivity (the destruction of commonality through dour principle).[6] As in the case of the futurists, humanity in any particular conception is mortified by the unhuman aesthetic agency, and hence the challenging misanthropy, enacted through the approach to art in movements such as these.

In humanist tradition, this unhuman agency in art has been called forth to explain its storied ideality, transcendence, and immortality, which we may laud only insofar as we are willing to mock ourselves even to the point of embracing death as the goal of life. Tradition turns into a certain kind of modernity, however, when the agency of death always implicit in art is brought into the foreground of aesthetics. As the futurists recognized, it then follows that iconoclasm is not the antithesis to a traditional love of art but rather its logical complement, a necessary homage to art's aggressive mockery, mimetic or otherwise, of humanity. Scratch the Taliban, tickle an aesthete. Violence, cruelty, and injustice define the medium through which the communications of these seeming opponents quite predictably take place. Were one inclined to the genre of the manifesto, one might sum up this situation by announcing, as the most crucial of aesthetic guidelines, the following rule: "Every day one must spit on the *Altar of Art!*"[7]

Famous in its own time, by the beginning of the twenty-first century Marinetti's proclamation about the nature of art had been virtually forgotten. By this time a more balanced statement made by one of his critics had become a commonplace of aesthetic theory, one so endlessly recited as finally to sound like the platitudinous voice of tradition itself: "There is no document of civilization which is not at the same time a document of barbarism."[8] This is a more measured account than Marinetti's and so enables one better to articulate, for instance, the differences among irredentist futurist demonstrations, the "capitalist realism" (in Sigmar Polke's famous jape) of pop art, and the dogmatic antihumanism of minimalism. Nonetheless, and precisely because of its bully-boy bluntness, Marinetti's proclamation was not all wrong. In its praise of the death-drive in civilization, it cuts to the chase, as the splendidly vulgar artists of a latter-day Hollywood would say. It jettisons the nuances of the past, as symbolized by Romanticism, sentimental love, museums, libraries, academics, and the finicky refinements of historicist thought in any form, in favor of a future incarnated in the volatile vitality of machinery.[9] In doing so it anticipates the "half grotesque, half barbaric fetishism of the machine" that Ernst Jünger described in "Total Mobilization" (1930) as well as the amalgam of G. W. F. Hegel, Friedrich Nietzsche, and fascism in Jünger's *The Worker* (1932).[10] Moreover, it looks forward to an era in which the unhuman nature of humanity has been so fully recognized as to give birth to the term *posthuman* as the sign of our marriage with technology. Although the image of the "multiplied body" that Marinetti appropriated from Mario Morasso did not catch on, he is our contemporary in his exuberance over the prospect of "*mechanical man with exchangeable parts*," a being that would be liberated even from death through its revolutionized sensibilities, ideas, and powers.[11]

The futurist machine was the product of a poetic materialism, a drive to "replace human psychology, now exhausted, with the *lyrical obsession of matter*."[12] The goal was "to create 'non-human' poetry" as well as other arts "foreign to humanity" by way of the transformations that would follow from the mechanization of humans.[13] "One must prepare, then," wrote Marinetti in *War, the Only Hygiene of the World* (1915), "for the imminent and inevitable identification of man with motor, facilitating and perfecting an incessant exchange of intuition, of rhythm, of instinct, and of metallic discipline absolutely unknown to the majority and yet divined by the spirits of the most enlightened." At one moment in this work he was even academic (and incautious) enough to cite "the transformational hypotheses of Lamarck" in his description of his hope for the "creation of a non-human type." For the most part, though, he was content to rely on his rodomontade to supply the sole and sufficient authority for his claims.[14] "We will vanquish the apparently irreducible hostility that separates our human flesh from the metal of motors," he wrote. The machine should be seen as a "product and consequence that in its turn produces infinite consequences and modifications in sensibility, in spirit, in life."[15] Futurist hearts, he announced, "feel no weariness, for they are nourished by fire, hate, and velocity!" In disdaining love and everything associated with it, futurists might even dream of being able "to create, one day, a mechanical son, the offspring of pure will, the synthesis of all the laws by which science is about to precipitate this discovery."[16] Following Marinetti's lead, Fortunato Depero noted that contemporary "experiments with amputees" involving the application of "mechanical elements to man" might well be "the first steps toward a future *of mechanical races*."[17]

With a fine poetic justice, Marinetti's statement about art as violence, cruelty, and injustice may be said to have foretold its own future oblivion.

As an aesthetic proclamation it reduces itself, along with all other manifestations of art, to a mechanically predictable death within the very
agony of which it tells, leaving no room for the hope held out by Walter
Benjamin's utopian historicist vision. The poetically just death of
Marinetti's proclamation is evident, for instance, in the fact that contemporary visions of hybridized human-machine entities proceed with a
marked absence of reference to futurism's pioneering declaration of a
cyborg era in the making. One telling example of this neglect is Martin
Heidegger's essay "The Question Concerning Technology" (1953), in
which he predicts that our decisive confrontation with the essence of
technology will take place in the realm of art without troubling to note
that some of his fascist confrères had announced this rencontre decades
earlier. More recently, an anthology titled *Virtual Futures: Cyberotics, Technology and Post-Human Pragmatism* (1998) made only a fleeting reference
to futurism, and there is no reference to it at all in Donna Haraway's
"Cyborg Manifesto" (1985), Hans Moravec's *Mind Child: The Future of
Robot and Human Intelligence* (1988), Bruce Mazlish's *The Fourth Discontinu-
ity: The Co-Evolution of Humans and Machines* (1993), Allucquère Rosanne
Stone's *The War of Desire and Technology at the Close of the Mechanical Age*
(1995), and N. Katherine Hayles's *How We Became Posthuman: Virtual
Bodies in Cybernetics, Literature, and Information* (1999). Similarly, in the
more popular *Flesh and Machines: How Robots Will Change Us* (2002), Rodney A. Brooks makes no mention of futurism, even though he does find
time to take cheerful note of Ronald Reagan's "Star Wars" program and
to conclude one chapter with a blithe prediction that Japan will use robots to keep its society "ethnically pure."[18] Despite its central concern
with fascism, even the *Anti-Oedipus* (1972) of Gilles Deleuze and Félix
Guattari found no room to mention the movement that first popularized the image of desiring machines and then dedicated these machines
to the service of Mussolini. Considering that futurism blazed the trail for
the investments made by Deleuze and Guattari in Nietzsche, anarchism,
avant-garde writing, madness, and theatrical cruelty, as well as in the poetic materialism of machinery, the silence in this last case is especially
deafening.[19]

Marinetti and the futurist movement were about as close to being all
wrong as it is possible to be, and yet they were on to something from
which avant-garde culture throughout the twentieth century would feel
licensed to steal. It is there in Andy Warhol's wish that "everybody
should be a machine," in Claes Oldenberg's identification with a "ma-
chinelike" nature, in Sol LeWitt's claim that in conceptual art the idea
"becomes a machine that makes the art," in minimalism's idealization of
factory facture, in the anarcho-machinism of schizoanalysis, and in the
more recent euphoria attendant upon cyberpunk transgressions and the

celebration of distributed agency in posthuman prosthetizations.[20] In these later movements what might be called the civilized side of futurism—its poetic adoration of modernity, machinery, and transformations in the human subject—would be embraced. Its barbaric nationalism, militarism, misogyny, racism, and fascism, along with its foreboding name, would simply—too simply—be erased.[21]

Despite the fitting violence, cruelty, and injustice of this defacing embrace, this characteristically postmodern iconoclasm, we are still haunted by futurism. A reflection on the significance of this situation might well begin with the most ironic aspect of Marinetti's movement, which lay in its birth rather than its prefigured appropriation and oblivion. For when this movement was first announced, the future with which it named itself was already an antique. Western culture had been confronting the proposition that humans are machines for more than two hundred years before the early twentieth century.

What are we to make, then, of the way the futurists and others after them have proposed the human-as-machine identification as if it were a radically new provocation? How are we to understand this preposterous construction of the *arrière* as the *avant*, of recollection as innovation, of nostalgia as utopian desire? What can we learn from the vividness of Marinetti's misanthropy, which has descendents as various as J. G. Ballard's *Crash* (1973), *Robocop* (1987), the music of Einstürzende Neubauten, the technoporn of Tom Clancy thrillers and Sharper Image catalogues, and the libertarian-tinged cult of extropianism, but which nonetheless has been repressed among the later cultural movements that have put a smiley face on futurist themes?

The machinery in question here ranges from the bicycles, locomotives, automobiles, planes, and factories of the earlier decades of the last century to the "killer apps" of computer technology that have dominated the public imagination more recently. In the present context such differences are of little moment, however, since in futurism and these later cultural movements it was the abstracted image of the machine that was of critical importance. Whether the things transforming humanity are pictured as futurist Bugattis or digitalized posthumanist entities—or, for that matter, as Cartesian springs, pulleys, and pumps— *machine* has generally been treated as a term that is fundamentally polemical in significance, with the details of particular technologies serving mainly to provide bits of anecdotal color.[22] Such being the case, it might yet be objected that the last century's appropriations of the machine, from the futurist era on, were genuine innovations insofar as they concerned art as a specific field of cultural activity. In the end, however, this response would simply direct us to the exhibitions of helicopters, Harley-Davidsons, and other industrial manufactures in museums of modern art in the late twentieth century—a curatorial breakthrough that is centuries behind the times, as any reader of the accounts of machinery in the *Encyclopédie*, for example, ought to be able to appreciate. It cannot be objected, either, that until recently the machine has been recognized only as an inessential part of or supplement to humanity, conceived of, for instance, as a bodily rather than a spiritual thing. In the propaganda of futurism, in the Symbolist works from which it borrowed some of its energies (such as Villiers de l'Isle-Adam's *Future Eve* [1886]), and on into the present, this straw man of an outdated humanism has been a useful foil to the projected machine men and women of the future, but it has been no less of an empty threat for all that. To give just one example, any reader of E. T. A. Hoffmann's "The Sandman" ought to have noted the author's judgment of how juvenile one had to be, in the modern era of 1816, to be affrighted by the similarities between human and mechanical things.[23]

Since the seventeenth century it has been commonplace to recognize the unhuman—the machine, in Descartes's formulation—within humanity. Bluntly represented as the foundation of statecraft in Thomas Hobbes's *Leviathan* (1651), the identification of the human body with machinery served Spinoza as a formula for reprobation when he said that skeptics "must be regarded as automata, completely lacking a mind"; caused some worry to John Locke, who was disturbed that "*Morality*" and "*Mechanism*" were "not very easy to be reconciled, or made consistent"; and was celebrated in the eighteenth century in the delirious materialism of Monsieur Machine himself, Julian Offray de la Mettrie.[24] Reactions, obviously, were various. Even Descartes's rigorously incomplete identification of humanity with machinery led many to regard as scandalous or, at best, needlessly provocative the human relations with machines that he did acknowledge. Once admit machinery into the conception of humanity and there might seem to be nothing to stop it from entirely assimilating this conception to itself, just as the hypermachinic Borg so quaintly and anachronistically threatened to do in the late twentieth-century television series *Star Trek: The Next Generation.* As Théophile Bordeu commented about Descartes in his *Researches in the History of Medicine* (1768), "One must admit that this was never the intention of this great man, but his system could offer room for falling into that error."[25] The example of Descartes, the physics of Robert Boyle and Isaac Newton, the iatromechanism of Hermann Boerhaave, and the wonderful androids of Jacques de Vaucanson, among other influences, had made *machine* a common synonym for *body*, in both French and English, by the mid-eighteenth century—just as it is in Marinetti's manifestoes, as when he refers, in good Enlightenment fashion, to "the human machine."[26]

By the 1700s it was unquestionable that humanity, as recognized by leading figures in European intellectual life, had entered into a different relationship with machinery and, having done so, was being forced to reconceive itself. The question Nietzsche raised in the following century—"Are there still human beings, one asks oneself, or perhaps only thinking-, writing- and speaking-machines?"—is both literally and figuratively, or materially and poetically, related to the androids that had fascinated Descartes in the seventeeth, La Mettrie in the eighteenth, and Hoffman earlier in the nineteenth century.[27] Not despite all the controversies over its participation in sentient life but because of them, the machine had become an inescapable reference point for statements on the nature and future of humanity. It took on this role in the superbly defensive final sentence of Immanuel Kant's "What Is Enlightenment?" (1784), with its hope for a humanity that does not consist of automatons, and it plays a similar role at crucial points in the works of David Hume, Nietzsche, the Symbolists, and many others.

The novelty of futurism, then, did not lie in its identification of humanity with machinery. On the contrary, in the case of Marinetti as in that of Andy Warhol, to want to be a machine could only be a form of willed naivité or, in other words, a manifestation of civilized barbarism. In the twentieth century this attitude expressed as desire what ought to have been known as a historical truism long institutionalized in military, industrial, and educational organizations and further attested to by centuries of tradition in science, medicine, philosophy, and art. Hundreds of years before Marinetti updated J. K. Huysmans's comparison of a locomotive to a woman, in *À rebours* (1884), by favorably comparing an automobile to the *Victory of Samothrace*, the proposition that human beings were a species of machinery had ceased to be novel.[28] As any *philosophe* worth his salt might have explained, to wish to be a machine must mean that one desires, absurdly, to be what one already is.

As is well known to all who have been stimulated by the shlock of the new in artworks such as the 1960s TV series *The Jetsons* and the 1982 movie *Blade Runner*, not to mention forebears such as the Depression-era *Buck Rogers* comics and radio shows, projections of the future are always anachronistic. (To get a sense of how antique our fetishization of computers will eventually appear, one need only consider the daring futurist comparison of the mind to . . . a typewriter!)[29] Yet this insight, however trivial in itself, holds a nontrivial implication for our understanding of futurism. Since the seventeenth century the machine has figured as that which holds within itself the future: the fullness of time wherein all metaphors have a chance to become literal. The machine, then, has also figured as a force that is bound to be disruptive of established conceptions of humanity. For thinkers engaged by this figure, the consequence has been a tendency to embrace a specified future—of Lockean experience, of Kantian Enlightenment, of Sadean desire, and so on—while effacing the metaphoricity of the machine and, along with it, the metaphysics of materialism. Therefore, to the futurist contempt for the nature of romanticism, which Marinetti and others saw as so much ideological machinery decked out in trembling foliage and moonlight, the Romantics might have replied *tu quoque.* There certainly was ideological machinery in the nature of romanticism, but it is of a kind with the ideological nature of the futurist machine, which can embrace its future only by effacing its past. Futurism provides a case study in the iconoclastic aesthetics that logically develop out of the early modern era in which the machine became a foundational term for humanity, and, as is shown by the cases of pop art and minimalism, among others, we have scarcely begun to appreciate the consequences of this consequence.

In its general misanthropy as in its specific adoration of the machine, futurism reproduced the past it disavowed. After all, misanthropy, too, has always figured as the naive desire to be the thing one already is. In fact, the conventional understanding of misanthropy as spoilt idealism demands this seeming contradiction. This understanding reassures us that one cannot really be a misanthrope, for the so-called misanthrope is simply one who is waiting to be reconciled to the humanity that he or she loves too well. From the *Phaedo* on through to Lucian's, Plutarch's, and Shakespeare's Timon, Molière's Alceste, and the furious works of Thomas Bernhard, this understanding has been codified as a tradition in the representation and psychological interpretation of character. It was most fully developed, perhaps, in the eighteenth century, in works ranging from Jonathan Swift's *Gulliver's Travels* (1726) to Henry Mackenzie's *Man of Feeling* (1766), August von Kotzebue's *Misanthropy and Repentance* (1788), and Friedrich Schiller's *The Misanthropist Reconciled* (1790). Loving not wisely but too well, in works such as these the misanthrope is commonly understood to be an exemplary representative of humanity even as he turns away from the world in utter disgust.

As Nietzsche suggested in his critical revision of this tradition, however, the conventional approach to understanding the misanthrope misunderstands just about everything. In the first place, this approach guarantees that all inquiries about humanity can only be pseudo-questions that have always already been answered. Just as importantly, this approach fails to recognize that the misanthrope by definition cannot be a timely figure—in other words, cannot be one's contemporary, a member of one's group or movement. To be contemporary would mean that one belonged within an established conception of humanity and thus was not really a misanthrope at all. In contrast, Nietzsche's portrayal is of a figure who is lost in the present, waiting for the past, and haunted by the future. In other words, his misanthrope is not a figure of humanity's disappointment with itself but rather an outsider to all its conventions, not excluding its conventional self-loathing and self-destructiveness. Like Bernhard's Glenn Gould, Nietzsche's *Übermensch* is a figure, above all, of art. More specifically, he is a figure of the anachronistic ontology of art, of the sublimity of the very notion of art, which does not advance in time with humanity.

It was with good reason, then, that Marinetti took pains to dissociate his movement from the example of Nietzsche's Zarathustra, for Marinetti was nothing if not conventional.[30] Despite his debts to the German philosopher, which were already noted by contemporary commentators such as René Huyghe and former adherents of the movement such as Gino Severini, F. T. Marinetti was no Friedrich Nietzsche.[31] Fiercely seizing on the supreme cultural commonplaces in the Europe of the last decades of the nineteenth century—the glory of war, nationalism, colonialism, manhood, and creative genius—he contributed to the invention of futurism by vociferously declaring his desire to be precisely what, in fact, well-established tradition declared that he was: a machine. Faithful to the conventional understanding of misanthropy, his unhuman machinery ultimately imaged the redemption of humanity, as when he called for the "magnification of the sense of the human and the urgent necessity to establish our relations with all of humanity at every instant."[32]

Of course, like every village atheist and tub-thumping patriot, Marinetti did not consider himself to be conventional. On the contrary, he was simple enough to believe that to embrace one's machine nature was to move toward liberation from oppressive social structures. He considered that the technological multiplication of desires and intuitions and sensations meant ever more and greater beauties were to be had in a future that had shaken the dust of the past off its angelically streamlined metal wings. Accordingly, in the "Technical Manifesto of Futurist Painting" (1910) signed by Umberto Boccioni, Carlo Carrà, Luigi Russolo, Giacomo Ballo, and Gino Severini, "the pain of a man is as interesting," we are told, "as that of an electric lamp, which suffers, and agonizes, and screams with the most heartrending expressions of pain."[33]

In other words, Marinetti was simple enough to believe that to be unhuman was a revolutionary act. It followed that he would also believe humanity was not unhuman in its traditional subordination of women, racial pride, identification with martial values, attachment to geographical father- and motherlands, and devotion to glorious destruction in art as in life. How could he have been so misguided as to consider his banalities the insights of genius? And how can it be that his profoundly arrière-garde positions continue today to swagger their way through works that sedulously avoid any mention of futurism?

Whatever mistakes he may have made (and of course there were many, both admitted and otherwise), Nietzsche never made this one of believing that humanity had ever not been unhuman. His difference from Marinetti in this respect is evident, for example, in the several ways *Thus Spoke Zarathustra* (1883–85) is designed to critique the conventional understanding of misanthropy. Early on, Nietzsche arranges for his protagonist to encounter a misanthrope of the most conventional kind, a religious hermit who has loved humanity only too much and so has left the world to live in solitude. In the wilderness he has transferred all his love to God as he has come to understand that man is "too imperfect a thing." "Love of man would kill me," he says. An eremitic Polonius, he tries to give Zarathustra advice, which Zarathustra politely sidesteps and parries until he takes his leave, marveling that the "saint in the forest" has not heard that God is dead.[34]

Nietzsche thus presents his readers with the figure of tradition to which his protagonist is most closely related and with which he is most likely to be confused. Having done so, he allows that figure its conventional interpretation, in which its misanthropy is attributed to misspent idealism. Then, however, Nietzsche moves him to demonstrate the incoherence of this interpretation through his own words, in which love comes to confess its hate and its devotion to death. Nietzsche continues this critique throughout the narrative, in which Zarathustra's expressions of love for humanity must continually struggle to differentiate themselves from contemptuous moods, thoughts, and actions. His love of solitude, similarly, must struggle not to be subsumed within a conventional understanding of misanthropy. "In solitude," he says, "whatever one has brought into it grows—also the inner beast. Therefore solitude is inadvisable for many. Has there been anything filthier on earth so far than desert saints? Around them not only was the devil loose, but also the swine."[35]

In addition to appearing to the hermit as an old acquaintance and fellow solitary, Zarathustra appears to him as an iconoclast and as an artist. Through these scrupulous differentiations Nietzsche further registers his protagonist's superficial associations with and profound rejection of the monk. Like Zarathustra, the monk is unhuman in his humanity; unlike Zarathustra, he does not know it. Like Zarathustra, he represents an aesthetics, of picturesque nature and melancholy Romantic solitude, suffused with death; unlike Zarathustra, he considers this situation to be moral and fitting. Like Zarathustra, he is a misanthrope; unlike Zarathustra, he does not recognize that to be a misanthrope is to be lost in the present, waiting for the past, and haunted by the future. Therefore, whereas the monk has no real questions about humanity, about which he offers Zarathustra his sententious advice, Zarathustra will ask, "if humanity still lacks a goal—is humanity itself not still lacking too?"[36]

Scratch the melancholy of a monk grubbing for roots in the wilderness, tickle the exuberance of a band of futurists speeding around the industrialized streets of Milan. To a certain extent, again, this is a trivial point: at the end of the day, the village priest and the local atheist lift a glass together at the café. One cannot be as fervently anti-clerical as Marinetti was—or, for that matter, as anti-feminine, anti-Romantic, anti-traditional, anti-Semitic, and so on—without clinging to an extremely literal, and hence credulous, conception of that which one supposedly opposes.[37] This semiotic, psychological, and sociological triviality also becomes a significant point, however, if one considers its implications for the futurist assumption that humans have yet to become machines. Could it be, we can imagine Zarathustra marveling, that they have not yet heard that *humanity is dead?*

In Nietzsche's conception, misanthropy, which is the ultimate in barbarism, is not to be distinguished from the highest pretensions of civilization or art: "Evil I call it, and misanthropic—all this teaching of the One and the Plenum and the Unmoved and the Sated and the Permanent. All the permanent—that is only a parable. And the poets lie too much."[38] Had the futurists recognized, as Nietzsche did, that art can be distinguished from life only through the perception within it of an unhuman agency, a "lie," disruptive of any given conception of humanity, they might still have seen something aesthetically new in modern machinery. They could not have vaunted their cars and airplanes, however, as harbingers of a future transformation of humanity. Nothing is more passé, Nietzsche might have told them, than looking to the future. In contrast to their expectant viewpoint, Zarathustra's encounter with the monk is designed to illustrate the definitively anachronistic ontology of any misanthropy, and any art, worthy of the name.[39]

Nietzsche's politics are scarcely more attractive than the futurists', and in any case it would be silly to argue for or against Marinetti's reading of Nietzsche as if its correctness were now a significant issue. In this comparison of the two, the point must rather be to clarify the particular kind of evil that attends upon the naïveté represented by the futurists in their cult of the machine.[40] As Nietzsche's work can show us, it was not only so that he might privilege his own genius and the genius of his movement that Marinetti had to disavow any relationship between the *Übermensch* of *Zarathustra* and the multiplied man of the future. Simple rivalry was surely a motive, as it was in the futurists' spats with the cubists, and Nietzsche's philological and historical interests, as well as his nationality and his attitude toward nationalism, presumably provided

Marinetti with others. Most important, though, is that a comparison to Nietzsche's *Übermensch* would not have allowed futurist misanthropy the novelty, the martial glory, it so desperately claimed for itself. What is more *civilized* than *misanthropy?* one can imagine Zarathustra asking, his mouth twisted in a sardonic grimace.

In conventional Enlightenment fashion, Marinetti presented himself as one who belonged to the present and who was committed to progress and thus to the transcendent future. If he had ever actually confronted his implication in his own time, and thus in his own misanthropic aesthetics, he would have been compelled to recognize how the anachronistic ontology of art dislocates the present within an anticipated past and a haunted future. He still might have misread Nietzsche, he still might have been a thoroughly nasty piece of hypermasculinity—haunted by the future as we all are, our counterfactual histories will ultimately prove speculative, just like the factual ones—but he could not have proudly identified his thinking with his times. To make him gloriously contemporary in spite of the violence, cruelty, and injustice of art was precisely the function, and remains the admonitory fate, of the futurist machine.

Marinetti could consign Nietzsche to the past because he read him, to the extent that he read him at all, with such historicidal literalness. Nietzsche belongs to the past, he concluded, because he mentions past things. Marinetti's view of machinery was just as literal: it changed things, and so it was progressive. Indeed, he did have an excited image of shiny metallic fast things, but Marinetti did not have the least understanding of what a machine might be, nor could he have had one, nor did he want one. As Marjorie Perloff has written, the machine per se was a "non-issue" in futurism.[41] What Marinetti actually wanted was a mechanism to seize upon the future and thus to cease being haunted by it, and he and his cohort designed a thing they called the machine to achieve this end.

The futurist machine was designed for the purpose of producing the futurist movement immediately, automatically, and necessarily, thus putting its art beyond question. Producing itself, the machine produced the literalism of a will responding to, or in fact demanded by, its times. To be demanded by the times was also, not incidentally, to be demanded by one's nation and race: to be the spontaneous development, as Boccioni put it, "of the profound will of a race" and of "its fundamental and characteristic sensibility."[42] As a matter of necessity, the machine would exempt itself and those who identified with it from the necessity of anachronism of which art tells. Thus would tradition become modern. The futurist movement, Marinetti wrote in 1940, "did not and still does not want to destroy the ancient inspirational motives of humanity but to

enrich and enlarge the sensibility of creators [and] by means of absolutely virgin motives to bring them to the same level as the motives
hitherto employed."[43]

As Giovanni Papini noted as early as 1914, Marinetti was inclined to
take literalist views of things in all the aspects of his aesthetics, not just in
its organizing conception.[44] As in his reading of Nietzsche, this literalism
would often be so simplistic as to appear flat-out stupid. Like a humor-
less John Waters (whose invention of Odorama was not meant as a send-
up of futurism, but could have been), Marinetti invented "Tactilism"
and other futurist arts with an energy frequently as witless as it was exu-
berant. He was enamored of onomatopoetic effects, for instance, because he thought they made poetry more direct and physical and so less
"literary," in the old-fashioned sense. Since futurist machines were also
characterized by their velocity, he experimented with syntax, punctua-
tion, and typography in an attempt to embody speed in the very form of
poetry. Since futurism was a revolutionary movement that disdained individuality as the fetish of an outmoded liberalism, one was enjoined to
avoid the first-person singular in one's writing and, along with it, all
"psychology."[45] In keeping with the futurists' identification with machinery, their oratory also should be mechanical: one should "completely dehumanize the voice" and "completely dehumanize the face" in the act of
declamation.[46] By eliminating romantic love, marriage, and the conventional family, Marinetti argued, his movement would finally abolish "the
mixing of the males and females" that "produces a damaging feminiza-
tion of males" through literal contact with girlie cooties, apparently.[47]
Futurist dance (long before the disco era's "Robot") should "imitate machines through gesture and movements" so as to "prepare for the fusion
of man with the machine."[48] Marinetti loyalists such as Luigi Russolo, with
his "art of noise," which was meant to reproduce the soundscape of the industrialized city, followed his literalist lead.

In Marinetti's manifestoes as in virtually all futurist proclamations and
demands, we are made witness to a way of thinking that might truly
seem mechanical and thus persuasive evidence of Marinetti's success in
turning himself into a machine. Futurist machines were not supposed to
be merely mechanical, however, as this trope is commonly understood.
Instead, they were supposed to be "furnished with the feline scent of
lightning calculation, of savage instinct, of intuition, of cunning, and of
temerity."[49] The literalism in evidence here can but serve further to illustrate the antiquity that disfigured the futurist movement. It is a literalism that could have no idea what it was being literal about, and so one
destined to be subject to the fantastic imaginary forces—as of art, mas-
culinity, nation, and race—being bruited about, with hellish consequences, at the time.

A similar literalism, similarly presented as an attack on bourgeois humanism, a commitment to progress, and a sign of the times, appeared in other twentieth-century cultural movements of the sort to which I have previously referred. Frank Stella, for instance, gave voice to this style of unthinking in describing the difference between "the old values in painting—the humanistic values" and his own work. "My painting," he said, "is based on the fact that only what can be seen *is* there. It really is an object."[50] In praising the virtues of three-dimensional objects, Donald Judd proclaimed that three dimensions "are real space" and, therefore, objects shaped to that space mean good riddance to the illusionism that is "one of the salient and most objectionable relics of European art." Furthermore, he explained that industrial materials could make art still more "specific," especially if they were used "directly," because "they are simply materials—formica, aluminum, cold-rolled steel, plexiglas, red and common brass, and so forth."[51] Similarly, in 1967 Robert Morris wrote, "The new three-dimensional work has grasped the cultural infrastructure of forming itself that has been in use, and developing, since Neolithic times and culminates in the technology of industrial production." Here, again, as in the case of Marinetti, we find a manifesto for an art seemingly demanded by the times, as exemplified especially by the machine and by the promise it might give of finally tossing out the "rotting sack of Humanism."[52] Although he used it in a somewhat different sense than mine here, it was with good reason that Michael Fried, in his famous essay on "Art and Objecthood," preferred the term "literalist art" to minimalism and the other labels then being mooted.[53]

In this 1967 essay Fried went so far as to hint at a significant relation between minimalist and fascist aesthetics.[54] I should note, then, that my reasons for comparing futurism to the later cultural movements I have mentioned, which efface its name and politics while embracing its machinic tropology, do not extend to suggesting anything of this kind. After all, long before futurism announced itself it was commonplace for artistic movements to create heuristics in the form of convictions: rules for production couched as the spiritual and material demands of one's time. Whatever else one may look to find in their words on their own art and that of others, one anticipates this sort of narcissism in artists' pronouncements, just as one does not expect artists such as Morris, Judd, and Stella to be rigorous thinkers. The literal turn of mind that they shared with Marinetti is the effect of a heuristic, an imaginary machine, that was designed to make their works possible, new, and revolutionary by snatching them away from the anachronistic ontology of art.

This tempting machine promises to make one's art a necessity of one's time, rather than yet another example of an immemorial necessity that participates in every aesthetic, including those of the posthumanist variety. Nonetheless, futurism and the later movements that have unwittingly followed it were not only beating a horse that was well and truly dead but one always already dead, thanks to the unhuman agency that makes the life of art, as well as its death, conceivable. In Marinetti's case in particular, he was simple enough to believe that it was something new for art to hate humankind even though art has figured immemorially as a hallowed desecration of humanity.

Morris and Judd and the others, like Marinetti, did not have a clue as to what a machine might be. They could not have used its image so polemically if their presumed contemporaneity had not in fact been passé, devoted despite itself to a dead image of humanity. Like Marinetti's, therefore, their attitudes toward machines had more in common with those of cargo cults than with those of scientists or engineers. That is why they could wish for a thoroughly misanthropic art and still make things perfectly suited for museum display. If instead they had recognized the misanthropic agency at work in the art to which they vainly sought to condescend, they still might have made the things they did. The motivations in, of, and around these things, however, would have made them look very different to people both then and now. One might mention the violence, cruelty, and injustice, for instance, that would have had to be figured into the dimensions of these things, disrupting the willed naïveté, the civilized barbarism, that gave them their contemporary glamor. One might say the same of the glamorous fetish that *Anti-Oedipus* became in certain vanguard circles and also of the techeuphoria that is currently devoted to suppressing the name and foreboding example of futurism.

The denegation of futurism in cultural movements devoted to machinic tropologies is as delusional as it is dangerous. For even though Benjamin was brilliantly insightful about the evil Marinetti represented, Marinetti's dictum about the nature of art has something to teach us about Benjamin, too. Benjamin's saying differs from Marinetti's in its treatment of violence, cruelty, and injustice as being coexistent with and yet, it might seem, incidental to art. Implicitly, he presents them as matters that are contingent or, in principle, remediable.[55] Marinetti's saying, on the other hand, gets at the platitudinous destiny of Benjamin's words about documents of civilization being also documents of barbarism. It suggests how traditional these words were bound to be, despite the radical intentions they were supposed to represent.

Marinetti certainly did not know better than Benjamin. If he had known better, he could not have lived such a stupid and despicable life both in and out of art. In spite of himself, however—even in spite of his own literalism—he recognized the necessity of misanthropy without which art is unimaginable unless or until it can become indistinguishable from life. So D. H. Lawrence praised him for his attention to the "non-human, in humanity," even as he excoriated the "crassly stupid" futurists for their pseudo-scientism. "Instead of looking for the new human phenomenon," Lawrence complained, "they will only look for the phenomena of the science of physics to be found in human being."[56] The contortions so many critics have gone through in trying to separate futurism from its fascist associations—from the brutal conventions to which it was so literally devoted from the beginning—are themselves evidence of the misanthropy people desire, and find, in art. And considering how the ancient desire for an art indistinguishable from life has repeatedly, mechanically, been rediscovered ever since the early twentieth century—as in surrealist aesthetics, Heidegger's rhapsodies over "that brief but magnificent time" in ancient Greece when he supposed that art had been all in all, Joseph Beuys's shamanism, the Situationist International, the Fluxus group, and recent paens to the liberatory potential of the Internet, to name just a few of its avatars[57]—it should become obvious, once again, that we have scarcely begun to appreciate the admonitory fate of the modern machine, whose future continues to haunt us.

Chapter Six

The Akedah on Blanket Hill

"Stones were thrown, then bullets fired": with these words the President's Commission on Civil Unrest introduced its account of the events that led to the slaughter of four students and the wounding of nine others at Kent State University on May 4, 1970.[1] In its conclusion the Commission's report did offer a more detailed evaluation, which deplored the violent behavior of some students while castigating in even stronger terms the roles played by National Guard troops, their officers, and university officials. Without assigning blame to anyone in particular, the report stated that the shootings of the students need not and ought not to have happened. It offered no opinion on the United States' invasion of Cambodia, which had provoked protests nationwide as well as at Kent State, including a demonstration during which police shot two students at Jackson State on May 14 of that same year. The Commission, however, was willing to go so far as to state that it was appalled by the outcome of the antiwar protests in this provincial Ohio town.

Still, that terse, haunting, almost poetic summary—"Stones were thrown, then bullets fired"—aptly conveys the sense of fatality in the Commission's final deliberations. Its report displays in an exemplary form the fetishistic attention to detail, numbing lack of affect, and savage devotion to neutrality characteristic of this sort of official document. We learn of the number of times one slain student was earlier observed giving the finger to the National Guard troops; of the stones found in another's pocket; of who among the victims was just trying to get to class; of a favorite student chant, over the course of that weekend, having been "One, two, three, four, we don't want your fucking war." We are offered quotations from interviews with guardsmen, students, faculty, administrators, and townspeople. Inexcusable mistakes were made, most assuredly, but still one is left with the impression that responsibility for what happened lay beyond any particular humans, even beyond humanity, in a realm transcending history that convention would assign to religion, philosophy, or art.

The disposition of the ensuing judicial proceedings was in accord with this judgment. Although three people were convicted of offenses related to the protests, all criminal charges against the guardsmen were summarily dismissed. Civil court cases were also pursued, but they led to nothing but a miserable payment of $675,000 to the plaintiffs, who also received a token expression of regret for the "tragedy" signed by the guardsmen and the governor of Ohio. It would seem that what happened was a concatenation of occurences from which we might draw some lessons in hindsight—suggestions as to future regulations, procedures, and preparations—but which at the time had simply spun out of human control. The determinedly responsible language of the report tells us that no one was really responsible. Stones were thrown, then bullets fired, as if by an unhuman power of their own. Reasonable readers of the report might well shake their heads and say that it was, indeed, quite a tragedy, to use the term promoted by Robert White, the President of Kent State University at that time, and by Richard Nixon, the crook then resident in the White House, before it was adopted by the ostensibly penitent guardsmen and governor.[2]

Years later, when he was commissioned to create a sculpture to commemorate that day's events, George Segal visited the campus, spoke with university officials, and read James Michener's book about the shootings. At the former chicken farm in New Jersey where he had his studio, he then came up with a design for the sculpture, which he constructed by his signature method of making plaster casts from live models. Segal was and remains best known for his depictions of so-called ordinary people in generic contemporary settings such as doorways, bedrooms, diners, buses, and shops. His works have often been compared to the paintings of Edward Hopper. Prior to the Kent State assignment, though, he had also been drawn to Biblical subject matter in an early piece (the 1958 *Legend of Lot*) and in a 1973 work made in response to a commission from the Tel Aviv Foundation for Literature and Art, *The Sacrifice of Isaac* (Figure 12).[3] In 1978 he returned to this last subject, fashioning a remarkably different image of the sacrifice for *Abraham and Isaac: In Memory of May 4, 1970, Kent State University* (Figure 13). A war of words then broke out when a new president of the university, Brage Golding, saw what Segal had wrought and refused to accept the sculpture for installation on campus, deeming it "inappropriate."[4]

"It seems preposterous that Biblical allegory was perceived as radical," the art critic and historian Lucy Lippard has written, and so indeed it may seem if one thinks in general terms of how the Abrahamic legend is officially hallowed in all three "religions of the book," Judaism, Christianity, and Islam.[5] In some of his own pronouncements on the matter, Segal professed a similar bewilderment. He described his work as "a call for compassion and restraint" and said, in response to suggestions that it

Figure 12. George Segal, *The Sacrifice of Isaac* (1973). Plaster. Art © The George and Helen Segal Foundation; licensed by VAGA, New York. Collection of the Tel Aviv Museum of Art. Gift of the Tel Aviv Foundation for Literature and Art

might provoke violence, "I don't ever remember seeing a work of art that inspired violence."[6]

As in these instances, Segal's public statements about art were often cast in a form that evoked a genially vague democratic humanism of a sort that was commonplace, if somewhat old-fashioned, in the intellectual and artistic circles he joined when he came into his mature style in the mid-twentieth century. Unsurprisingly, then, in one of his public statements about the Kent State controversy he took pains to point out that the "cruel story" of the sacrifice of Isaac has "a happy, compassionate ending," even though his sculpture dealt with "the terrifying moment just before the appearance of the angel and the ram" through which God intervenes to offer Abraham's knife an alternative to his boy's neck.[7] Before the president of KSU decided that any compromise would be insufficient, Segal even acceded to Golding's request that an inscription of the story from Genesis 22 be added to the sculpture so as to assure viewers that Isaac was spared.

Figure 13. George Segal, *Abraham and Isaac: In Memory of May 4, 1970, Kent State University*. Bronze. Art © The George and Helen Segal Foundation; licensed by VAGA, New York. Photo courtesy Princeton University Art Museum. The John B. Putnam, Jr., Memorial Collection, Princeton University. Partial gift of the Mildred Andrews Fund.

I have no reason to doubt the sincerity of the humanistic terms in which Segal defended this sculpture as well as other controversial works, such as Richard Serra's *Tilted Arc* (1981) or his own 1992 *Gay Liberation* (which Segal staunchly maintained was not a "political statement").[8] Nonetheless, Segal was not only a former chicken farmer but also a canny artist and a well-educated man, and so one cannot simply consider him to have been the aesthetic ambassador of unpretentious goodwill that he often cared to portray. When he claimed never to have seen a work of art that inspired violence, for instance, he must have momentarily forgotten all his knowledge of iconoclastic acts throughout history, from the Biblical smashing of pagan idols to the reformation-era destruction of Catholic icons and then on to and beyond the Nazi trashing of "degenerate art"—not to mention the violence immemorially incited by the propaganda of religious, nationalistic, and racist artworks. In fact, Judaic and Islamic tradition tells us that Abraham himself was a notable iconoclast.[9] Moreover, Segal had good reason to expect that the sacrifice of Isaac in particular would prove to be provocative in this context, despite the conventional sense of sacredness accorded to it. The related sculpture he had done for Israel had not been well received, he knew, because some saw it as condemning the ongoing oblation of Israeli youth in war.[10]

In this case, too, Segal claimed to have been misunderstood. "Those bureaucrats weren't willing to read the piece as a detached philosophical examination," he complained. Instead, "they were interpreting it on the simplest political level."[11] Be that as it may, this experience must have demonstrated to him that the sacrifice of Isaac was unlikely, to say the least, to be an innocuous theme for a work of public art. Like Søren Kierkegaard in *Fear and Trembling* (1843) and Bob Dylan in "Highway 61 Revisited" (1965), Segal chose Biblical subjects "because these old stories are so up-to-date"; such being the case, he certainly had no ground to fault others if they were struck by a sense of topicality that opened his work to contemporary conflicts.[12] Nevertheless, one can appreciate Segal's worry that topical applications might be too narrowly construed, thus drawing our eyes away from the full force of this artwork.

In the eerie realism of this sculpture, Abraham appears as a grim, hulking, bearded lout, his genitals prominent beneath his thin trousers, and yet also as a figure of disturbingly ambiguous gender. As Segal himself pointed out, Israeli critics were quick to note Abraham's matronly *embonpoint* and to draw forth its implications, asking why the sculptor had refashioned the patriarchal legend into a figure also suggestive of maternity.[13] With its large head and bulky trunk perched on skinny legs, Abraham's lumpy, unlovely, disproportionate body is unsettling in other respects, too. Advancing toward the supine figure of a fawn-like Isaac while holding his left hand clenched in a fist and clutching in his right a real, not a sculpted, knife, Abraham looks more like a stereotypical butcher than an example to the pious or Kierkegaardian knight of faith.

"I prefer impurity," Segal wrote in response to his own question as to whether Abraham's dedication to the value of human life had been "secular, political, military, economic, or religious," and its impurity must certainly be a strength of this work for those viewers who do not dogmatically reject it as some sort of offense.[14] For instance, anyone familiar with the Biblical story will note that Isaac's fabled obedience here seems more like enigmatic passivity, Abraham's attitude a fierce intent highly unlikely to communicate a sense of righteousness, if any such it may claim to possess. Segal said that he was drawn to stories from Genesis because he found them characterized by actions "full of impossible conflict," and the brilliance of this heterodox and impure work—so literal, in a sense, in its inclusion of a real knife and its casting of actual persons—lies in the way it allows our eyes to take in a representational scene in the very moment in which literal representation, or even perception of any kind, becomes impossible.[15]

Segal seems not to have done any special research into the interpretations historically given to the sacrifice of Isaac, contenting himself with reading Kierkegaard and with advocating (rather against Kierkegaard's teaching) "the openness of biblical interpretation."[16] Regardless, both his works on this subject appear deeply conversant with one of the most important features of this exegetical tradition: an insistence on the terrible incomprehensibility of Abraham's example. In the words of Philo of Alexandria, the Jewish philosopher of the first century, "one who gives his only darling son performs an action for which no language is adequate."[17] Like the medieval plays that would not hesitate to direct attention even to the most gruesome aspects of this story, such as the one that has Isaac asking if he must be decapitated—"Fader, shal my hed of also?"—Philo's commentary meticulously thinks through the possibility that, "following the law of the burnt offering, [Abraham] would have dismembered his son and offered him limb by limb."[18] Taking all such considerations into account, he concludes that Abraham is an utterly extraordinary figure: "Which of all the points mentioned is shared by others? Which does not stand by itself and defy description?"[19] According to Philo, Abraham must be followed and yet cannot be known, sympathetically or representationally, so awful is the experience he represents.

This emphasis became something of a topos in exegetical tradition. Even Maimonides, whose Abraham is an idealized type of righteous obedience to God, seems to contradict his own assurance about this characterization by saying, "[I]n this story he was ordered to do something that bears no comparison either with sacrifice of property or with sacrifice of life. In truth it is the most extraordinary thing that could happen in the world, such a thing that one would not imagine that human nature was capable of."[20] And long before Kierkegaard took this sacrifice as an instance of irremediable absurdity and Jacques Derrida, in discussing Kierkegaard, described it as a "most cruel, impossible, and untenable gesture," Martin Luther was so bold as to say that Abraham's trial "cannot be overcome and is far too great to be understood by us." The reason, he explained, referring to the promises God had earlier made to Abraham about the future course of Isaac's life, is that in Abraham's trial "there is a contradiction with which God contradicts himself." Our fleshly understanding "inevitably concludes either that God is lying—and this is blasphemy—or that God hates me—and this leads to despair." John Calvin similarly argued that this trial drew Abraham into "a contest with [God's] own word" and said that in Abraham's grief "the whole salvation of the world seemed to be extinguished and to perish."[21]

Luther's reflections are particularly interesting in the present context because he, like Segal, brought such an eerie realism to his conception of this event even as he insisted that it is unimaginable. On the one hand, he found it necessary to specify that "Abraham wanted to strike [Isaac's] throat, as butchers commonly kill calves." He opined as well that "Isaac was bound just as a butcher binds sheep or a goat with a rope and grasps the animal with one hand and holds the knife in the other." His account imagines how Abraham, after having received God's command, "sees nothing else. Everything fades out in him: Sarah, the domestics, his home, and Isaac." Even as he thus envisions the preparations for Isaac's sacrifice, however, he removes himself and his audience from any possible comprehension of Abraham's experiences. "I could not have been an onlooker, much less the performer and slayer," he says. "It is an astounding situation . . . and I surely admit that I cannot attain to these thoughts and sentiments either by means of words or by reflecting on them. We are not moved by these sentiments, because we do not desire to feel and experience them." In fact, as if warning his congregants not to try this at home, he takes care to insist that "the extraordinary example of Abraham should not be dragged along as a precedent to be followed." Offering himself as a comparison in place of the incomparable Abraham, he points out that he is in the habit "of praying God daily not to send any angel to [him] for any reason whatever." "But if one were to present itself," he adds, "I would not listen to him" and, in fact, "would turn away"—unless, he is punctilious enough to note, the angel were to speak of "an exigency of the state."[22]

Despite his animus toward the heretics, enthusiasts, and popes whom he fears might take Abraham as a precedent for their violence, Luther does not want to appear to be stubborn to the point of impious impracticality. In the event of pressing civil events, he would attend to an immortal who chose to drop by his place uninvited. Still, it is clear that he finds the sacrifice of Isaac to be profoundly troubling because it is an extraordinary event of the legendary past and yet, at the same time, so contemporary and ordinary that he can see in it all the unhuman forces that presently threaten to blind humanity, and he himself, as by a demonic angelic radiance against which prayers are useless.

By his own account, Luther was completely unable to take in the scene of Isaac's sacrifice and yet equally unable to turn entirely away from it, no matter how devoutly he prayed. This event was real to him, but eerily real, and so finally beyond perception and imagination. An example that one dare not take as a precedent, the experiences of Abraham nonetheless might serve as a reproach to those whom he saw as practising a false mortification, such as the anchorites of the early Christian era. Abraham's experiences, he argued, were "true mortifications. They do not happen in deserts, away from the society of human beings. No, they happen in the household itself." Yet we dare not imitate Abraham; we dare not even imagine that we can imagine him; and even as we judge that the sacrifice of Jesus Christ has rendered unnecessary any re-iteration of Abraham's experience, we still must pray to God to be spared the sort of angelic communication that helped make Abraham "the foremost and greatest among the holy patriarchs."[23]

Segal's sculpture, too, turns away from the angel, though not because the butcher's son shared Luther's fears of competing revelations, sects, and figures of apostolic and exegetical authority. What he shared with Luther, as with the strain of tradition that describes the sacrifice of Isaac as incomprehensible, is the sense that this story suspends us at the very limits of our ability to know what it might mean to be human. It is some such sense of things, too, that led Kierkegaard to discuss the sacrifice of Isaac in relation to the "hard saying" of Luke 14: 26: "If any one comes to me and does not hate his own father and mother and wife and children and brothers and sisters, yes, and even his own life, he cannot be my disciple."[24] We might remember how John Bunyan illustrated this saying in that scene early in *Pilgrim's Progress* (1678) in which Christian flees his home while clapping his hands over his ears so that he cannot hear the imploring cries of his wife and kids: an image of the Deadbeat Dad as the Knight of Faith. The patriarch bent on butchering his own son, of course, is a figure even more difficult to embrace. So Kierkegaard comments on the verse from Luke, "Who can bear to listen to it? This is the reason, too, that we seldom hear it. But this silence is only an escape that is of no avail." In contrast to the tragic hero, "who is the favorite of ethics" and who is "the purely human," in the sacrifice of Isaac Kierkegaard saw Abraham's confrontation with an unhuman paradox in which "the divine and the demonic" were joined and compelled our silence.[25]

The famous conclusion to Ludwig Wittgenstein's *Tractatus Logico-Philosophicus* (1921)—"Of that which we cannot speak, over that we must be silent"—takes on an especially dark import if we think of it in this context.[26] So, too, does the silence of Segal's sculpted figures. In the hesitation, the muteness, the aesthetic interruption of human being in which they stand, they body forth the sadomasochistic impasse toward which culture is driven through its every image, category, practice, law, and ideal. It is as if these figures are caught between Immanuel Kant's categorical imperative, which is unhuman in its contempt for the historical particularities of life, and Kierkegaard's teleological suspension of the ethical, which is unhuman in its devotion to the ahistorical singularity of the individual. Or, to be even more precise, one might say that Segal's sculpture captures only too well the reverence Isaac's sacrifice has so long enjoyed, which is a supreme instance of the power that generally accrues to cultural works in which love artfully confesses the hate, the desire for destruction, throbbing in its heart. Through the fierce series of aesthetic choices embodied in this sculpture, Segal asked, as Jean-François Lyotard did in *The Inhuman: Reflections on Time*, "What is not resolved in sacrifice, in offering, in being received?"[27]

Segal made of the sacrifice of Isaac an exemplary moral event that might also be called aesthetically sublime. True, Kant had illustrated the sublime by the commandment against graven images, but Segal's sculpture paralleled this commandment by leaving aside the consolations of the angel and the ram, cutting us off from knowledge of the supersensible. At once attractive and repulsive, this work is designed to compel our imagination to experience its limits and thus, in the sacrifice of its freedom, to dwell in the uncertainty of any sense of divine purpose, immortal destiny, and free will. At the same time, through the disturbingly prosaic nature of his graven figures, Segal's sculpture might well remind us of Friedrich Nietzsche's blunt suggestion as to how humans "venture to be inhuman *with a good conscience.*"[28]

It is not really so preposterous, then, that a biblical allegory should be perceived as radical; and in the version of the sacrifice of Isaac that Segal tried to present to Kent State, the conflict given sculptural form is no less impossible than in his first work on this subject. Perhaps it is even more so. In the case of the earlier sculpture, which was not associated with any particular event, viewers could at least suppose that one need not see any topical references in this new version of the ancient scene, which, after all, has been among those most frequently portrayed in the history of art. The situation was very different with the commission a private foundation had given Segal on behalf of Kent State. Here there could be no doubt of the allegorical tendency in this invocation of the story, even though there still might be, and was, great dispute as to just what was suggested by the comparison drawn between the ancient and the modern occasions.

Although Segal said the Kent State administration was informed of his chosen theme and gave it tacit approval early on, it is clear that the president of the university and his advisors had had something very different in mind. They suggested that a good substitute for the work the artist had made would be "a sculpture showing a soldier holding a gun, being accosted by a nude or nearly nude young lady using her feminine charms to deflect him from his military duty."[29] In proposing this kind of kitsch, the KSU administration might seem ridiculous or hopelessly provincial to Lippard and many others, not excluding myself; but this kind of reaction, much like Serra's godlike arrogance in responding to those who criticized his *Tilted Arc*, can be obtuse in its own way.

The memorial proposed by the KSU administration would have suggested, in effect, that the events of May 4 had never really happened. In making this proposal, the administration did have a certain sort of tradition and reason on its side. It might even have invoked the authority of Plato, who, in his ideal republic, refused to let Thetis tell of how Apollo "foretold the happy fortunes of her issue and yet became himself the slayer of [her] son."[30] As it was, however, the administrators were merely expressing their desire that this work should conform to what the public generally expects of all such memorials. Despite the controversy to which it initially gave rise, even Maya Lin's Vietnam Veterans Memorial was designed to satisfy these expectations. (To see its compliance, one need only consider what public reaction would have been if the winning design for this monument had not been Lin's minimalist black wall honoring "our" dead but rather, for example, a representational sculpture of an American Antigone giving a pious burial to a Vietnamese Polyneices.) As the KSU administration made clear in the architectural memorial it did eventually select for construction on campus, it expected this sort of thing to "contribute to the healing of a receding but still deep and collective wound in the University's and the nation's history." It should be designed so that visitors' reflections were "elevated" and so that all would be "reminded of the essential tenets which unite us, pondering their delicate yet precious nature."[31]

It is no wonder, then, that Segal's sculpture should have been rejected. Faithful to Kierkegaard's *Fear and Trembling* in at least one respect, it would not let this event settle into the comforting terms of the self-absolving sense of tragedy to which people such as Nixon had tried to confine it. As Harriet F. Senie has written, Segal's sculpture was "condemned for being too effective. It prodded a collective guilty conscience, rather than providing a distraction or a balm."[32] And it did still more. In a most uncompromising way, it raised questions about a foundational legend in Western civilization and, through this legend, about the fundamental conditions of art and culture.

There is no more terrifying story than that of Abraham's sacrifice of Isaac, and the fact that this story is reverenced in three powerful religions only makes it all the more difficult a subject for thought. Referring to its influence, Erich Auerbach wrote that "everyone knows it"; referring to its meaning, Kierkegaard said that it was unknowable. "Anyone who looks upon this scene is paralyzed," he maintained. As if that were not enough, "Anyone who looks upon this scene is blinded," he added, scorning those who would say, comfortably, as if in a mood for memorials, "We know it all—it was only an ordeal."[33] He saw this story as cause for fear and trembling, and he was far from being the first or last thus to regard it, as we can see from the reactions to Segal's Kent State Memorial.

The fear and trembling of the Kent State officials were obvious. In saying that "the inescapable first impression is that an older person is threatening to kill a younger person who is pleading for his life," however, these officials did not mischaracterize Segal's interpretation of the Abrahamic legend. It could scarcely seem a coincidence that this sculpture had in fact been made to memorialize the shooting of thirteen young people by National Guard troops under the command of older men.[34] The allegorical correspondences were not perfect; many members of the Guard were also young men. Nonetheless, these correspondences were clear enough and far more brutal than, for example, the Marquis de Sade's use of the sacrifice of Isaac as a justification for infanticide.[35]

Struck by this brutality, one need not turn for an alternative to the farcical piety of Robert McCoy, a KSU presidential assistant who seems to have had his material ghostwritten by Joseph Heller. "An act of violence about to be committed," he said, "is inappropriate to commemorate an act of violence."[36] Whatever one's response, though, it can scarcely be denied that in his choice of subject Segal was seeking something other than a conventional sense of uplift and healing. Whatever else it may call to mind, a comparison between Abraham preparing to sacrifice Isaac and National Guardsmen firing on students at Kent State must suggest, at least initially, that the latter event is a profanation of everything supposed to be sacred in the former. We might be reminded of a similarly brutal appropriation of this biblical story, in this case to characterize the First World War, in Wilfred Owen's "Parable of the Old Man and the Young" (1920), which concludes with an account of what happens when the angel interrupts Abraham:

. . . lo! an angel called him out of heaven,
Saying, Lay not thy hand upon the lad,
Neither do anything to him. Behold,
A ram, caught in a thicket by its horns;
Offer the Ram of Pride instead of him.
But the old man would not so, but slew his son,
And half the seed of Europe, one by one.[37]

If there were any doubt that we should see things in this way, Segal's work dispels it by portraying Isaac as a muscular young man, not as the child he appears to be in the Tel Aviv sculpture. To be sure, the Isaac of legend changes from a small child to a fellow in his teens, twenties, or thirties, depending on the accounts on which one chooses to rely, so there is authority for either representation. Making him a youth who appears to be the same age as the victims at Kent State, however, was bound to appear as a decision marked as much by political as by aesthetic and historical motives. Furthermore—if there could still be any doubt as to this tendency—the young man is portrayed on his knees, his face upturned to the figure of Abraham. He does not appear passive or peaceful, as in the earlier *Sacrifice of Isaac*. Instead he seems alert and robust, his flesh taut and vibrant with life even in the pallor of the plaster original to the later bronze casting.

In this particular, too, whether he was aware of it or not, Segal had ample precedent in tradition for his choices. Some midrashic commentaries on this story, like some medieval plays, emphasize Isaac's youthful vitality by having him implore the feebler Abraham to bind him and bind him well, lest he move involuntarily and thus spoil the offering.[38] In the context of the Kent State massacre, though, it is virtually impossible to see the healthy muscularity of this Isaac, who is comparable in size to his father, as anything but a reproach to the older figure about to strike him down. The expression on his face is not restful, as in Segal's other version of this story, but open-mouthed and, one might infer, supplicatory. In contrast, the bearded Abraham in this case is closed-mouthed, set, and determined, with his knife held at crotch level and pointing straight at Isaac's heart. The clothing of these figures, too, is more markedly contemporary than in the first *Sacrifice of Isaac*, with the barefooted Abraham wearing a collared shirt and what seem to be work pants, Isaac what looks like a pair of cotton shorts. In a surpassingly grotesque touch, Abraham's sleeves and trousers are rolled up as if to signify that he is ready to get down to business and would prefer not to soil his clothes, if he can help it, in doing so. It is difficult to imagine any other reason for this feature of the sculpture, which adds to the contemporary, informal, or working-class connotations of Abraham's clothing an atrocious hint of trivial self-regard that is utterly devastating toward any attempt to project a redemptive reading onto this scene. Isaac's near nakedness is unremarkable, for so he appears in virtually all versions of this legend. Abraham's bare feet, calves, and arms, however, suggest that at this moment, in his unquestioning obedience to divine commands no matter how they might grieve him, this patriarch sees no need to subject himself to the further unhappiness of messing up a perfectly fine outfit with his child's gore. Whatever sacredness we might strain to infer from this scene becomes utterly demonic once one notices this touch of finicky refinement, which all of eternity could not excuse.

Therefore, had it been sited on the Kent State campus as originally planned, *In Memory of May 4, 1970* would have stood as a powerful gesture not only against that day's killings but also against monumentality and all that monumentality conventionally is taken to connote. It would have opposed the vulgar idiom of elevation and healing but also every aesthetic rhetoric that, in claiming more sophistication, still wants monuments to embody some sort of deadly transcendent value. In the site at Kent State for which it was designed, Segal's work would have embodied impurity, profanation, accusation, irreparable distance, unbearable intimacy, and the utter impossibility of knowledge. Although Segal himself spoke of tragedy in describing the story depicted in this work, the sculpture repels the humanistic assurances of tragic motivation, scale, resolution, and tradition. Instead, what we see in the eerie realism of this piece of art—what blinds us—is the absence of the human in the human. We see something like what Antonin Artaud described as the "bloody and inhuman" nature of his desired theater, which would appear as such in order "to manifest and fix in us, unforgettably, the idea of a perpetual conflict and spasm by which life is divided every minute, by which all of creation raises and asserts itself against our established state of being," thereby communicating "in a concrete and immediate way the metaphysical ideas of various fables whose very atrociousness and energy suffice to demonstrate their origin and tenor in essential principles."[39] We might also compare what we see in Segal's sculpture to the immemorial sculptural figure, that tortured image out of Ovidian fable, at the center of Francisco Goya's "This is worse." In this work of eerie realism, we might add, as in the genre of the Gothic, we meet with the impossibility of society.

Through this sculpture we confront what happened at Kent State as an unhuman act that was willed not by suicidal rocks or self-motivated bullets but by human beings with ages of tradition supporting them. At the same time as it draws us into this insufferable representation of the

Kent State shootings, then, Segal's sculpture opens out onto a broader historical world, including the world of our present and of the future. It does so, first of all, by presenting its legendary figures in the moment before the sacrifice is supposed to have happened and in the absence of the usual iconic signs, an angel or a ram, that God will alter his decree and spare Abraham's son. Whereas many accounts emphasize that Abraham never hesitates, that he is absolutely and unquestioningly obedient, Segal's version sculpts the story into a pause, an interruption, that by the nature of his medium cannot end. There could be no more striking contrast to Abraham as the single-minded type of devotion that he is taken to be when his trial is used to prefigure Israel's historical deliverance and spiritual salvation. No less of a contrast appears when we turn to the interpretations of Abraham's trial, in Christian tradition, as representing the battle between flesh and spirit, the promise of resurrection, and God's offering of his own son to deliver humankind from the wages of sin.

We see one of these traditional versions of Abraham, for instance, in Philo's statement that "Abraham admitted no swerving of body or mind."[40] Similarly, in the *Targum Pseudo-Jonathan*, an Aramaic rendering of the Hebrew scriptures that appears to date from the seventh or eighth century, angels on high are made to exclaim, "Come, see two unique ones who are in the world; one is slaughtering, and one is being slaughtered; the one who slaughters does not hesitate, and the one who is being slaughtered stretches forth his neck."[41] Like some other commentators, Maimonides furthered this approach by actually praising Abraham as a coldblooded killer.[42] Following much the same tradition in this regard, at least, Calvin wrote, "The sum of the whole turns on this point; that Abraham, when he had to slay his son, remained always like himself."[43]

As against accounts such as these, which maintain that we must not think of Abraham hesitating, which may even see in his three-day journey to the place of sacrifice on Mount Moriah an image of his unquestioning devotion to the divine command, the hesitation wrought forth by Segal's sculpture calls to mind versions of this story that portray Abraham as a less monumental or, as some might think, more humanized character. After all, Segal seems to have followed Kierkegaard not only in allowing for the possibility of Abraham hesitating, but also in considering that it would be truly unhuman not to bring this story down to earth or, in other words, not to treat it anachronistically. Kierkegaard wrote, "My soul balks at doing what is so often done—talking inhumanly about the great, as if a few centuries were an enormous distance. I prefer to speak humanly about [the sacrifice of Isaac], as if it happened yesterday, and only let the greatness itself be the distance that either elevates or judges."[44]

It might be tempting to see Segal's updated version of this legend, then, as also being an attempt to realize this philosopher's claim that we must "express the sublime in the pedestrian."[45] Or if it is not Kierkegaard's influence that we see here, we might still think, for example, of medieval plays in which Abraham is given certain homely touches. In a play from Brome, Abraham falters, so stricken is he by pain and grief, and finally has to be urged on to his duty by Isaac, who feels tortured by the delay. In the version from the Towneley cycle of plays, Abraham not only hesitates but actually says, "To slo hym thus I thynk grete syn." Moments such as these serve to remind us that the idealized patriarch coexisted in tradition with Abrahams who were not so monumentally sure of themselves. We may remember that in the early Christian era Origen had argued that the significance of Abraham's three-day journey to Mount Moriah lay not in the example of cold reflection it provided but rather in the fact that "throughout the whole trip he might be torn to pieces with his thoughts."[46] As these examples may serve to indicate, centuries of exegesis existed to lend their support even to the decidedly down-to-earth Henry Fielding when, through the character of Parson Adams in *Joseph Andrews* (1742), he labored to humanize the figure of Abraham by putting the story of the sacrifice of Isaac into a comic context.[47]

Certain strains of Judaic and Christian tradition, then, would have authorized Segal as well to "humanize" the figure of Abraham and the story of the sacrifice of Isaac, had it been his intention to pursue this end. The hesitation embodied in his artwork, however, is never overcome. This irresolution cannot simply be attributed to the nature of the sculptural medium or to an accident of design, as with the absence of the sort of inscription to which Segal had reluctantly agreed. Eerily earthbound, the scene of *In Memory of May 4, 1970* very precisely does not image Kierkegaard's sublime movement of faith into and from infinity. Neither does it offer us the predictable piety of those mystery plays in which hesitation is only temporary, designed to illustrate the frailties of human emotion without compromising the tenets of faith. On the contrary, it is because he is so human in appearance that this Abraham appears unhuman in his purpose. In fact, one might imagine that the angel whose visitation Luther so devoutly, and comically, wished to avoid would have looked just this terribly ordinary—as the fearful reformer knew all too well.

Exegetical tradition offers some support even to the argument that the sacrifice of Isaac is an allegory of the sadomasochistic misanthropy, inescapable and incomprehensible, within that which we call love, whether human or divine. The rabbinic commentator from the third or fourth century who had Abraham ask God if the whole trial had been some sort of joke may have meant to emphasize the infinite distance between divine and human comprehension, but he still seems also to have indicated, whether intentionally or not, just how misanthropic the whole story is likely to seem to those of ordinary human feeling, sympathy, and mind.[48] To learn that some midrashic commentaries suggest "that Abraham got it all wrong," that "he misunderstood God's command," is only to learn what we must expect that *someone* must have ventured to suggest, is it not?[49] In fact, more than one scholar has pursued this sort of suggestion, including C. A. Schmidt, an eighteenth-century theologian who argued that God had never demanded the sacrifice of Isaac but instead had corrected Abraham's delusion on this point.[50] More recently, in complaining that Kierkegaard paid too much attention to the demand for sacrifice and too little to the voice recalling this command, Emmanuel Levinas seems also to have recoiled from the horror at the heart of this legend.[51]

The nineteenth-century editor of the second-century B.C.E. *Book of Jubilees*, R. H. Charles, supposed that in this Ethiopian retelling of Genesis and Exodus the incitement to try Abraham is attributed to the demonic figure of Mastema because the idea for this sport would have been "unworthy of God."[52] In a related observation, Louis H. Feldman has written that Flavius Josephus seems "to have found the manner in God's test of Abraham to be a bit embarrassing"; and Josephus, if he did indeed feel this way, certainly has not been alone in finding himself in that predicament.[53] Still more awful thoughts have occurred to some, such as one "Johannes Clericus," who suggested in 1733 that, contrary to common belief, Isaac had not willingly offered himself to the sacrifice.[54] Even more upsetting to conventional Judaic and Christian tellings of the story is the counter-tradition within Islam, whose adherents (as the outraged Luther put it) "tell the fictitious story that Ishmael was immolated in the place of Isaac, who, they say, ran away and did not obey his father."[55] In the light of these other interpretations and, as Derrida's account emphasizes, in the context of the ongoing conflicts in the Middle East, tradition finally does not leave us with any human center to the story except that which can be found in the experiences of bondage, exile, and violence within families and among peoples. Tradition thus returns us, again, to the cultural centrality of Segal's Kent State memorial. "The reading, interpretation, and tradition of the sacrifice of Isaac," Derrida writes, "are themselves sites of bloody, holocaustic sacrifice."[56]

Even in pious medieval drama, moments occur that are so eerily realistic, for lack of a better term, that, in the context of the play as a whole, they might blind and paralyze us, compelling us to hesitate, in stunned silence, rather than accept the comfort retrospectively offered to us by all that the familiar ending is supposed to signify. In the Northampton version of the Abraham play, for instance, Isaac pleads for his father to get on with his duty with an eloquence that seems more likely to disable a man who possesses any humanity at all: "A, fadir, ley me downe sofft and feyre/And haue ido nowe, and sle youre eyre/For I am hampred and in dispeyre/And almost at my lives ende."[57] Even more striking is the moment in the Brome *Abraham* after the angel has been sent, Isaac released, and a sheep secured for sacrifice in his stead. As Isaac bends down to blow on the fire that will burn this offering, he pauses and asks, "But fader, wyll I stowppe down lowe,/ȝe wyll not kyll me with ȝowre sword, I trowe?"[58] Whoever put that question in Isaac's mouth clearly saw that the events of this story, whatever else they may teach, do not liberate us from the suspicion of unaccountable violence. We might draw a comparison on this point between these literary portrayals and some of the images given us by the visual arts, such as the paintings on this subject by Rembrandt and Caravaggio (Figures 14 and 15). With its portrayal of a patriarch of gentle countenance who has mercifully covered his son's face in preparation for his sacrifice, Rembrandt's image of this scene was more conventional than Caravaggio's, in which Abraham is a sterner figure, his knife a crude utilitarian instrument, and his son a terrified child, by no means reconciled to his fate, whose eyes draw the viewer directly into his horror. Caravaggio's version, however, is no less faithful to tradition than Rembrandt's.

Missing from both Caravaggio's and Rembrandt's paintings, as also from Segal's Kent State sculpture, is any overt reference to the pathetic role played by Sarah in the traditional narratives of Isaac's sacrifice. To say so is not necessarily to identify a limitation or fault, since this ancient story might be interpreted as showing us the unbearable horror of a world of men without, or beyond, women.[59] It might be argued, in fact, that Segal's 1973 *Sacrifice of Isaac* is finally less impressive than the Kent State sculpture precisely because of this issue. Just as its more vague contemporaneity allows it to reach toward a conventional sense of tragic universality, so, too, does the quasi-hermaphroditic Abraham in this work, by recalling the traditional trope of patriarchs who nurse their dependents, suggest a generalized figure of authority rather than one who is categorically, historically, and ideologically masculine. This figure may then lead us to forget that in the legendary story Sarah's unwilling ignorance is as crucial an element as Abraham's silence.

A recurrent feature in medieval plays about the sacrifice of Isaac, as in Jewish and Christian commentaries on this story, is the image of Sarah as one who is kept in the dark about Abraham's plan. In the Northampton *Abraham*, for instance, when Isaac learns he is to be sacrificed, he asks if his mother knew that he was to be slain. "Crist forbede!" exclaims Abraham, who then goes on feelingly to describe the pathetic loss of appetite to which he expects her grief will lead once she learns of this

Figure 14. Rembrandt van Rijn, *Sacrifice of Isaac* (1635). Oil on canvas. Hermitage, St. Petersburg. Photo courtesy Scala/Art Resource, New York.

Figure 15. Caravaggio, *The Sacrifice of Isaac* (c. 1603–4). Oil on canvas. Uffizi, Florence. Photo courtesy Scala/Art Resource, New York.

event: "She wol ete affter but litel brede."[60] The Dublin version of the drama places even greater emphasis on Sarah's relegation to the background of this act, having her plead with Abraham much as a wife in a folk tale, full of vague forebodings, might seek to restrain her incautious child from wandering abroad: "Yea! But I pray you, gentle fere,/As ever you have loved me dear,/Let Isaac abide at home here,/For I kept not he went in the wind." In this version, in fact, Abraham's righteousness might seem severely strained by the disingenous way that he explains to Sarah and Isaac why the boy needs to accompany him: because he has not yet witnessed a sacrifice and so needs to learn "how God should pleased be"! When she finally learns the truth of what happens, Sarah—now the typical wife of folk tradition browbeating her husband—cries, "Alas, where was your mind?"[61] Of course, she is promptly brought to accept all that has happened as the issue of God's will, but still the way that she and the other Sarahs are confined to unknowing silence stands in marked contrast to the silence of Abraham that Kierkegaard labored to construe as the ultimate condition, test, and sign of faith. In some versions of the story, in fact, such as that of the *Targum Pseudo-Jonathan,*

Sarah dies during the course of Abraham's trial, never to see him or her son again. In glancing objections, imagined reactions, and pathetic details such as these a certain irreverence toward Abraham's implacable masculine identification with the law edges its way into these stories, and to such an extent that Abraham is even made defensively to protest to Isaac, in the Northampton play, that he loves him just as well as Sarah does.

As those nameless medieval dramatists so touchingly recognized, the importance of Sarah's enforced ignorance of and absence from this trial of Abraham is that it brings us to know that more is at stake in this sacrifice than Isaac's neck or Abraham's self-regard. Long before the ram presents itself, sacrifices have taken place in the form of more or less innocent dissembling, more or less justified assumptions of patriarchal authority, and more or less violent differences in the culture of feelings and in the definition of culture's boundary lines. If there were no human sacrifice in this story—if it in fact marked, as many commentators have wished to believe, a sacred injunction against ancient types of human sacrifice, for which animal offerings henceforth were to substitute—then these details of the mystery plays could never have had any effect, whether in the fourteenth century or today. Their apparent power to move audiences then as now is a measure of the extent to which these artworks registered a general sense of irreparable loss and a specific doubt about masculine authority even amidst their most sincere professions of faith in the established order of things. In telling of what is not resolved in sacrifice, these eerily realistic details tell of the many sacrifices that go unacknowledged within those few offerings of which we boast. They tell, in other words, of the hatreds that exist even in our dearest loves.

What Caravaggio so profanely highlighted, this specifically masculine spirit of destruction conveyed by the story of Abraham and Isaac, Kierkegaard sought to deflect from our attention by drawing an analogy between Abraham's trial and that of a mother weaning an infant, as well as by comparing it to the trial undergone by the Virgin Mary. At best, though, his attempt was rather perfunctory. In his telling, Sarah, like Hagar, remains forever in the background of Abraham's monumental silence. Sarah does not even appear in the background, however, of Segal's Kent State sculpture, in which the youthful figure of Isaac also does not register the fact that of the four people slain on May 4, 1970—Jeffrey Glenn Miller, Allison B. Krause, William K. Shroeder, and Sandra Lee Scheuer—two were young women. This aesthetic choice may owe much to the desire to make reference, within the Kent State context, to the broader context of the Vietnam War and to the many thousands of young men slaughtered there. Still, it might seem that this work thus perpetuates the patriarchal thrust of traditions related to the Abrahamic legend.

To regard the Kent State work in this way, however, might also mean that one is looking at it too literally or, as it were, too topically. Consider: Is it true to say that the National Guardsmen that day sacrificed both boys and girls, both sons and daughters? Or is it more true, more realistic, to say that in this situation Abraham was still sacrificing Isaac, no matter what the sex of the victims might be, fully confident as he was that any women worthy of the name were at home, in exile with Hagar, or—if they happened to be in the vicinity—approaching the soldiers in the fetching state of undress specified by the KSU administration as appropriate to memorialization? If the latter view obtains, then we have a different image. In place of a Kierkegaardian logic of absolutes, in which Abraham's intended sacrifice of Isaac is *either* a crime *or* a sanctified act of obedience, Segal's impure work then invites us to see it as simultaneously crime and sacred ritual, everyday act and extraordinary event, singular and utterly traditional drama, patriarchal exemplum and travesty.

True, despite all that I have argued here, there is nothing to stop those so inclined from imputing a therapeutic and uplifting effect to Segal's work, as in the heartbreaking encomium of Arthur Krause, father of one of the four slaughtered students: "I think that it shows that we, the older generation, and the younger generation share God's mercy, and that he can stop sacrifices."[62] In fearing that the installation of the sculpture on the KSU campus would lead to disorder and violence, however, the KSU administrators, despite their redoubtable obtuseness, were actually quite perceptive about this work's disturbing emphasis on the agony of culture, which is founded on sacrifice and in which sacrifice never ends. This is the great insight of Segal's sculpture, which KSU's President Golding rightly perceived could not be blocked even by an inscription assuring viewers that Isaac was and would be spared.

In Friedrich Schlegel's distinctively modern conception of the realm of sacrifice as the realm of signification, irony is the name for this omnipresent demand for sacrifice. For Schlegel, the consequence of human finitude in the face of a divine totality is that everything humanly perceived, imagined, or known is cut by, or sacrificed to, the rule of irony. Irony is "the freest of all licences, for through it one disregards oneself, and yet also the most law-abiding, for it is absolutely necessary." It is also—and here we can recognize the affinity with Kierkegaard's *Fear and Trembling*, despite Kierkegaard's fierce criticisms of Schlegel—"the form of paradoxes." It pervades everyday existence. As Schlegel puts it, it is "very much at home in the history of humanity." Therefore, art and life are necessarily symbolical or, what amounts to saying the same thing,

fragmentary. Irony is so pervasive, in fact, that it turns around upon itself and confronts us with "the irony of irony," which arises when "irony
runs wild and no longer allows itself to be governed at all."[63] The absurd
and paradoxical silence of Abraham on his way to sacrifice Isaac, as
Kierkegaard describes it, plunges us into this irony of irony, in which the
distinction between the demonic and the sacred proves to be beyond
human comprehension.

Many others besides Kierkegaard—T. S. Eliot, for one—are heir to
Schlegel's Romantic irony. Although it owes something to this background, however, Segal's *In Memory of May 4, 1970* seems more closely
akin to the post-Romantic conception of sacrifice found in the works of
figures such as Nietzsche, Sigmund Freud, Artaud, Georges Bataille, and
Derrida. For writers such as these, the wild license of irony—the cut of
the sacrificial knife—is not restrained by the presumptive rule of a
beneficent deity. To see the realm of signification as the realm of sacrifice is then to see idealization as the effect, not the cause, of sacrifice. In
other words, it is to see sacrifice not as an isolated act, sacred or ac-
cursed, as the case may be, but as the work of culture in its every aspect.
From the most fundamental postulations of identity to kinship relations,
economic structures, linguistic performances, and everything else, the
argument would run, sacrifice enables culture to be. This kind of approach would have it that without the demand for sacrifice, which cuts
into even our dearest loves in a way that is bound to suggest hatred,
there would be no art or culture of any kind. Far from simply threatening humanity, unhuman violence establishes its conception and tradition. So we learn from the motivation of culture "beyond good and evil,"
in Nietzsche's revisionary account of Judaeo-Christian history; from the
human necessity of an inhuman theater of cruelty, in Artaud's aesthetics; from the centrality of castration to the formation of identity and
symbolic structures of all sorts, in Freud's account; from the demand for
violent outbursts of useless expenditure, as in orgasms and wars, in
Bataille's; and from the connection Derrida draws between Abraham's
sacrifice of Isaac and the "incalculable sacrifice" that organizes society:
"I offer a gift of death, I betray, I don't need to raise my knife over my
son on Mount Moriah for that."[64] So, too, did Segal choose to design his
sculpture around the suspense, the instructive agony, in this tale of
Abraham and Isaac, rather than to subsume this agony into a humble
and reverent form of irony. In doing so he may even have made reference to Freud: certainly the way his Abraham wields the knife at crotch
level has the effect of inviting viewers to see an Oedipal narrative at
work in the Biblical tale.

To object to this work as being violently inappropriate, then, or even
as being a literal incitement to violence, is only to give obtuse notice to

the insight into modernity that Theodor Adorno expressed in one of his most famous statements: "Every work of art is an uncommitted crime."[65] Far from being epigrammatically hyperbolic, as it might seem at first glance (for where is the harm in Mozart or Monet?), Adorno actually understated the case. Telling us that humanity is other than itself, art raises the knife to our necks, holds us in suspense, imaging the unhuman stuff that we allow ourselves to see in it so that we need not find this so unbearable as we confront it in ourselves.

What the Kent State University administration wanted was art in its popular modern understanding: art as watered-down religion or, one might say, sanctified crime. What the faux-folksy Segal gave them instead was art, and religion, in all their criminal power. The irony of ironies in this work is that Segal, through ostensibly representational means—the casting of real human bodies—focused attention on the reality of culture as abstract figuration. In cutting the ancient legend into the contemporary world, in showing the realm of sacrifice as the realm of signification, he suggested that the world becomes world, reveals its originary foundation, through the work of culture, which is the work of substitution and delay, of displacement in time and space, which is epitomized in art. In the suspense into which he cast Abraham's knife we see the incisiveness of figuration, which cuts through the "literal" reference to the Biblical story, just as it does through the "literal" models for the sculpture. In doing so, Segal's figuration shows an agonizing recognition of the aesthetic nature of culture that Kierkegaard, following Schlegel, could not help but admit in every aspect of the very writings in which he tried so hard to deny it. Art, at its most unhuman, makes humanity possible. It is because of this paradox that Segal's eerie realism has the power to blind and paralyze.

To say so is not to propose that Segal's work is some sort of artistic equivalent to the theoretical writings of Schlegel, Kierkegaard, Nietzsche, Freud, Artaud, Bataille, Adorno, and Derrida, and I also do not mean to suggest that these writings are all more or less equivalent to one another. To associate Segal's sculpture with these various strains of modern and postmodern thought is merely to indicate some crucial contexts for the conceivability, pertinence, provocation, and importance of this work. The most important context of all, though, may be the Report of the President's Commission on Civil Unrest. Unlike this report, Segal's sculpture does not portray the fatality at work in the events of May 4, 1970 as some kind of inexcusable occurrence for which no one, in the end, is truly to blame. Segal's artwork insists that the ideal of sacrifice serves at once to maintain and obscure the relation between an agent of violence, on the one hand, and a victim, on the other. There is no pretense of evenhandedness in the outrage embodied in this work. It maintains that this inequitable structuring of power, far from being accidental or incidental in relation to the desire for humanity supposedly shared by all, is in fact generative of that desire and thus inseparable from the very conception of humanity. In other words, through his use of the legend of Abraham and Isaac, Segal pointed to the idealization of violence within the institutions of gender, family, nation, and religion, not to mention education. He portrayed his figures in such a way that we can neither comprehend nor look away from this violence, this sacrificial movement of temporal and spatial displacement, that is the realm of signification. In this respect Segal is quite unlike those of whom Philo complained, "quarrelsome critics who misconstrue everything" by arguing that Abraham's action was not "great or wonderful" but rather of a kind with many forms of sacrifice that all sorts of people have made in the past and still continue to make.[66] (To Philo, we may infer, Derrida might be such a critic.)[67] Unlike these carpers, Segal focused our attention on the extraordinary nature of Abraham's example, refusing to dissolve it in generalizations about sacrifice and thus making all the more appalling the comparison between the sacrifice of Isaac, which is traditionally reverenced, and the slaughter of the students at Kent State, which is also reverenced whenever and wherever it is made an occasion for elevation, for healing, or, in other words, for the recuperative idealizations of culture and the banal consolations of tragic art. In its iconoclastic and thoroughly religious approach, which rejects idolatrous monumentality, Segal's work emphasizes the unique nature of the Abrahamic legend in a way designed to be insufferable to those who pride themselves on their religion.[68]

It is ironic—even an irony of ironies, I dare say—that when Robert McCoy, the assistant to the president of Kent State University, went to see Segal in New Jersey in an attempt to dissuade him from his design, he brought with him a long study of the sacrifice of Isaac.[69] Whatever this might have consisted of, it evidently was sufficient to convince KSU president Brage Golding that an institution dedicated to the ideals of learning dare not invite thoughts about the possible relevance of Genesis 22 to its own contemporary history, in which humanity, as always, confronted the unhuman task of facing up to its own ungodly violence. I dare say that his decision was totally wrong, and yet he could not have been more right. The irony of ironies is that ages of tradition establish that we cannot hope to learn from this story; we can but strive, blinded and bound as we are, to survive it.

Chapter Seven

What Is It Like to Be an Artwork?

The question would seem to invite two lines of inquiry. One would ask what it is like to be a certain kind of object: the artwork kind of thing, image, artifact, or construction. The other would ask what it is like to be a certain kind of subject: one who is like the artwork kind of thing. In this case we might think of what it is like to be a famous model, for instance, a celebrity such as Michael Jackson, or a deadpan Warholian superstar; to be as the Sun King or as Cleopatra were; to be a beauty, a dandy, or, perhaps, what has come to be called a performance artist.

The first approach, asking what it is like to be a certain kind of object, would seem to be unpromising, to say the least. Any responses from such things would have to be ventriloquized by we who are doing the asking or by others like us who happen to be standing by with an opinion: artists, critics, collectors, philosophers, journalists, passersby, whoever. At best, then, in coming to any conclusions we would only be fooling ourselves. Frustrated, we would still have no idea what it is like to be an artwork.

Confronting this frustration, we might wish we could take a leaf from the book of Zeus and Juno. These divinities were able to call for the testimony of Tiresias, who had had it both ways, when they were debating whether men or women take more pleasure in sex. In a similar fashion, we would like to hear from Galatea, Pinocchio, those figures that step out of paintings in Gothic romances, the Dorian Gray of the famous portrait, and others of their ilk. Then we could learn what it is like to be the artwork kind of thing. Unlike the Olympian divinities, however, we who suffer our mortality will not be able to expect a meaningful reply from literary characters who, for better or worse, do not. We cannot help but know their utter difference from us, for it is the likes of us who have made it. With these cultural objects as with all others, the fact that we may not have known exactly what it was we were making only makes matters worse. *Ut pictura poesis* and similar strategies cannot be of use to us, for we will know that the one speaking is not the other from which we wished to hear. Again, or still, we come to a frustrating impasse. We cannot say what it is like to be an artwork.

It is curious, then, that the second approach to this question is traditionally assumed to derive from the first. When we think about what it is like for people to be like artworks, we act as if artworks had told us what it is like to be like them.

Art first appears as an object, we are inclined to think, and only then may it be figuratively appropriated to distinguish a great beauty ("She's like a work of art!"), a revered human icon, or postmodern projects of the sort that involve the artist's own person, as in the notorious instance in which Chris Burden had a friend shoot a .22 bullet into his arm (*Shooting Piece*, 1971). "I want to be a living work of art," said Luisa Casati, an early twentieth-century personality of studied decadence, and we recognize that her use of *living* as an adjective marks the presumed innovativeness of her aesthetic will in relation to traditional concepts of the artwork.[1] We still see this presumption in the words of Otto Muehl, one of the Vienna Actionists of the 1960s, when he characterizes his decision to use the body as "artistic material" as a crucial phase in his evolution.[2] Similarly, in a 1973 statement that her body was her "artistic material," Gina Pane implied that she was transferring to herself a preestablished notion of such material and of the works made from it.[3] "Why *not* be an artwork?" exclaimed Hannah Wilke, who also gained some fame in the 1970s not only for things she made but for what she made of herself; and even in this bold question we see the curious assumption that only after art was conceived in the form of an object had the idea arisen that a human being might be such a thing.[4] Yet how can that be if, as would seem to be the case, the objects supposed to be fundamental to our conceptions of art cannot tell us the first thing about what it is that we are presuming to derive from their example? How can humans be like objects of art if we cannot know what it is like to be like an artwork?

This confusing state of affairs arises because of a perennial and perhaps inescapable tendency to underestimate the art in humanity, to overestimate the humanity of art, and thus to obscure the unhuman motivation in both of them. As with so much else, one of the most brilliant explorers of this confusion was Denis Diderot. Through the dialogue about theatrical art in his *Paradox of the Actor* (c. 1773–77), he presented the counterintuitive argument that the greatest actor will be the one who possesses the least sensibility. The greatest art, in other words, will come from the person who is least human, or most like an object. With their focus on the object and the subject, my two lines of inquiry into what it is like to be an artwork are anticipated and knotted together in Diderot's paradoxical argument, which is devoted to explaining the logical impasses into which the experience of art leads us.

According to Diderot, one does not wish to see an actor distinguished by hypersensitive nerves, extreme delicacy of temperament, and immediate emotional responsiveness. On the stage such a one will prove too life-like, too human, and as a result will bring into disrepute "the dignity of his species" (61–62).[5] The desired aesthetic effect will be lost, as when "a woman who is unhappy, and truly unhappy, weeps without touching you at all" or, worse, makes you laugh because she looks ridiculous and appears vulgar. We would then see in this person what we find to be true with everyone else, that "excessive passions are almost all accompanied by grimaces that the artist without taste abjectly copies but that the great artist avoids" (61). Therefore, instead of a person of sensibility, one wants an actor with "a cool head" (64). The successful actor is one who "weeps like a faithless priest who preaches on the Passion; like a seducer on his knees before a woman whom he does not love but whom he wishes to dupe; like a beggar in the street or at the doorway of a church who turns insulting after he despairs of putting the touch on you; or like a courtesan who feels nothing and yet swoons in your arms" (57). In fact, one can go so far as to say that an "extreme sensibility makes actors mediocre, mediocre sensibility makes the great mass of bad actors, and an absolute lack of sensibility prepares actors to be sublime" (57). The great actor is an inspired "mannequin" (51) who is able to imitate any and all feelings while inwardly remaining completely unaffected by them.

To a considerable extent, of course, Diderot's argument was specifically related to the aesthetics, economics, and sociology of the eighteenth-century French theater. For instance, it bears reference to a taste for sublime emotions and idealized acting styles. Moreover, this famous dialogue strives to make a virtue of the déclassé condition of actors in an era in which the stage was "a resource, never a choice"—a resource, that is, for those afflicted by a "faulty education, poverty, or libertinism" (96). Diderot's argument also goes beyond these eighteenth-century circumstances, however, in its paradoxically sardonic and yet lighthearted suggestion that the exceptional actor typifies ordinary humanity.

Diderot prefigured Wagner's argument, in Johann Wolfgang Goethe's *Faust* (1808), that "an actor could instruct a priest."[6] The question, finally, is not who possesses the sort of *sang-froid* that Diderot attributes to the actor, but rather who does not. What Chateaubriand saw in Napoleon, an essentially cold man who played the part of himself, Diderot saw in people from all walks of life. Resembling such types as the infidel priest, the seducer, and the beggar, the actor also resembles all members of the public insofar as they, like the interlocuter in Diderot's dialogue, are ready to laugh at the misery of others.

Representing the soul of conventionality in this dialogue, this interlocuter, like those who converse with Socrates in Plato's dialogues, does try to express disagreements at various points. Even at these points, however, he never really objects to the miserable image of humanity conveyed by the main speaker. "One never becomes an actor through a love of virtue, through a desire to be useful to society and to serve one's country or one's family, through any of the respectable motivations that can transport an honest soul, a warm heart, a sensitive spirit toward a noble profession" (96), this speaker asserts. Here, what might seem to be a criticism of the actor is actually a satire on humankind. Through this speaker's sly irony we are given to understand that the motivations of humanity as a species are no more respectable than those of the actor as an individual. Just as the actor is a mannequin, an unhuman work of art, so, too, is the human species whose imaginary dignity is preserved by the theatrical wonders of insensibility; and so, too, are the honest souls, the warm hearts, and the sensitive spirits who flatter themselves on the nobility of their professions.

To see what we are like, then, we need to recognize ourselves in the mimicry of the actors who are characterized here as "tedious, wasted, wasteful, mercenary, more struck by our affectations than touched by our misfortunes; of an undisturbed spirit at the sight of a troubling event or at the telling of a sad story; loners, vagabonds, by the order of their superiors; lacking in morality, totally lacking friends, with almost none of the sweet and sacred relationships that bind us to the pains and pleasures of another who shares our own" (95). Such is the actor, and thus would we see ourselves acting were it not for all the moral, religious, political, sentimental, economic, and theatrical "artwork" that is created by our artful professions of humanity. In other words, we would see ourselves as just such base persons were it not for the dignity, so called, of our species, which is nothing but a theatrical effect.

So Diderot's actor is an ancestor of Charles Baudelaire's dandy. The dandy similarly "aspires to insensibility" while bodying forth a condition of exceptionally marked artifice that Baudelaire suggested to be, paradoxically, profoundly banal.[7] Many other figures have also belonged to this lineage. In terms of a specifically theatrical representation, though, this tradition may have come to its ne plus ultra in certain works of performance art in recent decades. One might think, for example, of the performance in which the French artist Orlan, on a live TV broadcast, underwent plastic surgery designed to sculpt her face into an appearance that would be, by conventional standards, not only unpretty but positively unhuman.

There is an important sense, however, in which Orlan is a very traditional artist and Diderot's argument, even in its own time, nothing new.[8] Indeed, one might say that its seeming novelty was a banality immemorially recognized as such in the everyday speech and behavior of priests and seducers, beggars and professionals, and, for all practical purposes, everyone.

The image of humans as artworks who are estranged from themselves in their self-defining art goes back at least to the "noble lie" in Plato's *Republic*.[9] Socrates explains this fiction, or outlandish "Phoenician tale," in the course of describing how he proposes that the guardians and rulers and other members of his ideal republic will be chosen, raised, and educated. In the end, his plan is "to persuade first the rulers themselves and the soldiers and then the rest of the city that in good sooth all [the] training and educating of them were things that they imagined and that happened to them as it were in a dream, but that in reality all that time they were down within the earth being molded and fostered themselves while their weapons and the rest of their equipment were being fashioned."[10] In short, the lie is that culture is nature. Although in fact their world, their roles within it, and their education for those roles were all artfully designed, they are to be brought to consider themselves as having been born into their roles, which will themselves appear to be born of nature, as will the entire cultural, social, political, and economic world of the republic. Art creates the republic, but through its art art itself is to be forgotten.

For thousands of years, in the theater of everyday life, this paradox and all that it entails have been reiterated. In the commonplace recognition that human beings, as cultural creatures, are not simply works of nature but works of art, we show our insight into the politics of Socrates's aesthetics. The tropes we still use were already familiar to Plato: children are to be mastered, molded, stamped, bred, led, cultivated, shaped, formed, disciplined, raised, guided, guarded, supervised, tested, refined, or, in a word, made. They are to become what they are not, what they would not have been without all sorts of cultural interventions, and thus transformed into adults the way artists make their materials into paintings or sculptures or such-like things. As Orlan has put it, alluding to the social theory of Michel Foucault, "Every culture disciplines, punishes, and fabricates the body."[11]

At the same time as it is recognized, however, this creative activity is made a secret. Just as in the *Republic*, the necessity of this artistry may be acknowledged but must also begin in a profound dissimulation. This dissimulation is so profound that humans come to believe that it is only in a secondary or derivative sense that they are artworks. Having been painted, sculpted, scripted, or in some other way made art, they still maintain a category of art for certain objects with which they recognize their affinity only figuratively. Though they are art, it is always with surprise or a sense of novelty that they come to see themselves as being like an artwork. The assertion that life imitates art seems like a paradox to them, and figures such as Diderot and Orlan seem untraditional. Predictably, they underestimate the art in humanity, overestimate the humanity in art, and thus obscure the unhuman motivations of both of them. In short, they create their nature through the conception of art as a noble lie.

Diderot's paradox of the actor is this paradox of the noble lie, and his insensible thespians are counterparts to Plato's dispassionate rulers. Accordingly, Diderot compared the realm of theatrical spectacle to that of a well-ordered society, with the actor who keeps a cool head in the one deemed analogous to "the just man" in the other.[12] To be sure, Diderot made a travesty of the good society as Socrates conceived of it. He virtually upended this conception by granting so much more value to actors on the stage, with their thoroughly dubious backgrounds, than he did to the human actors in the respectable professions and elite ranks of society. Precisely for this reason, however, he proved an insightful critic of Plato's noble lie and of all that is taken to follow from it. He saw that the logical incoherence of this famous paradox not only affects our conceptions of art and humanity but binds them together in a profoundly antipathetic and ultimately incomprehensible relationship.

In Plato's account, Socrates portrayed himself as a sculptor putting the finishing touches on those who would rule over the ideal state. Through their regulation of the social order, these ruler-artworks, in turn, were supposed to become political artists producing citizen-artworks in the various kinds made possible by the differing natural potential of individuals.[13] Socrates anticipated that this artistic image of himself and of the ideal rulers of the ideal state would appear counterintuitive to his audience. He regulated his discourse accordingly, introducing this image only gradually and showing great concern to control the probable reactions of his audience at every turn in his argument's design. Thus, in presenting himself as a kind of artist, like a sculptor, he also showed himself to be an actor. Inadvertently, then, despite all his precautions, he set the stage for Diderot's identification of the just ruler as a vulgar fraud.

For Socrates, education in its origins is fabulation, untrue stories.[14] In order to produce truth, the appearance of education must hide within itself the truth of this falsehood, along with other sorts of lies, so that students do not realize how they have been made to act.[15] Friedrich Nietzsche recognized this situation when he characterized pedagogy as "dissimulation" and the educator, who is "beyond good and evil," as an actor who "never says what he himself thinks, but always only what he thinks of a thing in relation to the requirements of those he educates."[16] Long before Nietzsche, though, Diderot drew the logical conclusion that, according to his own principles, Socrates could not possibly have known what he was talking about. Instead he was akin to the talented but thoroughly unrespectable actors on the stage in eighteenth-century France. Under the dignity of the ideal of humanity that Socrates sketched for his listeners lay a disturbing insensibility to the very qualities he portrayed as ideal. At the origin of the noble lie lay the lie of nobility, or the lying noble, who should therefore be seen as fit company for the faithless priest, the loveless seducer, the hostile supplicant, and, in general, all successful human actors.

So what is it like to be a work of art? It is like being human, Diderot suggested. To be more precise, it is like performing the lie of one's humanity. Dissimulation, not imitation, must be the keyword of this aesthetics, in which the being of a work of art is like a human being recognizing how unhuman he or she is. With his fables, his metaphors, his aesthetic reference points, his calculated acting within the genre of the dialogue— not to mention his godlike literary immortality—Socrates, Diderot saw, was a human work of art.

From this perspective, humanity constitutes itself by creatively positing the categorical priority of artworks over people, who then can only be "like" art. In order to maintain its self-constituting deception of itself, humanity needs to differentiate this category of art within culture and in distinction from its own being. Thus is created the paradox, the lie of noble dignity, in which our species lives and moves and has its being. Thus is nature made out of culture.

Consequently, when persons overtly make artworks of themselves, as in the case of Baudelaire's dandies or related figures such as Oscar Wilde and Andy Warhol, their activity is likely to prove disturbing to the general public. In such persons the public is confronted with a challenge to the presumed primacy of the artwork as an object in distinction from the human subject. Insofar as dandies, aesthetes, or the like are seen as a special case, however—that is, as persons only aspiring to be like art—the provocation need not be especially distressing. A real problem arises only when there might seem to be no difference between art and humanity in general. In bringing us to this insight, what Diderot left unexplored but marked out as the most provocative conclusion that might be drawn from his paradox of the actor was the possibility that ordinary, unimaginative, undistinguished persons should put themselves onstage in all their unmitigated vulgarity and call the resulting display "art."

Of course, rather than sounding provocative, this conclusion may remind some readers of reviews of performance art by dyspeptic cultural critics such as Robert Hughes and Hilton Kramer—or even of reviews by more thoughtful critics who have been confronted just once too often by the work of artists who are unable to live down to their pretensions. Paradoxes are a lot easier to come by, after all, than a work like Diderot's "Paradox of the Actor," and for a long time now so-called provocations in the arts have been a dime a dozen. Still, the question remains: what would happen if one tried to live out the recognition that art is not first in objects and only then, metaphorically, a condition that may be ascribed to human beings? What would happen if one tried to live out the implications suggested by Diderot's unknotting of Socrates' noble lie? What is it like to be an artwork once *artwork* is seen to be, first and foremost, the work that makes humans? What is it like to be made human by a fable, a lie—an unhuman motivation that forever escapes the very notion of humanity it creates?

Orlan's attempt to answer these questions is particularly interesting because it does seem to take the implications of Diderot's paradox to the logical extremes of theatrical representation. For instance, in a 1993 performance titled *Omnipresence*, which was part of a series of such works collectively titled *The Reincarnation of Saint Orlan* (1990–95), she underwent an operation that consisted, in part, of the insertion of implants under the flesh above her eyebrows. (The implants were of a type normally used to enhance the appearance of cheekbones.) Like her other plastic surgeries, this one was conducted in elaborately theatricalized surroundings. Orlan wore an Issey Miyake gown and read from a text on her art by a Lacanian analyst, Eugénie Lémoine-Luccione, as well as from writings by Julia Kristeva, Michel Serres, and Antonin Artaud. She performed in the manner of an actor or a performance artist, on a live video feed and while fully conscious, keeping a cool head, even as the flesh on her face was being sliced away and resculpted (Figure 16).

Through this performance Orlan commented on her existence as a work of art. The plastic surgery was designed to reproduce in her flesh a morphed image (created through a computer program) in which her original appearance would be combined with "the visage of Leonardo da Vinci's *La Joconde*, Sandro Botticelli's *Venus*, the *Diana* sculpted by an anonymous artist of the school of Fontainebleu, François Gérard's *Psyche*, and Gustave Moreau's *Europa*."[17] As Orlan explained it, her aim was to act "against the standards of beauty and against these models" by reworking them, keeping in mind the positive associations they also had for her. Diana, for instance, "was chosen because she is insubordinate to gods and men," Mona Lisa "as a guiding light in the history of art" and as an image of "a problem of identity," given the theory that her appearance corresponds to Leonardo's own.[18] Completing the whole were the features created on her forehead: "the two little bumps that go beyond these times, two volcanoes in eruption over the dominant ideology."[19] Although Orlan planned her remodeled brow to be related to Mona Lisa's, these features correspond to no conventional physiognomy in art or in life. Having often proclaimed that "the body is obsolete," Orlan effectively explained this statement by thus incarnating the anachronistic and unhuman nature of art in her own flesh.[20] Other people now sometimes look upon her as if she were an alien from the universe of *Star*

Figure 16. *Orlan* (2002). Photo courtesy Philippe Leroux/SIPA.

Trek; no wonder David Cronenberg, the director of *Scanners* (1981), *Dead Ringers* (1988), and *Crash* (1996), among other films about the unhuman, is said to have wanted her to play herself in one of his movies.[21]

To regard Orlan as she appeared in the aftermath of this performance is to see demonstrated the noble lie of the artwork's precedence over its dissimulations in humanity. Her quasi-Nietzschean "going beyond" shows up the tendency to underestimate the art in humanity, to overestimate the humanity of art, and thus to obscure the unhuman motivation in both of them. As Linda S. Kauffman has commented, Orlan "gives new meaning to an 'anatomy of criticism.'"[22] Like Burden, the American artist who arranged to have his body modified by a .22 rifle bullet, Orlan crossed the barrier between symbolic and real violence, a distinction wrought in the making of art and the unmaking of humanity, in order to suggest that it is ultimately a distinction without a difference. So she has written, "It would be false to distinguish my operation-performances from my *Self Hybridations* [produced through computer-manipulated images] as that which arises uniquely from the real, on the one hand, and, on the other, from the purely virtual."[23] Like Burden's, her work has stimulated the most basic sort of questions as to whether she "really" did it, whether the art in question is "really" real. Orlan reports that when Barbara Rose sought to publish an article on her work in *Art in America*, the editor-in-chief demanded videotaped evidence in order to be certain that these surgical operations had really happened.[24]

Yet Orlan's artistry is, in fact, quite traditional. Like Napoleon's gesture of crowning himself, Orlan's self-nomination marks her recognition and acceptance of the presumptuous nature of modern identity, that noble lie. Like the Gothic tradition that remade Descartes's demonic and yet eminently modern theater of identity, Orlan defines thinking by way of the unhuman in an art that willfully "swings between defiguration and refiguration."[25] Moreover, like Goya's reworking of Ovidian metamorphoses, Orlan's retracing of art history brings out an immemorial violence, especially against women, that has led her to resist and transform the distinctions of gender. While opposed to the example of the futurists by virtue of her staunch feminism and her thoroughgoing recognition of the anachronistic nature of art—"Today is already formerly"[26]—she yet resembles them in her identification with cutting-edge technology, her resistance to the image of art as an inherited body of sacred tradition, her related opposition to the Catholic tradition that she blasphemes in her role as Saint Orlan, and, most generally, in her drive to project an image of herself as a being that has moved beyond humanity. We see this projection, for instance, when an enthused critic exclaims, "Orlan is fundamentally a mutant actually recognized as such."[27]

In the foregoing respects Orlan's self-sculpting aesthetic might seem to be the antipodes of the sculptural aesthetic of George Segal, who saw himself as a humanist and whose work has generally been seen as devoted, even to a fault, to the image of ordinary human bodies. To come to such a conclusion, however, would be to forget the eerie realism, the instructive agony, in Segal's Kent State memorial, which suspends us at the very limits of our ability to know what it might mean to be human.

Orlan, too, is just this traditional. As the sacrificial nature of art, in Segal's portrayal, is designed to blind and paralyze us, so, too, does Orlan follow her very different designs to a similar end. "My work situates itself," she has written, "between the madness of seeing and the impossibility of seeing."[28] Despite all their differences, which are obviously many and significant, these cases all lead us to confront the unhuman culture that we try in so many ways to deny.

What is it like to be an artwork? This is the question of all culture, of all education, of the very making of humanity. Therefore, it is also the question of the unhuman and thus of all monstrosity, as Mary Shelley recognized in *Frankenstein: Or, the New Prometheus* (1817).[29] Fittingly, then, one of Orlan's artworks is a 1990 photograph of herself with her hair designed to look like Elsa Lanchester's in *The Bride of Frankenstein* (1935). This concern to display the paradox of the artwork has animated her career from the beginning. One of her earliest photographic works, for instance, was *An Attempt to Come out of the Frame* (1965), in which a naked Orlan emerges from a picture frame that we would ordinarily expect to hold, undisturbed, a flat image. Similarly, in a 1968 exhibition, *The Grand Odalisque*, she reconstructed this art-historical chestnut by using her own body to usurp the place of the familiar voluptuous image. She thus symbolically displaced all works of art insofar as their materiality has figured, in imagination, as the passive female object to be manipulated by male subjects possessed of creative power. In addition, just as her appearances under the name of Saint Orlan allude to works such as Giovanni Lorenzo Bernini's seventeenth-century Saint Theresa, so, too, has she impersonated other such figures, including the Madonna and Botticelli's Venus, thus pointing to the age-old denigration of women by means of their spiritualization or idealization. In suggesting that Orlan is, as Parveen Adams has put it, "an image trapped in the body of a woman," all these works look forward to their culmination in the metamorphoses made real in the computer and in the operating room.[30] She has even had reliquaries made from the flesh removed in her surgeries, thus calling attention to the culturally pervasive nature of the Lacanian *corps morcellé* at the same time as she shortcircuits culture by crossing the wires of the sacred and the profane.

In relating Orlan's art to that of Marcel Duchamp and Andy Warhol, Christine Buci-Glucksmann (borrowing a Duchampian catchphrase) has characterized it in terms of "the beauty of indifference."[31] One can understand the motivations for this remark, but it is, perhaps, too redolent of dated avant-garde attitudes, such as those among Baudelaire's dandies, that are really quite foreign to Orlan's work. This remark would seem more appropriate, for instance, if applied to Duchamp himself or to someone like Guillaume Apollinaire, who stated, "More than anything,

Figure 17. Hannah Wilke, *Give: Hannah Wilke Can—A Living Sculpture Needs to Make a Living.* © 2005 Donald Goddard. Courtesy Ronald Feldman Fine Arts, New York. Photo Donald Goddard.

artists are men who want to become inhuman."[32] Dissemblence is not the same as indifference, after all, and there is good reason to take seriously Orlan's characterization of her work as "carnal art": that is, as an art moved by and meant to communicate passion. Like Diderot's actors, Orlan is, in an important sense, unhuman, but this is not to say that she is inhuman or indifferent. It is rather to say that she disrupts the noble lie of humanity and thus, necessarily, the art through which that humanity has historically sought to dissimulate its imaginary identity. A better comparison is to an artist such as Wilke, who referred to herself as a living sculpture in one of her works ("Give: Hannah Wilke Can—A Living Sculpture Needs to Make a Living" [1978]—Figure 17) and who titled another "I Object: Memoirs of a Sugargiver" (1977–78). "Object" in this last title is both a verb and a noun, conveying a sense of resistance even as it mocks traditional objectifications of women and points to the artist as a new sort of object, an "I Object," an embodied performance of identity.

Like the art of Wilke, an approximate contemporary, Orlan's work arises, in part, from an idiosyncratic take on the feminist movements of the 1970s and has benefited, in terms of its reception, from the cultural changes effected by those movements. Again like Wilke, however, she has never been what one would call a politic feminist, a good person to draft for a committee or to entrust with a position as the public face of an organization. Opposing her work to the fourfold police of "religion, psychoanalysis, money, and art history," she is more like an unreconstructed *soixant-huitard* than a positive role model whom one should seek out to sign a petition.[33] As Wilkes's was, her work is as disturbing toward the humanistic strains in post-70s feminism as it is toward the patriarchal infrastructure of humanism in general. In this respect her art is also related to that of other women artists of the 1960s and 1970s such as Carolee Schneeman, Gina Pane, Eleanor Antin, Ana Mendieta, and Adrian Piper.[34]

Orlan's art is further related to that of other artists from this era, such as the Viennese Actionists, Burden, Gilbert and George (especially in their "living sculpture" period), and Marina Abramovic, whose work was not markedly feminist but was clearly preoccupied with the contemporary discovery, as it were, of the body as an art object. In the case of Abramovic, this led to works such as her 1975 *Rhythm O*, in which the artist provided seventy-two objects on a table—ranging from a gun, a bullet, a whip, a knife, a lipstick, a feather, a bandage, a book, and a hammer to honey, salt, sugar, cake, and an apple—while providing herself as well, declaring, "I am an object. During this period I take full responsibility." She also created "instructions for the public," which consisted of the sentence, "There are seventy-two objects on the table that one can use on me as desired."[35] Surviving this as well as other performances that might be considered to have risked her life, Abramovic has generally characterized her aesthetics in terms that are mystical, optimistic, and primitivist, teetering on the edge, if not falling right over into, New Age earnestness. Nonetheless, as with Orlan's work, which can also at times seem fuzzy-minded and simplistic in her accounts of it, Abramovic's works have always carried with them a powerful recognition of the unhuman motivations in art, as in the ongoing series of sculptures she has collectively titled *Transitory Objects for Non-Human Use* (1991-present). This series includes, for instance, the 1995 *Chair for Non-Human Use* (Figure 18), the legs of which are impossibly high, regarded from a conventional human standpoint.

It is also important to see Orlan in the context of certain others who are not artists, properly speaking, but who, as the result of work like Orlan's, Abramovic's, Wilke's, and Burden's—not to mention Warhol's and Duchamp's—may well be seen as morphing the supposedly proper definitions of artists and artistry into hitherto unthinkable forms. These would include not only Michael Jackson, considered now as a body artist rather than as King of Pop and alleged pedophile, but also less famous persons who have nonetheless gained a certain popular recognition. We might think of Jocelyn Wildenstein, the New York socialite who had her

Figure 18. Marina Abramovic, *Chair for Non-Human Use* (1995). © 2005 Artists Rights Society (ARS), New York/VG Bild-Kunst, Bonn. Photo courtesy Marina Abramovic and Sean Kelly Gallery, New York.

face remodeled to resemble a jungle cat's, or Cindy Jackson, who remodeled her face and body in her quest to resemble a Barbie doll.

Persons such as these might seem to be degrading company for Orlan, with her university affiliations, aesthetic manifestos, readings from Lacanian psychiatrists and poststructuralist philosophers, and allusions to the traditions of high art. To regard this comparison as degrading, however, would be to fall into the error of which Diderot wrote more than two centuries ago: the error of confusing performance with refined sensibility and, thus, with personhood. Michael Jackson, Jocelyn

Wildenstein, Cindy Jackson, and innumerable other practitioners of "body mod" will not seem to be artists in the same sense in which Orlan is—may seem more like actors in the offstage condition described by Diderot, uncultivated and unimportant—only to those who imaginatively clean up Orlan's art, purifying it of its scattershot politics, narcissism, blood, vulgarity, and extremity, so that it will still bespeak a noble sense of humanity. Whether they appreciate her work or not, those who do not wish to engage in this sort of policing will recognize that one cannot insult such an actor by comparing her performances to those of the miserable generality of the species. It is precisely this sort of comparison that her art demands, just as Diderot's art did. Keeping a cool head as she directs and undergoes her operations, dressed in designer fashions and reading from cool works of theory, too, Orlan may incarnate a kind of dignity, but it is not one that can be claimed by the species, by humanity. It belongs, rather, to the work of art.

What is it like to be a work of art? Those bumps above the artist's eyebrows provide a response. It is like being the foreign body of humanity: the body that must appear foreign, like a déclassé actor or a détourné implant, so that humanity may feel at home in its skin. Therefore, it is also like being at odds with oneself: expressive by virtue of inexpressiveness, natural by virtue of cultivation, sophisticated by virtue of ignorance, self-identical by virtue of dissimulation, and so on. To be like a work of art is then also to be like an image of society unable to comprehend itself as such, destined instead to seem paradoxical, as if founded on antagonism rather than unity: at once real and unreal, like and unlike, material and ideal, existing in truth and represented in rhetoric. It is like being differentiated by gender, sexuality, race, class, status, wealth, and other categories of being while yet suffering a metamorphic power above, beyond, and through such differences. In other words, to be like a work of art is to be like a simultaneous experience of desire and disavowal that is bound to seem unhuman and yet profoundly and intimately unhuman. It is, in short, very much like being all too human.

Like Diderot's paradox, Orlan's brows, thus considered, can lead us to a better understanding of the essay by Thomas Nagel that I have deliberately deformed in the title of this essay. In "What is it like to be a bat?" Nagel writes about the mind-body problem, which he characterizes in terms of "the subjective character of experience" (116). He is concerned to argue that this character of experience explains the limitations of materialist philosophical explanations or, in other words, the would-be physicalist reduction of mind to body with which contemporary philosophers are much concerned. Nagel argues that "every subjective phenomenon is essentially connected with a single point of view, and it seems inevitable that an objective, physical theory will abandon that point of view" (167). The titular bat, then, finds its way into the essay to represent an exemplary, because especially striking, case of subjectivity. (Martians, whom he also brings into the essay, could also have served his purposes.) As "a fundamentally *alien* form of life" (168), this bat is supposed to teach us that, because we cannot adequately imagine its point of view, we ought not to hope for an ultimate reduction of subjective experience to objective explanation.

This essay has become so famous—among other effects, it has inspired a pop CD—that it might be considered something of an artwork itself. In fact, it may be more cogent as a work of art than as a philosophical argument. If taken in the latter character, this essay is perhaps most notable for its avoidance of any reference to culture. Something like this term needs to be in the essay because culture is both subjective and objective, both inside and outside, both what defines us as human and what divides us from other humans that we judge to be as alien as animals or extraterrestrials.[36] It is not in the essay, however, because its inclusion would have required its author to grapple with the falsity of the stark opposition he poses between subjectivity and objectivity. In other words, it would have taken Nagel out of the realm of Anglo-American philosophical discourse and into the realm of art.

Instead, driven by immemorial cultural tradition to underestimate the art in humanity, Nagel writes as if the question "What is it like to be a human?" were a simple one. This is not to say that he is unaware of complexities: he knows perfectly well that the problem he addresses "is not confined to exotic cases . . . for it exists between one person and another" (170). Moreover, he notes the relationship between the problem addressed in his thought experiment and the long-standing philosophical problem of "other minds" (178n). So Nagel's human beings do have some of the bat and the Martian, some Gothic monstrosity, in them. Nonetheless, he constructed his essay on the premise that, for the purposes of argument, he could assume that we all share the same subjectivity: "By 'our own case' I do not mean just 'my own case', but rather the mentalistic ideas that we apply unproblematically to ourselves and other human beings" (169n). This is how the art in humanity is underestimated, through this noble lie of the unproblematic species that makes a philosopher think he must turn to another species to find a sufficiently compelling example for the question of metaphysical difference that he is raising.

At the same time, this is how the humanity in art is overestimated: through the assumption that an aesthetic (in this case, of the exotic) can be invoked merely for the purpose of emphasis without there being any other effects on one's argument. Yet such power as this essay has had is largely owing to this aesthetic, without which it would have appeared as little more than a restatement of the opposition, which has been commonplace at least since Wilhelm Dilthey, of the human and physical sciences—an opposition that ultimately goes back to the Platonic distinctions between spiritual and earthly realities that eventuate in the art of the noble lie. As Nagel's essay itself establishes, the invocation of the bat proves nothing, after all, that could not, in principle, have been established by referring to other minds, to other animals, or to other beings hitherto unknown to us, such as Martians.

The choice of this one example over all the conceivable others lends the essay a vivid, outlandish, surrealistic—in a word, exotic—effect. In a work designed to prove the sublimity in subjectivity, beyond any physicalistic accounting, this Gothic bat is Nagel's sublime actor. All those who find the bat exotic, who identify unproblematically with one another by way of this image, compose the audience in his theater. It is fitting, then, that Nagel's essay has become something of a cult object, for through it the audience to which it is designed to appeal can experience an image of an ideal society based on the noble lie that disclaims art. Just as the craze for the Gothic in the late eighteenth and early nineteenth centuries enabled some enthusiasts to make a stand, however perverse, against the demystification of reality promised by modern science, so, too, does Nagel's Gothic serve a similar purpose almost two centuries later. Eerily, this neo-Cartesian essay repeats literary and cultural history in the form of philosophy and thus reminds us of the continuing importance of René Descartes as the first Gothic novelist.

What it is like to be a work of art is like that.

Conclusion: The Necessity of Misanthropy

> *I am not a friend of man and not at all proud of being a man. Confidence in man actually represents a menacing danger; belief in man is a great folly, a madness.*
> —E. M. Cioran

The notion that art is unhuman ought to be a great thumping platitude, and perhaps it is. Compelling philosophical, religious, economic, political, and psychological traditions bring us to see the misanthropic agency of art in cultural history. You must not make images of things, we have been sternly warned, for that golden calf we polish may become an idol before which we abase ourselves, embarrassing posterity. Banish your poets, burn your romances, and switch off *Baywatch*, we are admonished, lest we find ourselves starving to death as we feast on pie-in-the-sky illusions. We all know that art is likely to estrange us from humankind, putting us out of sympathy with our fellows. We expect the aesthete to be cold at heart and parasitic in character, like Waldo Lydecker in Otto Preminger's *Laura* (1944) or one of his contemporaries, Leni Riefenstahl, in Adolf Hitler's Third Reich. In the fiction of Thomas Bernhard the misanthrope himself will be brought to admit that art may displace human beings but cannot replace them: "with all those old masters we have always only had a mocking relationship."[1] Consuming resources that might otherwise be used to fight for justice, feed the poor, and keep IT networks humming along at maximum efficiency, art is a useless luxury, the first course to be cut when schools get back to basics. Its purposiveness, after all, is purposeless. Mad people make it, and it is akin to madness, and it may make us mad.

At the same time, many traditions image art as the epitome of human nature, the pinnacle of human civilization, and the very vehicle of humanization. These images also show our recognition that art is unhuman.

Paeans to art's divinity can comfortably coexist with hostility to it, as in persons such as Hilton Kramer and programs such as the National

Endowment for the Arts, because the assumption in both cases is that the fundamental motivations of art do not belong to humanity but to powers beyond it, which humanity can experience but cannot own. Transcendent or transgressive, ennobling or corrupting, however these powers may be described, an emphasis remains on the unhuman agency of art. Far from being in conflict, these differing images support each other now just as they have through thousands of years of aesthetic reflection. Art in any given instance may seem emancipatory or oppressive, depending on who is doing the talking, because in either case we take its motivations ultimately to lie beyond us. We recognize that it is "irretrievably irrational," as Thierry de Duve says, an "agonistic value" in which "disagreement is the rule."[2] As Georg Lukács put it, alluding to the legend of Galileo's *sotto voce* riposte to the authority of the Inquisition, "Art always says 'And yet!' to life."[3] The Gothic literature in which we see the unhuman agencies of rank, wealth, family, religion, and nationality sadistically lord it over human beings is but one genre of artistic testimony to the impasses into which we are driven if we remain reluctant fully to admit the unhuman nature of art.

If it is a fact, nevertheless, that it is odd to see art termed unhuman, then that fact deserves our consideration.

* * *

I always thought that artists are compassionate. That they create art out of compassion. But that was stupid.[4]

Through the figure of the misanthrope we image to ourselves the unhuman nature of art.

In his version of the legend of Timon the Misanthrope, which was also recorded by Plutarch, among others, Lucian took care to establish this point. To sum up Timon's vow to have nothing more to do with human beings, Lucian had him say, "In short, they shall be no more than statues of stone or bronze in my sight."[5]

To regard others as artworks is to treat them as unhuman and in doing so to establish one's own unhuman nature. One might say that Timon is assuming a role akin to that played by the capricious gods who rule over Ovid's *Metamorphoses* and Francisco Goya's *Disasters of War*: a role in which one can choose to change humans into stones or trees or heaps of other things. In his thorough rejection of everything associated with the human world, however, Timon has already cast off the possibility even of this identification. "I hate all alike, both gods and men," he says.[6] Lucian chose instead to situate Timon's misanthropy in the realm of the aesthetic, trusting his audience to understand what Ovid and Goya also would come to know: that the misanthrope, by definition, is imaginable only as a figure of art.

For Timon in the second century as for Dorian Gray in the late nineteenth, the misanthrope is a figure of art defined through a recognition of humanity as the aesthetic species. Humanity is the species betrayed by art, in both senses of that word: the species at once revealed and undone through the agency of art. What Percy Bysshe Shelley said of incest, that it is "a very poetical circumstance," is true also of misanthropy, and for the same reason.[7] It situates us on the very boundary of culture, there where it and we are being made, artfully.

In Plutarch's early second-century account as in Shakespeare's early seventeenth-century *Timon of Athens*, Timon most fully reveals himself by composing his own poetic epitaph. This apotropaic artwork demands anonymity for its author, promises curses to its readers, and thus further emphasizes the unhuman agency encrypted in art.[8] The figure of Timon suggests that humanity is definitively at odds with itself: identifiable only through disidentifications. Humanity would not be itself were it not also unhuman and thus truly recognizable only in art, as opposed to so-called human life. A comparable line of reasoning would lead Arthur Schopenhauer to the conclusion that to be alive and human is of necessity to be misanthropic, such being the consequence of life's divisive *principium individuationis*. The only exceptions to this rule, as he saw it, were those who have completely renounced the will to live and so may look upon things as if from the viewpoint of the dead. For these saintly or ascetic sorts, Schopenhauer said, the world is like an artwork. At certain moments, as when we lose ourselves in beauty, human beings in general may also see the world in this way. At such moments one "looks back calmly and with a smile on the phantasmagoria of this world which was once able to move and agonize even his mind, but now stands before him as indifferently as chess-men at the end of a game, or as fancy dress cast off in the morning, the form and figure of which taunted and disquieted us on the carnival night."[9] Not quite an object and too much of an object, at once falling short of and exceeding reality by objectifying reality's insufficiency, the artwork is the measure of the misanthrope and the proof of this figure's necessity.

Knowing what we know of the history of humanity, who can fail to realize that the trope of misanthropy is the hope of society?

*   *   *

. . . he had to support police and the good of society, which, he remarked very quietly, would take care, down in Surrey, that these unsocial impulses, bred more than anything by the lack of good blood, were held in control.[10]

The misanthrope's aesthetic nature is symbolized above all else by his presentation as an extreme and exceptional figure.

At first glance it must seem absolutely absurd that it should be so. After all, it is not only surrealist anthropologists such as Georges Bataille who tell us of "the immeasurable hate that divides mankind."[11] Bataille was no more eloquent on this point than was Christopher Marlowe's damned Faustus or, for that matter, the eminent humanist Guillaume Budé:

I might almost say we are bound to admit that this is the real end of legal training and the profession of the civil law: to make each man act with ingrained and calculated malice towards the neighbour to whom he is linked by ties of citizenship and sometimes of blood. He is always grabbing something, taking it away, extorting it, suing for it, squeezing it out, breaking it loose, gouging it away, twisting it off, snatching it, snitching it, filching it, pinching it, pilfering it, pouncing on it—partly with the tacit complicity of the laws, partly with their direct sanction, he carries off what he wants and makes it his own.[12]

In our own time, even a mind as ordinary as Margaret Thatcher's could recognize that "there is no such thing as society."[13] For Thatcher this misanthropy at the heart of social life was to be celebrated; she seemed to take quite seriously the notion of compassion advanced by the professional mope Oscar Levant, who once quipped, "It's the quality I expect in everyone except myself."[14] The men and women of Britain applauded this misanthropy right along with Thatcher insofar as they lent their support to a motto, that people must "look to themselves first," that placed this proud daughter of the middle classes into the venerable tradition of Social Darwinist speculation, Hobbesian political theory, and Ovidian theophany.[15] Thus do we, as Petrarch said, "unlearn humanity among men."[16] We might also recall the famous example of Niccolò Machiavelli, who, like Thatcher, offered token expressions of respect for humanity while advocating policies that were misanthropic through and through. Possessed of a much finer mind than Thatcher's, however, Machiavelli was much better able to comprehend the implications of his position, as when he managed slyly to identify Dante, the divine poet, with his own pitiless pragmatism. Often, Machiavelli wrote, the common people,

deceived by an illusive good, desire their own ruin, and, unless they are made sensible of the evil of the one and the benefit of the other course by some one in whom they have confidence, they will expose the republic to infinite peril and damage. . . . Dante says upon this point in his discourse "On Monarchy," that the people often shout, "Life to our death, and death to our life!"[17]

Margaret Thatcher provides us with but a single modern instance, of course, of how decidedly unexceptional misanthropy is. From their own simmering resentments or their casual watching of the evening news, one's fellow humans can be trusted to come up with any number of other examples. After all, from its beginnings the legend of Timon has invited us to see this sort of figure as saturated with irony, with its hatred and rejection of humankind actually conveying an eminently human sort of love. Such is the case, for instance, with another character from Thatcher's era, the protagonist of Dennis Potter's scabrous masterpiece *The Singing Detective* (1986).

To become the extraordinary figure of the misanthrope, this irony tells us, one must fail to comprehend the most elementary lesson one encounters in life. Far from destroying the ideal of humanity, this lesson informs us, mutual hostility actually serves to constitute it. As we learn from his rude behavior, from the flashbacks to his childhood, and from his quasi-cinematic fantasies, this is the lesson Potter's Philip Marlow is forever trying to accept. This familiar irony explains why the supposedly extraordinary misanthrope can figure as society's ultimate aesthetic achievement, as William Thackeray had pointed out in the preceding century when he portrayed that gleeful "young misanthropist," Becky Sharpe, as the artist and artwork virtually demanded by the times.[18] It also explains why an avid and miserly approach to money, as with Thackeray's Becky, Charles Dickens's Scrooge, and George Eliot's Silas Marner, is often associated with the misanthrope. In cases such as these, this character is shown to be betrayed by, or simultaneously obsessed with and repelled by, the economic conflicts that are at the center of social life for everyone. Similarly, the frequent association of misanthropy with misogyny, in *The Singing Detective* no less than in Friedrich Schiller's *The Misanthropist Reconciled* (1790), pins this figure, wriggling with obsession and repulsion, to sexual conflicts so common as to be banal. For instance, the gold standard for inhumanity in eighteenth-century England was the history of the Spaniards' genocidal behavior in the New World; and it is as a result of the most banal cause imaginable, her betrayal by men, that the character of Millwood in George Lillo's *London Merchant* (1731) becomes so deeply misanthropic as to identify with this behavior of her nation's historic enemy.

Through the figure of the misanthrope we are impressed with what Jean-Luc Nancy calls the exposition of community: the spacing of singularities, or alterity, in society.[19] The excommunication of the misanthrope by society, or vice-versa, exposes the fallacy that community is founded on communication. As with Schopenhauer's *principium individuationis*, we see instead the constitutive and ultimately incommunicable role of dissension in all things.

We pretend that the misanthrope is an unusual figure in the same way we pretend that peace within and among nations is the normal state of affairs in relation to which all outbreaks of violence are deviations, mistakes, or surprises. In other words, the misanthrope is an abnormal figure in the same sense in which it is normal to name a military campaign "Operation Infinite Justice."[20] The King of Brobdingnag knew as much, as we can see in his shocked reaction to Lemuel Gulliver when this Yahoo offers to help him acquire gunpowder, cannons, and related armaments:

The King was struck with Horror at the Description I had given of those terrible Engines, and the Proposal I had made. He was amazed how so impotent and groveling an Insect as I (these were his Expressions) could entertain such inhuman Ideas, and in so familiar a Manner as to appear wholly unmoved at all by the Scenes of Blood and Destruction, which I had painted as the common Effects of those destructive Machines; whereof he said, some evil Genius, Enemy to Mankind, must have been the first Contriver.[21]

What René Descartes had celebrated as the recipe for modernity, the definition of thought by way of the unhuman, the King sees in its full Gothic horror, as a formula for misanthropy. Following Descartes but well in advance of the Gothic lesson, Jonathan Swift saw that this misanthropy actually constitutes the human species. Yahoos, the Master Houyhnhnm tells Gulliver, "were known to hate one another more than they did any different Species of Animal."[22]

Despite this kind of recognition, the absurdity in the presentation of the misanthrope as an extreme and exceptional figure does make a certain kind of sense. As art disavows the imaginable limits of humanity through the figure of the misanthrope, we see how unimaginable the reality of social life is. "There is no such thing as society," the misanthrope tells us; and even though we know the truth of this saying perfectly well, our predictable response is to see this figure as a spoiled idealist, an extreme and exceptional figure, whom art humanistically enables us to patronize. So we get works in which the misanthrope is ritually brought to appreciate art, such as Ferdinand Raimund's 1828 play *The Alpine King and the Misanthrope*, in which the protagonist's economic anxieties and distrust of humankind are manifested in his rejection of his daughter's suitor, a young artist, until the magic of art corrects his temperament. Like the popular eighteenth-century theme of the misanthrope reconciled to society, this play marks a specifically modern attempt to unite art and life in the name of humanity. This attempt could succeed, however, only by reducing both art and life to sentimentality, the opiate of the bourgeoisie. This reconciliation through the magic of art dramatizes the modern attempt to master art by denying its unhuman nature or, in other words, by erasing the social conflicts without reference to which art is, indeed, senseless "magic." At the same time, though, this plot represents the traditional understanding of the misanthrope that has one of its origins in Plato's *Phaedo*, that is taken up in conventional readings of characters such as Molière's Alceste in *The Misanthrope* (1666) and William Wycherley's Manly in *The Plain Dealer* (1676), and that is still commonplace today. Through this understanding we deny the unhuman nature of art so that the reality of social life may remain, as we so passionately wish it to be, absolutely unthinkable.

In fact, it is almost as if the whole idea of the misanthrope must be so unthinkable that it deserves to be treated as something of a joke. Accordingly, in literary and cultural history it is common for those who obviously appear to be misanthropes to deny that they are any such thing. Lord Byron's Childe Harold, for instance, takes pains to assert that he does not view the throng of humankind "with misanthropic hate"; Bernard Mandeville denies he is "a Man-hater"; and E. M. Cioran, who wrote *On the Inconvenience of Being Born* (1973), among other titles, still insisted, "People horrify me, but I am not a misanthrope."[23]

Misanthropes say such things because they are misanthropic enough to have confidence that their audience will believe them.

Perhaps they say them as well because they remain human enough to take their own words at face value.

*   *   *

I exist on the earth as on a strange planet to which I have fallen from the one I used to inhabit.[24]

We might see the misanthrope as a character type and then trace the histories, complexities, associations, and influences of this *hosti humani generis*. Then we would say something like the following: "Before the misanthrope became the sociopath, the infamous loner of whom neighbors tell after someone on a killing spree is finally taken into custody, he had many other careers: hermit, anchorite, devil, scholar, hypochondriac, Wandering Jew, Romantic hero, ironist, anarchist, narcissist, existentialist anti-hero." Tracing a genealogy back to figures such as Menander's "Dyskolos," or "bad-tempered man" (c. 317 B.C.E.), we would draw on a lexicon of terms such as *bitter, dour, bilious, dyspeptic, joyless, angry, mordant,* and *choleric.* We would trace careful distinctions among subtypes so as to distinguish, for example, the biomedical concept of the sociopath from the psychoanalytic concept of the narcissist or from the theological treatment of the devil as the proverbial enemy of man.

This would represent an eminently human approach, one in which everything becomes thinkable—save for reality and art.

Michael Haneke makes this point in his masterpiece of misanthropy, the 1998 film *Funny Games,* in which two young men invade a lake house and gratuitously torture and kill the Spielbergian mother, father, and son vacationing there. This work is obviously motivated by the pleasure audiences take in the suspense offered by family hostage films such as *Desperate Hours* (1955) and *Straw Dogs* (1971), but it speaks as well to every cinematic device that invites us to explore the supposed depths of human nature. *Funny Games* demands that the members of its audience recognize the sadomasochistic nature of suspense, take responsibility for the pleasure they take in this mechanism, and thus come face to face with their own implication in this film's misanthropic design, which refuses to pay society off in the end with a conventional offering of innocence or knowledge. Its conclusion—that all this torture and death has indeed been a peculiar game—marks Haneke's attempt to get at the unimaginable reality of social life and the unthinkable viciousness of the popular conception of art as a trivial vacation from that reality.

In "The Age of the World Picture" (1938) Martin Heidegger similarly saw such a trivializing of art as an "essential phenomenon of the modern period" deserving our unequivocal rejection. What happens, he wrote, when art moves "into the purview of aesthetics" is that "the art work becomes the object of mere subjective experience, and . . . consequently art is considered to be an expression of human life." He added that "human activity," concomitantly, "is conceived and consummated as culture," and he meant his readers to understand that this was an absolutely scathing description of the present state of affairs.[25] It would be pretty to think that Heidegger's terrible complicity with Hitler's regime should invalidate this misanthropic picture of the world and restore to his readers the simple relation of art to humanity that we nostalgically imagine always to have existed, or at least at some time to have existed somewhere, before the barbarians arrived. Walter Benjamin, however, no less than Heidegger, would tell us a different story.

Insightfully seeing exactly what was wrong with the modern conception of art, Heidegger came to exactly the wrong conclusion as to what was to be done to rectify it. He proved himself to be more like the vulgar Sam Peckinpah than the artful Michael Haneke, and his aesthetic spawn are the Chapman brothers, with their cheap trivializations of Nazi imagery.

Heidegger might have been one of the greatest misanthropes of the twentieth century. Instead, dramatically and disgustingly, like the thugs in *Funny Games*, he showed himself to be all too human.

* * *

The community of lovers—no matter if the lovers want it or not, enjoy it or not, be they linked by chance, by "*l'amour fou*," by the passion of death (Kleist)—has as its ultimate goal the destruction of society. There where an episodic community takes shape between two beings who are made or who are not made for each other, a war machine is set up or, to say it more clearly, the possibility of a disaster carrying within itself, be it in infinitesimal doses, the menace of universal annihilation.[26]

Contrary to the conventional understanding of this figure, an understanding that always serves to foreclose any fundamental questions about humanity, the opposite of the misanthrope is not the well-adjusted member of society. The opposite of this figure is the utopia: the totalitarian state in which art, no longer allowed to be misanthropic, is compelled to be healthy, satisfied, fully human.

Because his conception of futurism failed to recognize this opposition between misanthropy and utopia, Filippo Tommaso Marinetti was easy prey for Mussolini.

*   *   *

Ourselves with noise of reason we do please
In vain: humanity's our worst disease.[27]

In his narrative Lemuel Gulliver defends himself against the people who have charged him with "degrading human Nature, (for so they still have the confidence to stile it)."[28] Yet he does say that he expressed a wish, to the Portuguese captain who rescued him, for "some desolate place where to pass the Remainder of his unfortunate Life."[29] As a correlative to the figure of the misanthrope, alienated from or dead to the world, we have the image of this sort of utopian place, which takes the form of art because it bears both human and otherworldly references. Later in the eighteenth century, for instance, Schiller's Hutton would make a *hortus conclusus* of his estate, within which he would seek to make of his daughter a perfect work of art. The lake house in *Funny Games* is a later variant of this place. Timon's grave may be taken as the symbolic original of all such sites, as Thomas Hardy recognized when he alluded to it in the perfectly desolate scene of Michael Henchard's death and burial in *The Mayor of Casterbridge* (1886).

Yet misanthropic retirement, such as that of which Gulliver dreams, is but a markedly aesthetic version of all the retirements that structure social life. These include the walls of manners and manors alike. Retirements are made of formal behavioral codes; the legal structuring of conduct, identity, experience, and the material world; the physical architecture of barriers, gates, doors, and rooms; and the informal traditions that give life to concepts such as freedom, peace, understanding, and love. To convey this lesson, Swift designs his narrative so that no sooner is he rescued by those presumed to be his fellow humans than

Gulliver is forced to plead that he is not their enemy. Although his native land and Portugal are currently at war, as he has now learned, he notes that they were still friendly when he set out on his adventure five years earlier. He asks to be regarded as an anachronistic figure, effectively outside of social space and time, and thus more misanthrope—or Yahoo—than man.

Swift's view of human nature, so called, is then further illustrated when the worldly Portuguese captain tells the poor Yahoo that he should forego his dream of an exotic island and instead return to England, there to live with his wife and children. In the bosom of his family, the worldly captain assures Gulliver, he can count on finding all the desolation he could possibly desire.

$$* \quad * \quad *$$

Do you know if you ripped the fronts off houses you'd find swine?[30]

As Nathaniel Hawthorne warned, with a mixture of moralistic gravity and sneaking pleasure, in "Wakefield" (1835) and "The Birth-mark" (1843), among other writings, misanthropy takes form in the interruption by desire of an imaginary immediacy: an interruption that provides the minimal condition for our recognition of both humanity and art. Hawthorne showed desire as being moved by a will to enjoy the world as an aesthetic phenomenon, as Aylmer does when he strives to remove his beloved's blemish and as Wakefield does when he steps outside his door one day and does not return for twenty years, passing his time in the interim just one street over. Hawthorne thus showed his recognition that misanthropy, like art, is traditionally characterized in terms of an aspiration for transcendence, escape, or metamorphosis. No wonder Herman Melville became his admirer and friend. "Alone among the millions of the peopled earth, nor gods nor men his neighbors," misanthropic Ahab is a profoundly aesthetic subject, and an artist as well, one who seeks to make his mark not with pen or paintbrush but with a harpoon.[31] With misanthropy as with art, in this case as in others, we are likely to speak of a commitment to the ideal even as we also conceive of it in terms of alienation, uncompromising criticism, or the assertion of radical individualism in the face of pressures for conformity. Like Alceste, Aylmer and Ahab are demonically sincere because they make sincerity a transcendent value.

So the disillusionment with Brook Farm to which Hawthorne gave artistic form in *The Blithedale Romance* (1852) should have been predictable. From the outset of his career Hawthorne was drawn to demonic utopias, including the part of the New World that eventually became the United States, because he knew that misanthropy cannot be eliminated from social life any more than it can be from sexual desire or the ontology of art. The very will to eliminate it, he suggested, is not a solution to but a sign of misanthropy. That is why we need art: so as not to commit the unforgiveable sign of despair, which is all that remains of humanity in the absence of art's transformation of the human species through the yearning of formal differences and displacements. That is why we need misanthropy: so as not to close our hearts to the cultural hope that is to be found, both within and without us, only in what appears at any given moment to be unhuman.

As we are shown in works as disparate as Ovid's tale of Pygmalion, Charles Robert Maturin's *Melmoth the Wanderer* (1820), and Oscar Wilde's *Picture of Dorian Gray* (1890), the vitality we see in art is the stirring of our desire in it. This is the unhuman desire through which we are forever willing ourselves to be a different species, a more perfect work of art.

*   *   *

Man is not the "lord of creation," but the exterminator of the species.[32]

In Villiers de l'Isle-Adam's *The Future Eve* (1886), when Lord Ewald recoils from the android, Hadaly, that Thomas Edison has designed to be the woman of his dreams, Hadaly accuses him of being a "slave to [his] species."[33] This is the misanthropy of art speaking, hilariously and profoundly heedless of any possibility of self-contradiction. Imperturbably founded on contradiction, on the agony of culture, art can be better or worse, Hadaly shows us, but never logically incoherent.

Misanthropy reveals the masochism in the pride that we take in our humanity. By its very existence misanthropy highlights all the ways that we are, indeed, slaves to our species. Not the least of the ironies built into Pieter Bruegel's *Misanthrope* (c. 1568) is that the human figure in this painting, that thieving, grinning lout, is humbly bent over within the boundaries of the world while the misanthrope, who is presumably outside of it, is able to walk upright. The misanthrope seems to stand at the primitive and otherwise inaccessible origin of judgment, where everything may be called into question, and everything is, so that one may be as free, and as unhuman, as art.

We take pleasure in the image of misanthropy because we identify with this assumed superiority of the misanthropic figure. The converse is true as well. The figures we see as superior or heroic will have something misanthropic about them, as in the case of Homer's sulky Achilles, William Shakespeare's spluttering Lear, Byron's Childe Harold, Patricia Highsmith's Ripley, or John Ford's John Wayne. The misanthrope's global rejection of humankind is an unsurpassable and incontrovertible act of judgment, as Melville so brilliantly showed through the character of Bartleby. In all other respects Bartleby is the most unheroic human conceivable and yet, in the perfection of his retirement—"I prefer not to"—he is possessed of a sublimity that opens fathomless chasms within the walls and expressions of our everyday life.

As all the Bartlebys, Timons, and Alcestes find, this uprightness that makes them attractive also makes them hateful. To relieve us of our subjection, they must also remind us of it; to release us from our masochism, they must first rub our noses in the shit we eat in every moment of our social equanimity. It is not surprising, then, that misanthropic rebellion is popularly interpreted as representing, fundamentally, a kind of despair. If we did not denigrate it in this way, how could we live with our despairing selves as we go through each day busily pursuing life so as to avoid having to face the challenge of art?

It is to despair, in particular, that we owe one of the most popular images of misanthropy: that it is more profound than geniality, affability, or simple happiness. This impression might be called the adolescent version of misanthropy, or the J. D. Salinger brand, although this is not to say that it is found only among adolescents. There is something of this in the fiction of Thomas Hardy, for instance, as in a reference in *Tess of the D'Urbervilles* (1891) to "that cold accretion called the world, which, so terrible in the mass, is so unformidable, even pitiable, in its units."[34] We can also see this brand of misanthropy in Peckinpah's sophomoric didacticism: *this*, he smirks, is what the college professor *really* wants, deep in his tweedy heart. In this version misanthropy is a shortcut to knowingness. Sentimental in its cynicism, as the comedy of W. C. Fields is sentimental in all the splendor of its curmudgeonly sarcasm toward mom, apple pie, and children who deserve to be baked into mom's apple pies, this wised-up attitude is another way of communicating the demand that any conception of misanthropy as a genuine questioning of humanity must be unthinkable.

Yet this is not to say that the mature or adults-only version of misanthropy, as it is commonly conceived, is any more free of bathos. This version speaks with greater sobriety and sublimity, in the manner of Arsenius, the fourth-century church father who explained his departure for eremitic solitude by saying, "I cannot be with God and with men."[35] Cioran provides a modern echo: "The more we detest humanity, the more we are ripe for God, for a dialogue with no one."[36] As Nietzsche suggested through his send-up of such monkish seriousness in *Thus Spoke Zarathustra* (1883–85), this version of misanthropy is still a typically human form of consolation and thus no real questioning of culture at all. Like the adolescent version, this is still a glorification of egoism: of the image of individual consciousness, though which one lives and suffers alone, as Holden and Cioran complain. Both of these versions, then, are still dependent on the most commonplace conception of humanity imaginable: the gloomy conception, as Zarathustra might sneer, of the human being as the *deep* animal.

Wherever and if ever it can be thinkable, misanthropy is not at all profound, for it does not take us inside humanity or human concerns with knowledge. Transforming the human to the aesthetic species, as if by a god's whim, it does not even accept the profound pleasure of dissatisfaction that the adolescent in all of us takes for wisdom. Misanthropy really begins to matter only when we come to the end of despair and find what lies beyond it.

What lies beyond despair: this is the misanthropic definition of art, perhaps the most precise one humanly imaginable.

Notes

Preface

1. John Keats, "Ode to a Nightingale" (1820), *The Poetical Works of John Keats*, ed. H. W. Garrod (London: Oxford University Press, 1956), 207.

2. Friedrich Nietzsche, *Daybreak* (1881), ed. Maudemarie Clark and Brian Leiter, trans. R. J. Hollingdale (New York: Cambridge University Press, 1997), 333 (translation modified).

3. Zora Neale Hurston, *Their Eyes Were Watching God* (New York: Harper and Row, 1990), 57.

4. Theodor W. Adorno, *Aesthetic Theory*, ed. Gretel Adorno and Rolf Tiedemann, trans. Robert Hullot-Kentor (Minneapolis: University of Minnesota Press, 1997), 197.

5. Adorno, *Aesthetic Theory*, 226, 81.

Introduction: To Love to Hate

1. C. Carr, "This Is Only a Test: Chris Burden," *Artforum* 28 (September 1989): 121. See also Max Kozloff's reference to what he calls the "lumpen terrorism" of body art (for which Burden is one of his main exemplars) in "Pygmalion Reversed," *Artforum* 14 (November 1975): 32; the comparison of Burden to a terrorist (the work specifically addressed here is his 1971 ski-masked appearance in *You'll Never See My Face in Kansas*) in Frank Perrin, ed., *Chris Burden* (Paris: Blocnotes Éditions, 1995), 9; and the reference to body art like Burden's as "a kind of aesthetic terrorism" in Lea Vergine, *Body Art and Performance: The Body as Language* (1974; Milan: Skira, 2000), 26.

2. On this point see the argument of Amelia Jones, *Body Art/Performing the Subject* (Minneapolis: University of Minnesota Press, 1998), 130–32.

3. See also Frazer Ward's emphasis on the significance of the Vietnam War to *Shoot* (1971), the piece in which Burden had a friend fire a rifle bullet into his arm. In "Gray Zone: Watching *Shoot*," *October* 95 (Winter 2001): 114–30, Ward suggests that *Shoot* "refused to exempt its public from its acquiescence in spectacular representations of violence" (129).

4. Holland Carter, "Dislocating the Modern," *Art in America* 80 (January 1992): 102.

5. Although he gives no source for his claim, which is at odds with what Burden has said in the public records of his performances, Herbert Blau reports that the photo is a kind of illusion because, according to Burden, he had not seen the airplane when he fired the gun. See Blau, "Les rhétoriques du corps et la guerre des nerfs," *Cahiers du musée national d'art moderne* 51 (Spring 1995): 24.

6. Robert Horvitz, "Chris Burden," *Artforum* 14 (May 1976): 31n.

7. Samuel Beckett, *Watt* (New York: Grove Press, 1970), 202.

8. Theodor W. Adorno, *Aesthetic Theory*, ed. Gretel Adorno and Rolf Tiedemann, trans. Robert Hullot-Kentor (Minneapolis: University of Minnesota Press, 1997), 39, 50.

9. Dorothy Parker, "Books: A Hymn of Hate," *Complete Poems*, ed. Colleen Breese (New York: Penguin, 1999), 289; Burden, quoted in Suzanne Muchnic, "Wrestling the Dragon," *Artnews* 89 (Dec. 1990): 129.

10. T. E. Hulme, "Romanticism and Classicism," *The Collected Writings of T. E. Hulme*, ed. Karen Csengeri (Oxford: Oxford University Press, 1994), 62.

11. Sébastien-Roch-Nicolas Chamfort, *Maximes et pensées, Oeuvres complèts de Chamfort*, ed. P. R. Auguis, 5 vols. (Paris: Chaumerot Jeune, 1824–25), 1: 393. On this point, see the analysis of "the tradition of benevolent misanthropy" in Thomas R. Preston, *Not In Timon's Manner: Feeling, Misanthropy, and Satire in Eighteenth-Century England* (University: University of Alabama Press, 1975), 2.

12. Jean-Jacques Rousseau, "Lettre à D'Alembert," ed. Bernard Gagnebin and Jean Rousset, *Oeuvres complètes*, ed. Bernard Gagnebin and Marcel Raymond, 5 vols. (Paris: Gallimard, 1995), 5: 35.

13. Immanuel Kant, *Critique of the Power of Judgment*, ed. Paul Guyer, trans. Paul Guyer and Eric Matthews (Cambridge: Cambridge University Press, 2000), 157.

14. Thomas Love Peacock, *Nightmare Abbey, The Works of Thomas Love Peacock*, ed. H. F. B. Brett-Smith and C. E. Jones, 10 vols. (New York: AMS Press, 1967), 3: 73.

15. Friedrich Schiller, *Der Versöhnte Menschenfeind* (1790), ed. Herbert Kraft, Claudia Pilling, and Gert Vonhoff with Grit Dommes and Diana Schilling, in *Schillers Werke*, ed. Julius Peterson, Hermann Schneider, et al., 42 vols. (Weimar: Hermann Böhlaus Nachfoler, 1943-), 5: 268.

16. Arthur C. Danto, "The Abuse of Beauty," *Daedalus* 131 (Fall 2002): 35.

17. Beckett, *Watt*, 81, 82–83.

18. See Robin Wilson, "Going Out with a Bang: Gunplay as Performance Leads Two UCLA Professors to Quit," *Chronicle of Higher Education* 51 (February 4, 2005): A9. The other professor in question here was the artist Nancy Rubins.

19. Jorge Luis Borges, "The Babylon Lottery," trans. Anthony Kerrigan, in *Ficciones*, ed. Anthony Kerrigan (New York: Grove Press, 1962), 65.

20. Johann Wolfgang Goethe, *Faust*, ed. Gotthard Erler (Berlin: Aufbau-Verlag Berlin und Weimar, 1986), 73.

21. That is, until God sent a dream to terrify them into bringing him back. I take this account from Antonius, *La vie et les miracles de Saint Syméon Stylite l'ancien*, ed. and trans. M. Chaîne (Cairo: Institut Français d'Archéologie Orientale, 1948).

22. Sander L. Gilman, *Franz Kafka: The Jewish Patient* (New York: Routledge, 1995), 237.

23. See Breon Mitchell, "Kafka and the Hunger Artists," in *Kafka and the Contemporary Critical Performance: Centenary Readings*, ed. Alan Udoff (Bloomington: Indiana University Press, 1987), 236–55.

24. For the story of Theodore's cage, see *Three Byzantine Saints*, ed. and trans. Elizabeth Dawes and Norman H. Baynes (Oxford: Basil Blackwell, 1948), 106–07. On the problem of ambition, see, e.g., the near-contemporary account of the fourth-century Father Apollo in *The Lives of the Desert Fathers: The Historia Monachorum in Aegypto*, ed. and trans. Norman Russell and Benedicta Ward (London: Mowbray, 1981), 78–79: "He severely censured those who wore iron chains and let their hair grow long. 'For they,' he said, 'make an exhibition of themselves and chase after human approbation, where instead they should make the body waste away with fasting and do good in secret.' "

25. See William Langland, *Piers Plowman: The C Version*, ed. George Russell and George Kane (London: Athlone, 1997), 380–84 and *The Myrour of Recluses: A Middle English Translation of* Speculum Inclusorum, ed. Marta Powell Harley (Madison, N.J.: Farleigh Dickinson University Press, 1995), 4. For Antony, see St. Athanasius, *The Life of Saint Antony*, ed. and trans. Robert T. Meyer (Westminster, Md.: Newman Press, 1950).

26. Philip Rousseau remarks upon this trouble with curiosity seekers in *Ascetics, Authority, and the Church in the Age of Jerome and Cassian* (Oxford: Oxford University Press, 1978), 59–60.

27. See Horst Bredekamp, *Kunst als Medium sozialer Konflikte: Bilderkämpfe von der Spätantike bis zur Hussitenrevolution* (Frankfurt am Main: Suhrkamp Verlag, 1975), 187–88.

28. See St. Jerome, "The Life of S. Hilarion" (c. 391–92), *Letters and Works*, trans. W. H. Fremantle, G. Lewis, and W. G. Martley, in *A Select Library of Nicene and Post-Nicene Fathers of the Christian Church* 2nd ser., ed. Philip Schaff and Henry Wace (Grand Rapids, Mich. Eerdmans, 1954), 310–14.

29. See Bede, *Ecclesiastical History of the English People* (c. 731), ed. and trans. Thomas Miller (London: N. Trübner, 1890), 369; Petrarch, *The Life of Solitude* (c. 1346–56), ed. and trans. Jacob Zeitlin (Urbana: University of Illinois Press, 1924), 188; and Dante Alighieri, *The Inferno, The Divine Comedy* (c. 1307–21), trans. Charles S. Singleton, 3 vols. (Princeton, N.J.: Princeton University Press, 1970), 1: 29.

30. Thomas De Quincey, "On Murder Considered as One of the Fine Arts," *Collected Writings*, ed. David Masson, 14 vols. (Edinburgh: Adam and Charles Black, 1889–1890), 13: 9–51. In addition to the original 1827 essay, De Quincey published supplementary articles in 1839 and 1854; I concern myself here only with the first piece.

31. De Quincey, "On Murder Considered as One of the Fine Arts," *Collected Writings*, 13: 48.

32. De Quincey, "On Murder Considered as One of the Fine Arts," 13: 42.

33. V. A. De Luca, *Thomas De Quincey: The Prose of Vision* (Toronto: University of Toronto Press, 1980), 44. A much better analysis of De Quincey's "misappropriations" in "On Murder Considered as One of the Fine Arts" is offered in Joel Black, *The Aesthetics of Murder: A Study in Romantic Literature and Contemporary Culture* (Baltimore: Johns Hopkins University Press, 1991).

34. Charles Baudelaire, *Fusées, Oeuvres complètes*, ed. Y.-G. Le Dantec, rev. Claude Pichois (Paris: Gallimard, 1961), 1258.

35. This work has also been referred to under other titles, including *The Perfidy of the World*. For more information on this and other points, see Sally Elizabeth Mansfield, "*The Misanthrope* by Pieter Bruegel the Elder," M. A. Thesis, (University of Virginia, 1978).

36. Kant, *Critique of the Power of Judgment*, 157.

37. Rousseau, "Lettre à D'Alembert," *Oeuvres complètes*, 5: 34.

38. Johann Georg Zimmermann, *Über die Einsamkeit*, 4 vols. (Leipzig: Weidmanns Erben und Reich, 1784–85), 4: 92.

39. Robert Burton, *The Anatomy of Melancholy*, ed. Thomas C. Faulkner, Nicols K. Kiessling, and Rhonda L. Blair, 3 vols. (Oxford: Oxford University Press, 1994), 1: 245.

40. Heinrich von Kleist, "Empfindungen vor Friedrichs Seelandschaft," *Sämtliche Werke und Briefe*, ed. Ilse-Marie Barth, Klaus Müller-Salget, Stefan Ormanns, and Heinrich C. Seeba, 4 vols. (Frankfurt am Main: Deutscher Klassiker Verlag, 1990), 3: 543–44.

41. Flannery O'Connor, "A Good Man Is Hard to Find," *The Complete Stories* (New York: Farrar, Straus and Giroux, 1972), 133.

42. Rousseau, "Lettre à D'Alembert," *Oeuvres complètes*, 5: 35.

43. Lord Byron, "The Giaour," *The Complete Poetical Works*, ed. Jerome J. McGann, 7 vols. (Oxford: Oxford University Press, 1980–93), 3: 41.

44. On the relations among misogyny, aesthetics, and misanthropy, see *Misogyny, Misandry, and Misanthropy*, ed. R. Howard Bloch and Frances Ferguson (Berkeley: University of California Press, 1989).

45. Angela Carter, *The War of Dreams* (New York: Harcourt Brace Jovanovich, 1972), 240. In England this book first appeared under a much better title, *The Infernal Desire Machines of Doctor Hoffman*.

46. Carter, *The War of Dreams*, 244.

47. I have taken the translation from Wolfgang Stechow, *Pieter Bruegel the Elder* (New York: Harry Abrams, 1969), 134–37.

48. A calthrop was a military implement, a kind of spike used to disrupt the advance of enemy soldiers; some scholars have identified the objects in the picture as such implements.

49. Jonathan Franzen, in "The Talk of the Town," *New Yorker* (24 September 2001): 29.

50. Marshall Berman, "Missing in Action: Death and Life in New York," *Lingua Franca* 11 (November 2001): 9.

51. See Marianne Hirsch, "The Day Time Stopped," *Chronicle of Higher Education* (January 25, 2002), B: 12–14.

52. Herbert Muschamp, "The Commemorative Beauty of Tragic Wreckage," *New York Times* (November 11, 2001), 2: 37.

53. Quoted in Thomas Vinciguerra, "For Author of 'Prozac Nation,' Delayed Film Is a Downer," *New York Times* (November 9, 2003), 9: 6.

54. Philip Nobel, quoted in Andrew Rice, "The Commerce of Commemoration," *The Nation* (January 31, 2005): 26.

55. David Joselit, "Terror and Form," *Artforum* 43 (January 2005): 45.

56. Susan Buck-Morss, "Aesthetics and Anaesthetics: Walter Benjamin's Artwork Essay Reconsidered," *October* 62 (Fall 1992): 4.

Chapter 1. Crowning Presumption

1. All references to and quotations from Marlowe's works are taken from *The Complete Works of Christopher Marlowe*, ed. Roma Gill, David Fuller, and Edward J. Esche, 5 vols. (Oxford: Oxford University Press, 1987–98). References are given within the text.

2. Michel Foucault, *Discipline and Punish: The Birth of the Prison*, trans. Alan Sheridan (New York: Vintage, 1979), 217.

3. After first agreeing to have the Pope crown him, Napoleon reconsidered and decided to crown himself, with the Pope's apparent agreement. See Frédéric Masson, *Le sacre et le couronnement de Napoléon* (1905; Paris: Albin Michel, 1978), 159–61.

4. Chateaubriand, *Mémoires d'outre-tombe* (1849–50), ed. Maurice Levaillant and Georges Moulinier, 3 vols. (Paris: Gallimard, 1951), 2: 348; Walter Scott, *The Life of Napoleon Buonaparte*, 3 vols. (Philadelphia: Carey, Lea, and Carey, 1827), 2: 61.

5. Chateaubriand, *Mémoires d'outre-tombe*, 2: 354.

6. Quoted in Warren Roberts, *Jacques-Louis David, Revolutionary Artist: Art, Politics, and the French Revolution* (Chapel Hill: University of North Carolina Press, 1989), 156.

7. See Daniel Wildenstein and Guy Wildenstein, *Documents complémentaires au catalogue de l'oeuvre de Jacques-Louis David* (Paris: Fondation Wildenstein, 1973), 174–75.

8. Ben Jonson, "Timber, or Discoveries" (1640), in *Marlowe: The Critical Heritage, 1588–1896*, ed. Millar Maclure (London: Routledge and Kegan Paul, 1979), 50.

9. La Rochefoucauld, *Réflexions ou sentences et maximes morale* (1678), *Oeuvres complètes*, ed. L. Martin-Chauffier, rev. Jean Marchand (Paris: Gallimard, 1975), 409. Hereafter *Maximes*.

10. Niccolò Machiavelli, *The Prince* (1532), trans. Luigi Ricci, rev. E. R. P. Vincent, *The Prince and The Discourses* (New York: Modern Library, 1940), 89.

11. La Rochefoucauld, *Maximes*, 418.

12. Bernard Mandeville, *The Fable of the Bees, or Private Vices, Publick Benefits* (1714–28), ed. F. B. Kaye, 2 vols. (Oxford: Oxford University Press, 1924; rep. Indianapolis: Liberty Classics, 1988), 1: 235.

13. La Rochefoucauld, *Maximes*, *Oeuvres complètes*, 489. On the relation between La Rochefoucauld's writings and the "assumptions and methods of the modern science of his day," see Henry C. Clark, *La Rochefoucauld and the Language of Unmasking in Seventeenth-Century France* (Geneva: Librairie Droz, 1994), 123.

14. La Rochefoucauld, *Maximes*, 490.

15. La Rochefoucauld, *Maximes*, 491.

16. This section had first been published in 1660, as an individual essay, in an anthology of writings by various authors.

17. W. G. Moore, among others, has recounted how shocked some of La Rochefoucauld's contemporaries were by his work. See *La Rochefoucauld: His Mind and Art* (Oxford: Oxford University Press, 1969).

18. Jonathan Dollimore, *Radical Tragedy: Religion, Ideology and Power in the Drama of Shakespeare and His Contemporaries* (New York: Harvester Wheatsheaf, 1984), 114.

19. *The History of the Damnable Life and Deserved Death of Doctor John Faustus*, in *Christopher Marlowe: The Plays and Their Sources*, ed. Vivian Thomas and William Tydeman, trans. P. F. (London: Routledge, 1994), 191, 192.

20. Cleanth Brooks, "The Unity of Marlowe's Doctor Faustus," in *Marlowe: Doctor Faustus: A Casebook*, ed. John Jump (London: Macmillan, 1969), 218. See also Lawrence Danson's remarks about Faustus being "the kind of legalist he himself contemptuously describes." Danson, "The Questioner," in *Modern Critical Views: Christopher Marlowe*, ed. Harold Bloom (New York: Chelsea House, 1986), 200–201.

21. Marjorie Garber, "'Here's Nothing Writ': Scribe, Script, and Circumspection in Marlowe's Plays," in *Christopher Marlowe*, ed. Richard Wilson (London: Longman, 1999), 47.

22. William Hazlitt, quoted in *Marlowe*, ed. Maclure, 78. On this point see also Stephen Greenblatt's argument that Marlowe's protagonists "imagine themselves set in diametrical opposition to their society where in fact they have unwittingly accepted its crucial structural elements" in "The Will to Absolute Play: *The Jew of Malta*," in *Staging the Renaissance: Reinterpretations of Elizabethan and Jacobean Drama*, ed. David Scott Kastan and Peter Stallybrass (New York: Routledge, 1991), 120.

23. For the demonological significance of Faustus's signature, see Gareth Roberts, "Marlowe and the Metaphysics of Magicians," in *Constructing Christopher Marlowe*, ed. J. A. Downie and J. T. Parnell (Cambridge: Cambridge University Press, 2000), 66.

24. This universality is closely related to the "secularization of space" that Greenblatt describes in Marlowe's drama in his *Renaissance Self-Fashioning: From More to Shakespeare* (Chicago: University of Chicago Press, 1980), 195.

25. Johann Wolfgang Goethe, *Faust* (1808), ed. Gotthard Erler (Berlin: Aufbau-Verlag Berlin und Weimar, 1986), 171.

26. Scott, *Life of Napoleon Buonaparte*, 2: 63. Scott's argument had long been a commonplace.

27. Thomas Hobbes, *Leviathan* (1651), ed. Edwin Curley (Indianapolis: Hackett, 1994), 464.

28. Machiavelli, *The Prince*, 62.

29. With reference to this point, see Garber's argument about the "encapsulated artifacts, literal works of art" (15), in Marlowe's writing, in " 'Infinite Riches in a Little Room': Closure and Enclosure in Marlowe," in *Two Renaissance Mythmakers: Christopher Marlowe and Ben Jonson*, ed. Alvin Kernan (Baltimore: Johns Hopkins University Press, 1977), 321. See also Janet Clare's analysis of the "shift of emphasis to the aesthetic" in Marlowe's work in "Marlowe's Theater of Cruelty," in *Constructing Christopher Marlowe*, 74–87; and Patrick Cheney, *Marlowe's Counterfeit Profession: Ovid, Spenser, Counter-Nationhood* (Toronto: University of Toronto Press, 1997).

30. Max Bluestone, "*Libido speculandi*: Doctrine and Dramaturgy in Contemporary Interpretations of Marlowe's *Doctor Faustus*," in *Reinterpretations of Elizabethan Drama*, ed. Norman Rabkin (New York: Columbia University Press, 1969), 71.

31. Paul Emil Thieriot, *Timon ganz allein*, in *Zeitung für die elegante Welt* 23 (1 February 1841) and 24 (2 February 1841): 89–96. Page references are given within the text.

32. For the relation between automatons and the Enlightenment, see my *Cannibals and Philosophers: Bodies of Enlightenment* (Baltimore: Johns Hopkins University Press, 2001), Chapter 3, "The Work of Art in the Age of Mechanical Digestion," 65–98.

33. Fred Botting, *Making Monstrous:* Frankenstein, *Criticism, Theory* (Manchester: Manchester University Press, 1991), 176.

34. Mary Shelley, *Frankenstein; or, The Modern Prometheus* (1818), ed. D. L. Macdonald and Kathleen Scharf (Peterborough, Ontario: Broadview Press, 1994). Page references are given within the text.

35. Theodor W. Adorno, *Aesthetic Theory*, ed. Gretel Adorno and Rolf Tiedemann, trans. Robert Hullot-Kentor (Minneapolis: University of Minnesota Press, 1997), 226, 183, 81.

36. Adorno, *Aesthetic Theory*, 53.

37. See Friedrich Nietzsche, *Daybreak* (1881), ed. Maudemarie Clark and Brian Leiter, trans. R. J. Hollingdale (New York: Cambridge University Press,

1997), 483: "Learn to know! Yes! But always as a man! What? Always to sit before the same comedy, act in the same comedy? Never to be able to see into things out of any other eyes than *these*? And what uncountable kinds of beings may there not be whose organs are better equipped for knowledge! What will mankind have come to know at the end of all their knowledge—their organs! And that perhaps means: the impossibility of knowledge!"

38. See Lee Sterrenburg, "Mary Shelley's Monster: Politics and Psyche in *Frankenstein*," in *The Endurance of* Frankenstein: *Essays on Mary Shelley's Novel*, ed. George Levine and U. C. Knoepflmacher (Berkeley: University of California Press, 1979), 143–71.

39. Giorgio Agamben, *The Open: Man and Animal*, trans. Kevin Attell (Stanford, Calif.: Stanford University Press, 2004), 76–77.

Chapter 2. I Think; Therefore, I Am Heathcliff

1. On this topic of art becoming life in the Gothic, see Maggie Kilgour, *The Rise of the Gothic Novel* (New York: Routledge, 1995), 85–87, 156–58.

2. G. W. F. Hegel, *Aesthetics: Lectures on Fine Art*, trans. T. M. Knox, 2 vols. (Oxford: Oxford University Press, 1998), 1: 11.

3. On this point, though not on all others, I am in agreement with the entertaining polemic against "a continuing consensus" that "subsumes the Gothic into an anti-Enlightenment rebellion" (215) in Chris Baldick and Robert Mighall, "Gothic Criticism," in *A Companion to the Gothic*, ed. David Punter (Oxford: Blackwell, 2000), 209–28.

4. See the valuable argument about the creation of "an autonomous realm of the aesthetic" in relation to "the historical coincidence of the expanding taste for commercial fictions of the supernatural and the project of a supernaturalised theory of capitalism," in E. J. Clery, *The Rise of Supernatural Fiction, 1762–1800* (Cambridge: Cambridge University Press, 1995), 9.

5. See the "Fifth Set of Objections" in the "Objections and Replies" published with the *Meditations* in René Descartes, *Meditations on First Philosophy, The Philosophical Writings of Descartes*, trans. John Cottingham, Robert Stoothoff, and Dugald Murdoch, 2 vols. (Cambridge: Cambridge University Press, 1984), 2: 179–240.

6. Matthew Lewis, *The Monk*, ed. Howard Anderson (Oxford: Oxford University Press, 1980), 107.

7. Descartes, *Meditations, Philosophical Writings*, 2: 12.

8. Descartes, *Meditations, Philosophical Writings*, 2: 12.

9. See, e.g., the danger of appearing impious suggested by the theologian Antoine Arnauld in the "Fourth Set of Objections" in Descartes, *Meditations, Philosophical Writings*, 2: 151–53.

10. Descartes, *Meditations, Philosophical Writings*, 2: 15.

11. Descartes, "Fifth Set of Objections," *Meditations, Philosophical Writings*, 2: 180.

12. Descartes, "Second Set of Objections," *Meditations, Philosophical Writings*, 2: 88. The editors note that these replies were collected and largely composed by Marin Mersenne.

13. Descartes, "Author's Replies to the Second Set of Objections," *Meditations, Philosophical Writings*, 2: 109.

14. On the question of how the aesthetic conventions of the meditation figure in Descartes's work, see the volume edited by Amélie Oksenberg Rorty, *Essays on Descartes' Meditations* (Berkeley: University of California Press, 1986).

15. Robert Miles, *Gothic Writing 1750–1820: A Genealogy* (New York: Routledge, 1993), 3.

16. Mary Wollstonecraft, *Maria, or The Wrongs of Woman* (New York: W. W. Norton, 1975), 114.

17. Wollstonecraft, *Vindication of the Rights of Woman*, ed. Carol H. Poston, 2nd ed. (New York: W. W. Norton, 1988), 5.

18. See the "Second Set of Objections" and Descartes's response in Descartes, *Meditations, Philosophical Writings*, especially 2: 98, 109.

19. See the discussion of a partial "collapse of Cartesian dualism" in the writings of Ann Radcliffe and Edmund Burke in Steven Bruhm, *Gothic Bodies: The Politics of Pain in Romantic Fiction* (Philadelphia: University of Pennsylvania Press, 1994), 99–100.

20. Emily Brontë, *Wuthering Heights*, ed. Ian Jack (Oxford: Oxford University Press, 1995). (Page numbers to this work are given within the text.) In relation to this point, see the chapter on "The Spectralization of the Other in *The Mysteries of Udolpho*" in Terry Castle, *The Female Thermometer: Eighteenth-Century Culture and the Invention of the Uncanny* (New York: Oxford University Press, 1995), 120–40.

21. Ann Radcliffe, *The Italian*, ed. Frederick Garber (Oxford: Oxford University Press, 1981), 18, 19, 367. The first quotations here are initially made in reference to an unknown tormentor, but Schedoni soon comes to be suspected either of being this person or, as eventually turns out to be the case, of being the agent behind his actions.

22. Radcliffe, *The Italian*, 239.

23. Radcliffe, *The Italian*, 52.

24. Lewis, *The Monk*, 130.

25. Descartes, "Author's Replies to the Second Set of Objections," *Meditations, Philosophical Writings*, 2:102.

26. Thomas Love Peacock, *Nightmare Abbey, The Works of Thomas Love Peacock*, ed. H. F. B. Brett-Smith and C. E. Jones, 10 vols. (New York: AMS Press, 1967), 3: 41.

27. Sophia Lee, *The Recess*, 3 vols. (New York: Arno Press, 1972), 3: 11.

28. Lewis, *The Monk*, 51, 53.

29. Charles Robert Maturin, *Melmoth the Wanderer*, ed. Douglas Grant (London: Oxford University Press, 1968), 39, 303.

30. See the commentary on Charlotte Brontë's "Editor's Preface," on her editing of her sister's work, and on her "Biographical Notice" of Emily (which is described as being "shaped by a dynamic similar to that of *Wuthering Heights* itself") in U. C. Knoepflmacher, *Wuthering Heights: A Study* (Athens: Ohio University Press, 1994), 111–13, 4.

31. The sadomasochistic aspects of Gothic literature have been much remarked, but see, e.g., William Patrick Day, *In the Circles of Fear and Desire: A Study of Gothic Fantasy* (Chicago: University of Chicago Press, 1985).

32. Terry Eagleton, *Myths of Power: A Marxist Study of the Brontës* (London: Macmillan, 1975), 107–8. See also Nancy Armstrong's argument that *Wuthering Heights* "locates desire elsewhere, in an extrasocial dimension of human experience," in *Desire and Domestic Fiction: A Political History of the Novel* (New York: Oxford University Press, 1987), 196.

33. Johannes Caterus, "First Set of Objections," in Descartes, *Meditations, Philosophical Writings*, 2: 67. I owe the identification of the allusion to Terence to the translators of this work.

34. See the analysis of issues of textuality in *Wuthering Heights* in Carol Jacobs, *Uncontainable Romanticism: Shelley, Brontë, Kleist* (Baltimore: Johns Hopkins

University Press, 1989), 61–84; the argument about how "the book" in this novel figures "as a complex image, the nexus of multiple associations linking cultural order and the control of language with sublimation and the self-control of desire," in James H. Kavanagh, *Emily Brontë* (Oxford: Blackwell, 1985), 19; and Robert C. McKibben, "The Image of the Book in *Wuthering Heights*," *Nineteenth-Century Fiction* 15 (September 1960): 159–69.

Chapter 3. Immemorial

1. Jean-Luc Nancy, "On Being-in-Common," trans. James Creech, in *Community at Loose Ends*, ed. Miami Theory Collective (Minneapolis: University of Minnesota Press, 1991), 5.

2. Cf. Maurice Blanchot's description of disaster as "forgetfulness without memory, the motionless retreat of what has not been treated—the immemorial, perhaps," in *The Writing of the Disaster*, trans. Ann Smock (Lincoln: University of Nebraska Press, 1986), 3.

3. See André Malraux, *Saturn: An Essay on Goya*, trans. C. W. Chilton (London: Phaidon, 1957), 93. For a view closer to the one for which I am arguing here, see Theodor Hetzer's characterization of Goya's "reporter-like realism" (94) in "Francisco Goya and the Crisis in Art around 1800," *Goya in Perspective*, ed. Fred Licht (Englewood Cliffs, N.J.: Prentice-Hall, 1973), 92–113. Hetzer's argument that Goya's art disrupts Baroque tradition because "it does not serve to transform the particular into part of the general" (111) is also relevant to my argument here.

4. Ronald Paulson, *Representations of Revolution (1789–1820)* (New Haven, Conn.: Yale University Press, 1983), 294.

5. Cf. Roberto Alcala Flecha's comments on the "radical pessimism" of Goya's art from the *Caprichos* on, which he sees as having been shared by many of his contemporaries, in *Literatura e ideologia en el arte de Goya* (Zaragoza: Diputación General de Aragón, 1988), 12.

6. Arthur C. Danto, *Encounters and Reflections: Art in the Historical Present* (New York: Farrar Straus Giroux, 1990), 254. The immediate reference of this passage is to the *Caprichos*, but it is also clearly intended to characterized the *Disasters*.

7. On the question of mythological themes in Spanish art, see José Luis Morales y Marín, *Pintura en España: 1750–1808* (Madrid: Ediciones Cátedra, 1994), 45–48.

8. Claude Bédat, *L'Académie des beaux-arts de Madrid: 1744–1808* (Toulouse: Association des Publications de L'Université de Toulouse, 1973), 12–13.

9. See Bédat, *L'Académie des beaux-arts de Madrid*, 280. The works to which I refer here would include the Ovidian "Fall of the Giants" (1764) that Goya's brother-in-law, Francisco Bayeux, created for Madrid's Palacio Real, as well as paintings such as the "Apollo and Daphne" by Cornelis de Vos given to the Madrid Academy by Charles IV in 1792.

10. In *Goya y el mundo a su alrededor* (Buenos Aires: Editorial Sudamérica, 1947), 15–16, José López-Rey also points to the popularity of the pseudo-science of physiognomy as a source for Goya's images of human-animal transformations.

11. See also Janis Tomlinson's suggestion that this image contains "an ironic visual reference, as the impaled body recalls the Hellenistic fragment of the Belvedere Torso," in *Francisco Goya y Lucientes: 1746–1828* (London: Phaidon, 1994), 193. In *Goya: The Last Carnival* (London: Reaktion Books, 1999), 96,

Victor I. Stoichita and Anna Maria Coderch argue as follows: "By impaling the *Belvedere Torso* on a dead tree, Goya chose the most disturbing way to produce a link between the degradation of the notion of the human and that of classical form."

12. On the relationship between Ovidian aesthetics and violence, especially sexual violence, and on its implications for issues of gender in the *Metamorphoses*, see Lynn Enterline, *The Rhetoric of the Body from Ovid to Shakespeare* (Cambridge: Cambridge University Press, 2000).

13. In noting that "Agustina de Aragón is the only person who can be identified," Eleanor A. Sayre suggests that the *Disasters* is concerned with "the effects of war on nameless individuals" in her "Introduction to the Prints and Drawings Series," *Goya and the Spirit of Enlightenment*, ed. Alfonso E. Pérez Sánchez and Eleanor Sayre (Boston: Little, Brown, 1989), cx.

14. Hugh Thomas, *Goya: The Third of May 1808* (New York: Viking Press, 1972), 64.

15. See Alfonso E. Pérez Sánchez and Julián Gállego, *Goya: The Complete Etchings and Lithographs*, trans. David Robinson Edwards and Jenifer Wakelyn (Munich: Prestel Verlag, 1995), 115: "The inscription 'The one at Chinchón' on a trial proof, retouched by the artist before the final impression was taken, suggests that he himself witnessed the scene." Tomlinson, however (*Francisco Goya y Lucientes*, 193), casts doubt on the notion that any of the images in this series were based on Goya's personal experience.

16. Cf. Charles Martindale's comparison of Ovid's *Metamorphoses*, with their "combination of cruelty with a certain wit and detachment and the unruffled stylishness with which acts of violence are described," to Titian's *Flaying of Marsyas* in his "Introduction" to *Ovid Renewed: Ovidian Influences on Literature and Art from the Middle Ages to the Twentieth Century*, ed. Charles Martindale (Cambridge: Cambridge University Press, 1988), 4–5.

17. Licht, *Goya: The Origins of the Modern Temper in Art* (New York: Universe Books, 1979), 146.

18. An exception is number 45, a tableau of three female refugees seemingly being guided in their flight by a lean pig; if we view the image from left to right, the profiled women are progressively weighed down by their increasingly unrecognizable burdens, with the third woman being so overwhelmed as to be almost indistinguishable from what she carries, thus becoming, in effect, an animate heap of things.

19. As Tomlinson points out (*Francisco Goya y Lucientes*, 200–201), some of these images also appear to allude to Giambattista Casti's poem "The Talking Animals," to which specific reference is made in plate number 74.

20. See Stendahl [Henri Beyle, pseud.], *La Chartreuse de Parme*, ed. Henri Martineau (Paris: Fernand Hazan, 1948), 116.

21. See Stendahl, *La Chartreuse de Parme*, 68.

22. Thomas Hardy, *The Dynasts*, *The Complete Poetical Works of Thomas Hardy*, ed. Samuel Hynes, 5 vols. (Oxford: Oxford University Press, 1995), 4: 17, 5: 14, 4: 248, 4: 59, 5: 167, 4: 160, 5: 64.

23. Thomas Hobbes, *Leviathan*, ed. Edwin Curley (Indianapolis: Hackett, 1994). Page references to this work are given within the text.

24. Giorgio Agamben, *Homo Sacer: Sovereign Power and Bare Life*, trans. Daniel Heller-Roazen (Stanford, Calif.: Stanford University Press, 1998), 35.

25. John Wilmot, Earl of Rochester, *The Complete Poems of John Wilmot, Earl of Rochester*, ed. David M. Vieth (New Haven, Conn.: Yale University Press, 1968), 99.

26. I am thinking here of Quentin Skinner's valuable work, *Reason and Rhetoric in the Philosophy of Hobbes* (Cambridge: Cambridge University Press, 1996).

27. Carl Schmitt, *The Concept of the Political*, ed. and trans. George Schwab (1932; New Brunswick, N.J.: Rutgers University Press, 1976), 65.

28. Michel Foucault, "Truth and Power" and "The Confession of the Flesh" in *Power/Knowledge: Selected Interviews and Other Writings 1972–77*, ed. Colin Gordon, trans. Colin Gordon, Leo Marshall, John Mepham, and Kate Soper (New York: Pantheon, 1980), 97, 208.

29. Michael Hardt and Antonio Negri, *Empire* (Cambridge, Mass.: Harvard University Press, 2000), 353, 388.

30. For examples of this kind of work, see the essays gathered in *Hobbes*, ed. Robert Shaver (Aldershot: Ashgate, 1999).

31. Christopher Marlowe, "Hero and Leander" (1593), *The Complete Works of Christopher Marlowe*, ed. Roma Gill, David Fuller, and Edward J. Esche, 5 vols. (Oxford: Oxford University Press, 1987–98), 1: 192.

32. Cf. Skinner's comparison of Hobbes and Ovid, *Reason and Rhetoric in the Philosophy of Hobbes*, 233.

33. Ovid, *Metamorphoses*, ed. E. J. Kenney, trans. A. D. Melville (Oxford: Oxford University Press, 1986), 17 [1: 550], 35 [2: 355, 361–62].

34. The second edition of Brooks Otis's *Ovid as an Epic Poet* (Cambridge: Cambridge University Press, 1970) focuses on this vexed question of Ovid's Augustan or anti-Augustan attitudes, with an emphasis on his depiction of "the mercilessness of absolute power" (145). See also the wonderful analysis of the "uncertain and problematic dividing lines between poetics and politics in Ovid" (43) in Alessandro Barchiesi, *The Poet and the Prince: Ovid and Augustan Discourse* (Berkeley: University of California Press, 1997).

35. For a relevant argument about the amorality of the metamorphoses in Ovid's work and about the relation between these metamorphoses and his conception of art, see Joseph B. Solodow, *The World of Ovid's Metamorphoses* (Chapel Hill: University of North Carolina Press, 1988), esp. 157–232.

36. G. W. F. Hegel, *Hegel: The Letters*, trans. Clark Butler and Christiane Seiler (Bloomington: Indiana University Press, 1984), 113.

Chapter 4. The Injustice of Velázquez

1. Mary R. Richardson, *Laugh a Defiance* (London: Weidenfeld and Nicolson, 1953), 167.

2. "National Gallery Outrage," *Times* (March 11, 1914): 9. Page references to this article are given in parentheses in the text.

3. Richardson, *Laugh a Defiance*, 168.

4. Emmeline Pankhurst, *My Own Story* (New York: Hearst's International Library, 1914; reprint New York: Kraus Reprint Company, 1971), 343. In *The Suffragette Movement: An Intimate Account of Persons and Ideals* (London: Longmans, Green, 1931), 268, Sylvia Pankhurst noted that *My Own Story* "was produced by Rhita Childe Dorr from talks with Mrs. Pankhurst and from Suffragette literature."

5. Robert Adams, *The Lost Museum: Glimpses of Vanished Originals* (New York: Viking, 1980), 22.

6. Anthony Julius, *Transgressions: The Offences of Art* (Chicago: University of Chicago Press, 2002), 194.

7. "Comedian Faces Jail for Art Attack," *Guardian Unlimited* (October 31, 2003) http://www.guardian.co.uk/arts/news/story/0,11711,1074708,00.html

8. Richardson, *Laugh a Defiance*, 165. In an interview in the 1950s, Richardson also said, "I didn't like the way men visitors to the gallery gaped at it all day long." Quoted in David Freedberg, *Iconoclasts and Their Motives* (Maarssen, Netherlands: Gary Schwartz, 1985), 15.

9. The "Cat-and-Mouse Act," or Prisoner's Temporary Discharge for Ill-Health Act, was a measure the government had adopted in response to the suffragettes' hunger-strike tactics. Prisoners whose health was judged to be in danger would be released so that they could recuperate, with the expectation that they might be taken into custody again at any time to serve out the remainder of their sentences.

10. Adams, *The Lost Museum*, 24.

11. Tertullianus, *De Idolatria* (c. 198–208), ed. and trans. J. H. Waszink and J. C. M. Van Winden (London: E.J. Brill, 1987), 25. This argument would be revived in the era of the Reformation by Erasmus, among others; see Margaret Aston, *England's Iconoclasts* (Oxford: Oxford University Press, 1988), 1: 343.

12. Tertullianus, *De Idolatria*, 27.

13. Immanuel Kant, *Critique of the Power of Judgment* (1790), ed. Paul Guyer, trans. Paul Guyer and Eric Matthews (Cambridge: Cambridge University Press, 2000), 156. See also Jean-Joseph Goux's analysis of the iconoclasm of the Kantian sublime in relation to Sigmund Freud and Karl Marx, whom he discusses as iconoclasts in the Jewish tradition, in *Les Iconoclastes* (Paris: Editions du Seuil, 1978), esp. 7–64.

14. Kant, *Critique of the Power of Judgment*, 156.

15. The phrase "war of women against men" is taken from Emmeline Pankhurst; see her "Foreword" (unpaginated) to *My Own Story*.

16. David Freedberg, *The Power of Images: Studies in the History and Theory of Response* (Chicago: University of Chicago Press, 1989), 388.

17. Freedberg, *The Power of Images*, 388.

18. Louis Réau, *Histoire du vandalisme: les monuments détruits de l'art françois*, 2 vols. (Paris: Librairie Hachette, 1959), 1: 18. See also P.-J. Proudhon's comment on eighth-century Byzantine iconoclasm in *Du principe de l'art et de sa destination sociale* (c. 1863–65), ed. Jules L. Pusch (Paris: Marcel Rivière, 1939), 80: "The people who proved to be the most fervid devotees of beauty were also those who, under the influence of Christian revivalism, proved to be the most implacable destroyers of images."

19. Horst Bredekamp, *Kunst als Medium sozialer Konflikte: Bilderkämpfe von der Spätantike bis zur Hussitenrevolution* (Frankfurt am Main: Suhrkamp Verlag, 1975), 11, 112.

20. W. J. T. Mitchell, *Iconology: Image, Text, Ideology* (Chicago: University of Chicago Press, 1986), 207, 198.

21. Aston, *England's Iconoclasts*, 4.

22. See Bruno Latour and Peter Weibel, eds., *Iconoclash* (Cambridge, Mass.: MIT Press, 2002).

23. Victor I. Stoichita, "'Cabinets d'amateurs' et scénario iconoclaste dans la peinture anversoise du XVIIe siècle," in *L'art et les révolutions* vol. 4 *Les iconoclasmes*, ed. Sergiusz Michalski (Strasbourg: Société Alsacienne pour le Développement de l'Histoire de l'Art, 1992), 182–83.

24. They have characterized their work in this way in numerous interviews, but see, e.g., Alan Riding, "Goya Probably Would Not Be Amused," *New York Times* (April 6, 2003), Section 4: 2.

25. See Francis Haskell, "La Venus del espejo," in *Velázquez*, ed. Noemí Sobregués (Barcelona: Fundación Amigos del Museo del Prado, 1999), 223.

26. See Edmund Gosse, *Father and Son: Biographical Recollections* (New York: Charles Scribner's Sons, 1907), 278–79.

27. See Hilda Keen, "Suffrage Autobiography: A Study of Mary Richardson—Suffragette, Socialist and Fascist," in *A Suffrage Reader: Changing Directions in British Suffrage History*, ed. Claire Eustance, Joan Ryan, and Laura Ugolini (London: Leicester University Press, 2000), 180.

28. Pankhurst, *The Suffragette Movement*, 579–80.

29. See Kean, "Suffrage Autobiography," 182–84.

30. See Gerhard Jaritz, "Von der Objektkritik bis zur Objektzerstörung: Methoden und Handlungsspielräume im Spätmittelalter," in *Bilder und Bildersturm im Spätmittelalter und in der frühen Neuzeit*, ed. Bob Scribner (Wiesbaden: Otto Harrassowitz, 1990), 37–50.

31. Thomas More, *A Dialogue Concerning Heresies: Part 1* (1529), ed. Thomas M. C. Lawler, Germain Thomas More, Marc' Hadour, and Richard C. Marius, in *Complete Works of St. Thomas More*, ed. Louis L. Martz, Richard S. Sylvester, Clarence H. Miller, Franklin I. Baumer, George K. Hunter, Fred C. Robinson, Richard J. Schoeck, and Daniel R. Watkins (New Haven, Conn.: Yale University Press, 1963-), 6: 121.

32. See Aston, *England's Iconoclasts*, 146.

33. More, *A Dialogue Concerning Heresies*, 46.

34. More, *A Dialogue Concerning Heresies*, 47, 40.

35. "The Sixth Session of the Seventh Ecumenical Council," in Daniel J. Sahas, *Icon and Logos: Sources in Eighth-Century Iconoclasm* (Toronto: University of Toronto Press, 1986), 68.

36. More, *A Dialogue Concerning Heresies*, 46.

37. More, *Utopia*, ed. George M. Logan, Robert M. Adams, and Clarence H. Miller, trans. Robert M. Adams (Cambridge: Cambridge University Press, 1995), 235.

38. Richardson, *Laugh a Defiance*, 174.

39. Richardson, *Laugh a Defiance*, 179.

40. See the symposium on "Destruction in Art," *Art and Artists* 1 (August 1966).

41. See Lynda Nead, *The Female Nude: Art, Obscenity and Sexuality* (London: Routledge, 1992), 41.

42. Mikhail Bakhtin, *Rabelais and His World*, trans. Helene Iswolsky (Bloomington: Indiana University Press, 1984), 439. This passage refers specifically to the writings of François Rabelais but also reflects Bakhtin's analysis of folk culture, carnival, and festive laughter in general.

43. Joseph Leo Koerner, *The Reformation of the Image* (Chicago: University of Chicago Press, 2004), 11.

44. See Bredekamp, *Kunst als Medium sozialer Konflikte*, 79.

45. Lee Palmer Wandel, "Iconoclasts in Zurich," in *Bilder und Bildersturm im Spätmittelalter und in der frühen Neuzeit*, 134.

46. See E. Sylvia Pankhurst, *The Suffragette: The History of the Women's Militant Suffrage Movement, 1905–1910* (London: Gay and Hancock, 1911; reprint New York: Source Book Press, 1970), 358.

47. See Rowena Fowler, "Why Did Suffragettes Attack Works of Art?" *Journal of Women's History* 2 (Winter 1991): 109–25; and for the role of art and artists in suffragette protests, see Lisa Tickner, *The Spectacle of Women: Imagery of the Suffrage Compaign 1907–14* (Chicago: University of Chicago Press, 1988).

48. Dario Gamboni, *The Destruction of Art: Iconoclasm and Vandalism since the French Revolution* (New Haven, Conn.: Yale University Press, 1997), 132.

49. Freedberg, *Iconoclasts and their Motives*, 24.

50. Pankhurst, *My Own Story*, 345.

51. Jake Chapman, quoted in Lynn Barber, "Brothers in Art," *Observer* (March 29, 1999), Section: "The Observer Page."

52. Pablo Picasso, quoted in Christian Zervos, "Conversation avec Picasso," *Cahiers d'art* (1935): 173; Thomas Messer, quoted in Gamboni, *The Destruction of Art*, 167.

53. George Eliot, *Middlemarch*, ed. W. J. Harvey (New York: Penguin, 1965), 251, 252.

54. Pankhurst, *My Own Story*, 265.

55. Pankhurst, *My Own Story*, 213–14.

56. Quoted in Fowler, "Why Did Suffragettes Attack Works of Art?" 115.

57. Quoted in José Alvarez Lopera, "Iconoclastia y recuperacion de la herencia artistica durante la guerra civil española," *L'Art et les révolutions*, 241.

58. Theodor W. Adorno, *Aesthetic Theory*, ed. Gretel Adorno and Rolf Tiedemann, trans. Robert Hullot-Kentor (Minneapolis: University of Minnesota Press, 1997), 57.

59. Caroline Arscott and Katie Scott, "Introducing Venus," in *Manifestations of Venus: Art and Sexuality*, ed. Caroline Arscott and Katie Scott (Manchester: Manchester University Press, 2000), 5.

60. Jonathan Brown, *Velázquez: Painter and Courtier* (New Haven, Conn.: Yale University Press, 1986), 187.

61. Andreas Prater, *Venus and Her Mirror: Velázquez and the Art of Nude Painting* (Munich: Prestel, 2002), 109.

62. Brown, *Velázquez*, 183.

Chapter 5. The Illusion of a Future

1. F. T. Marinetti, "Fondazione e Manifesto del Futurismo" (1909), *Teoria e Invenzione Futurista*, ed. Luciano De Maria, *Opere di F. T. Marinetti*, 3 vols. (Milan: Arnoldo Mondadori, 1968), 2: 13.

2. Valentine de Saint-Point, *Manifeste de la femme futuriste suivi de Manifeste futuriste de la luxure, Le théâtre de la femme, La métachorie* (Paris: Editions Séguier, 1996), 14.

3. Thomas Bernhard, *The Loser*, trans. Jack Dawson (New York: Knopf, 1991), 92, 75. Translation slightly altered.

4. Marinetti, *Futurismo e Fascismo* (1924), *Opere*, 2: 430; "Prefazione futurista a 'Revolverate' di Gian Pietro Lucini" (c. 1910), *Opere*, 2: 24.

5. Marinetti, *Al di là del Communismo* (1920), *Opere*, 2: 424.

6. I am not the first to remark upon the connections among futurism, minimalism, and pop art; see, for instance, Enrico Crispolti, "Tre frammenti sul mito della machina," in *La macchina mito futurista*, ed. Floriana Viesti (Rome: Edizioni d'Italia, 1986) (unpaginated). For a major study that portrays futurism as a forerunner of the "technological sublime" in these later movements, see Caroline A. Jones, *Machine in the Studio: Constructing the Postwar American Artist* (Chicago: University of Chicago Press, 1996).

7. Marinetti, "Manifesto tecnico della letteratura futurista" (1912), *Opere*, 2: 47.

8. Walter Benjamin, "Theses on the Philosophy of History," *Illuminations: Essays and Reflections*, ed. Hannah Arendt, trans. Harry Zohn (New York: Schocken Books, 1969), 256.

9. Although it bore specific reference to Italian cultural and national history, the futurists' anti-museum attitude was already a long-standing trope in avant-garde polemics at the time when they arrived on the scene. See Dario Gamboni, *The Destruction of Art: Iconoclasm and Vandalism Since the French Revolution* (New Haven, Conn.: Yale University Press, 1997), 255–56.

10. Ernst Jünger, "Die Totale Mobilmachung," *Werke*, 10 vols. (Stuttgart: Ernst Klett Verlag, 1960), 5: 145.

11. Marinetti, "Manifesto della danza futurista" (1917) and "Manifesto tecnico della letteratura futurista," 126, 48. The image of machines "multiplying" human forces is recurrent in Mario Morasso's writing, as are other themes that evidently influenced Marinetti, such as an emphasis on "the relation between beauty and velocity" (38). See Morasso's 1905 work *La nuova arma (la macchina)* (Turin: Centro Studi Piemontesi, 1994).

12. Marinetti, "Manifesto tecnico della letteratura futurista," 44.

13. Marinetti, "Il Poema non umano dei tecnicismi" (1940), *Opere*, 2: 1041–42.

14. Marinetti, *Guerra sola igiene del mondo*, *Opere*, 2: 256.

15. Marinetti, "Manifesto tecnico della letteratura futurista," 48; "Introduzione a 'I nuovi poeti futuristi' " (c. 1925), *Opere* 2: 164.

16. Marinetti, "Fondazione e Manifesto del Futurismo," 13; *Guerra sola igiene del mondo*, *Opere*, 2: 254.

17. Fortunato Depero, "W la macchina e lo stile d'acciaio" (1927), *Prose futuriste*, ed. Riccardo Maroni (Trento: Voci della Terra Trentina, 1973), 46.

18. Rodney A. Brooks, *Flesh and Machines: How Robots Will Change Us* (New York: Pantheon, 2002), 135–37.

19. At least one contemporary commentator was quick to notice the relations between the anarchistic and Nietzschean tendencies of 1960s youth movements and similar tendencies in futurism; see Maurizio Calvesi, *Il futurismo* (Milan: Fratelli Fabbri Editori, 1970), 14–15. The similarities between futurism and *Anti-Oedipus* were obvious enough to have been noted with pleasure in an enthusiastic 1975 study by Umberto Artioli, *La scena e la dynamis: immaginario e struttura nelle sintesi futuriste* (Bologna: Pàtron Editora, 1975), 67. Andrew Hewitt's study of futurism in *Fascist Modernism: Aesthetics, Politics, and the Avant-Garde* (Stanford, Calif.: Stanford University Press, 1993) is also keyed to the work of Deleuze and Guattari in *Anti-Oedipus* (see esp. 92–94).

20. Andy Warhol, quoted in Gene R. Swenson, "What Is Pop Art?" in *Pop Art: The Critical Dialogue*, ed. Carol Anne Mahsun (Ann Arbor, Mich.: UMI Research Press, 1989), 118; Claes Oldenberg, quoted in Lucy R. Lippard, "Eros Presumptive" (1967), in *Minimal Art: A Critical Anthology*, ed. Gregory Battcock (New York: E. P. Dutton, 1968), 216; Sol LeWitt, "Paragraphs on Conceptual Art" (1967) in *Sol LeWitt*, ed. Alicia Legg (New York: Museum of Modern Art, 1978), 166.

21. A notable exception to this erasure of the case of futurism, however, can be found in the writings of Paul Virilio; see, e.g., Virilio, *The Aesthetics of Disappearance* (1980), trans. Philip Beitchman (New York: Semiotext(e), 1991), 66, 91, 94; and *The Art of the Motor*, trans. Julie Rose (Minneapolis: University of Minnesota Press, 1995), 203–4, 129–30.

22. There are exceptions, of course, one of the most notable being Manuel DeLanda's *War in the Age of Intelligent Machines* (New York: Swerve Editions,

1991). Another is Hayles's *How We Became Posthuman* (Chicago: University of Chicago Press, 1999), which provides important insights into the historical motivations and infelicities of reasoning that have led to human-machine identifications in science and literature. See also R. L. Rutsky's comment, in *High Techne: Art and Technology from the Machine Aesthetic to the Posthuman* (Minneapolis: University of Minnesota Press, 1999), 155, on how "the attitudes of this kind of high-tech vanguardism are often strikingly similar to the Italian Futurists' self-serving glorification of autonomous technology."

23. Villiers de l'Isle-Adam underlines this point when he has Thomas Edison refer to Hoffmann's story, among other works, as an inspiration for his female android. See Villers de l'Isle Adam, *L'Eve-future* (1886), ed. Alan Raitt (Paris: Gallimard, 1993), 125.

24. Benedictus de Spinoza, *Treatise on the Emendation of the Intellect* (c. 1662), *The Collected Works of Spinoza*, ed. and trans. Edwin Curley, 2 vols. (Princeton, N.J.: Princeton University Press, 1985), 1: 22; John Locke, *An Essay Concerning Human Understanding* (1690), ed. Peter H. Nidditch (Oxford: Oxford University Press, 1975), 77.

25. Théophile Bordeu, *Recherches sur l'histoire de la médecine, Oeuvres complètes*, 2 vols. (Paris: Caille et Ravier, 1818), 2: 667.

26. Marinetti, "Tattilismo" (1921), *Opere*, 2: 153. It should be noted that, although it became a commonplace in the eighteenth century, the use of "machine" as a synonym for "body" antedated it; it already appears, for instance, in *Hamlet* (2. 2. 124).

27. Friedrich Nietzsche, "On the Uses and Disadvantages of History for Life" (1873), in *Untimely Meditations*, trans. R. J. Hollingdale (Cambridge: Cambridge University Press, 1983), 85.

28. See Marinetti, "Fondazione e Manifesto del Futurismo," 10.

29. See Bruno Corradini and Emilio Settimelli, "Pesi, misure e prezzi del genio artistico: manifesto futurista" (1914) in *Archivi del futurismo*, ed. Maria Drudi Gambillo and Teresa Fiori, 2 vols. (Rome: De Luca Editore, 1958–62), 1: 41–42.

30. This observation that Marinetti's ideas were old hat—or, in the futurists' idiom, passéist—goes back to the very founding of futurism in 1909. On this point, see, for example, Paul O'Keefe, "Art, Action and the Machine," in *Dynamism: The Art of Modern Life Before the Great War*, ed. Penelope Curtis (Liverpool: Tate Gallery Likverpool, 1991), 45; Shirley W. Vinall, "Marinetti, Soffici, and French Literature," in *International Futurism in Arts and Literature*, ed. Günter Berghaus (Berlin: Walter de Gruyter, 2000), 17; and in the same volume, Günter Berghaus, "Futurism, Dada, and Surrealism: Some Cross-Fertilisations among the Historical Avant-gardes," 281. In 1913, Giovanni Papini (who later allied himself with the futurists for a brief time), pursued this line of criticism in the writings eventually collected under the title *L'esperienza futurista* (1919). See Papini, *L'esperienza futurista, Opere*, 10 vols. (Milan: Arnoldo Mondadori Editore, 1958–66), 2: 845. See also George L. Mosse's comments about how the "misanthropic and masculine ideal as the principle of creativity" in futurism is indebted to the racist and misogynist work of Otto Weiniger in "Futurismo e culture politiche in Europa: una prospettiva globale," in *Futurismo, cultura e politica*, ed. Renzo De Felice (Turin: Edizioni della Fondazione Giovanni Agnelli, 1988), 22.

31. See René Huyghe, "Introduction to 'Les Pays Latins,'" and Gino Severini, "L'Italie et le futurisme," in *Histoire de l'art contemporain*, ed. René Huyghe with

Germain Bazin (Paris: Félix Alcan, 1935; rep. New York: Arno Press, 1968), 469, 476.

32. Marinetti, "Distruzione della sintassi—Immaginazione senza fili—Parole in libertà" (1913), *Opere*, 2: 60.

33. Umberto Boccioni et al., "La pittura futurista: manifesto tecnico," in *Archivi del futurismo*,1: 66.

34. Nietzsche, *Thus Spoke Zarathustra: A Book for All and None*, ed. and trans. Walter Kaufmann (New York: Modern Library, 1995), 11–12.

35. Nietzsche, *Thus Spoke Zarathustra*, 292.

36. Nietzsche, *Thus Spoke Zarathustra*, 60.

37. Inexplicably, scholars of futurism have generally absolved Marinetti of any taint of anti-Semitism, noting especially his defense of avant-garde art against Nazi accusations of degeneracy in the 1930s. In fact, Marinetti's strategy for defending such art was to save it by throwing Jews to the wolves; he argued that Jews had never been important as its creators or as members of avant-garde movements, going so far as to make a long list of important contributors to modern art in which, after each name, he noted, "Not a Jew." See the documents provided by Enrico Crispolti in *Il mito della macchina e altri temi del futurismo* (Traponi: Editore Celebes, 1969), 685, 719, 737–40, 792–96.

38. Nietzsche, *Thus Spoke Zarathustra*, 86.

39. Hewitt addresses the issue of anachronism more specifically in relation to modernism and the avant-garde in "Fascist Modernism, Futurism, and Postmodernity," in *Fascism, Aesthetics, and Culture*, ed. Richard J. Golsan (Hanover, N.H.: University Press of New England, 1992), 38–55.

40. For a thoughtful study of the futurist machine as fetish and myth, "a model of the supine imitation of alienated technological 'values'" (224), see Roberto Tessari, *Il mito della machina: letteratura e industria nel primo novecento Italiano* (Milan: Mursia, 1973), 209–76.

41. Perloff, *The Futurist Moment*, 228. As David Cundy points out in "Marinetti and Italian Futurist Typography," *Art Journal* 41 (Winter 1981): 350, "It is noteworthy that Marinetti's innovations did not make use of the advances of modern printing technology."

42. Umberto Boccioni, *Pittura e scultura futurista* (1912), *Opera completa*, ed. F. T. Marinetti (Foligno: Franco Campitelli, 1927), 78–9.

43. Marinetti, "Il poema non umano dei tecnicismi," 1041–42.

44. See Giovanni Papini, "Il cerchio si chiude," *Archivi del futurismo*, 1: 189–90.

45. Marinetti, "Manifesto tecnico della letteratura futurista," 44.

46. Marinetti, "La declamazione dinamica e sinottica" (1916), *Opere*, 2: 106.

47. Marinetti, "Contro il matrimonio" (1919), *Opere*, 2: 319. On this point and related issues, see Barbara Spackman, *Fascist Virilities: Rhetoric, Ideology, and Social Fantasy in Italy* (Minneapolis: University of Minneapolis Press, 1996). See also the analysis of the sexual fantasies in Marinetti's writing, including the theme of release from all sexual differences, in Hal Foster, *Prosthetic Gods* (Cambridge, Mass.: MIT Press, 2004), 118–28.

48. Marinetti, "Manifesto della danza futurista" (1917), *Opere*, 2: 126.

49. Marinetti, *Guerra sola igiene del mundo*, *Opere*, 2: 263.

50. Frank Stella, in an interview with Bruce Glaser, "Questions to Stella and Judd" (1966), ed. Lucy R. Lippard, in *Minimal Art*, 157–58.

51. Donald Judd, "Specific Objects" (1965), in Judd, *Complete Writings 1959-1975* (Halifax,: Nova Scotia College of Art and Design/New York: New York University Press, 1975), 184, 187. Stella's attitude later came to be considerably more

complicated; on this and other points relevant to this essay, see James Meyer, *Minimalism: Art and Polemics in the Sixties* (New Haven: Yale University Press, 2001), esp. 119–27.

52. Robert Morris, "Notes on Sculpture, Part 3: Notes and Non Sequitur" (1967) and "Introduction" (1993) in Morris, *Continuous Project Altered Daily: The Writings of Robert Morris* (Cambridge, Mass.: MIT Press, 1993), 27, x.

53. Michael Fried, "Art and Objecthood" (1967), in *Minimal Art*, 117.

54. Commenting on the relation he saw between minimalism and surrealism, Fried referred to a remark made by Tony Smith in an interview: "it is perhaps not without significance that Smith's supreme example of a Surrealist landscape was the parade ground at Nuremberg." See Fried, "Art and Objecthood," in *Minimal Art*, 145n; and for Smith's remark see, in the same volume, Samuel Wagstaff, Jr., "Talking with Tony Smith," 386.

55. I say "it might seem" because the German original offers itself to a somewhat darker rendering than Zohn's famous version: "There is never a document of civilization [*Es ist niemals ein Dokument der Kultur*] that is not at the same time a document of barbarism." In this regard see Thierry de Duve's interesting comments on futurism's hideous career, and on the inadequacy of Benjamin's response that one should politicize art, in *Kant after Duchamp* (Cambridge, Mass.: MIT Press, 1996), 362–63.

56. D. H. Lawrence, "To Edward Garnett, 5 June 1914," *The Letters of D. H. Lawrence*, ed. James T. Boulton, 8 vols. (Cambridge: Cambridge University Press, 199–2000), 2: 182–83.

57. Martin Heidegger, "The Question Concerning Technology" (1953), in Heidegger, *The Question Concerning Technology and Other Essays*, trans. William Lovitt (New York: Harper and Row, 1977), 34.

Chapter 6. The Akedah on Blanket Hill

1. *The Report of the President's Commission on Campus Unrest* (New York: Arno Press, 1970), 233.

2. See Scott L. Bills, ed., *Kent State/May 4: Echoes through a Decade* (Kent, Ohio: Kent State University Press, 1982), 26, 35, 37.

3. Segal's other biblically themed works include *The Expulsion* (1986/87), *Abraham's Farewell to Ishmael* (1987), and *Jacob and the Angels* (1984–85).

4. Quoted in Martin Friedman and Graham W. J. Beal, *George Segal: Sculptures* (Minneapolis Minn.: Walker Art Center, 1978), 84.

5. Lucy R. Lippard, *A Different War: Vietnam in Art* (Seattle Wash.: Whatcom Museum of History and Art/Real Comet Press, 1990), 92.

6. George Segal, quoted in Friedman and Beal, *George Segal: Sculptures*, 84, and in Sterling Victor Fleischer, "Public Sculpture, Public Debate and the Politics of Commemoration: The George Segal Controversy and the Memorialization of May 4, 1970, at Kent State University," M.A. thesis, Kent State University, 2000, 114.

7. Segal, "On Public Sculpture," in Jan Van Der Mark, *George Segal*, rev. ed. (New York: Harry Abrams, 1979), 242.

8. Segal, quoted in Joseph Disponzio, "George Segal's Sculpture on a Theme of Gay Liberation and the Sexual-Political Equivocation of Public Consciousness," in *Critical Issues in Public Art: Content, Context, and Controversy*, ed. Harriet F. Senie and Sally Webster (New York: HarperCollins, 1992), 210.

9. See Carol Delaney, *Abraham on Trial: The Social Legacy of Biblical Myth* (Princeton, N.J.: Princeton University Press, 1998), 172.

10. In *Abraham on Trial*, 130, Delaney points out that after the Six Day War some Israeli soldiers had explicitly linked their antiwar protests to a rejection of the Akedah model of sacrifice.

11. Segal, quoted in Phyllis Tuchman, *George Segal* (New York: Abbeville Press, 1983), 91.

12. Segal in Tuchman, 95.

13. See Segal, "Postscript 1974," in Van Der Mark, *George Segal*, 67–68.

14. Segal, "Postscript 1974," 68.

15. Segal, quoted in Nancy M. Berman, ed., *George Segal: Works from the Bible* (Los Angeles: Skirball Cultural Center, 1997), 6.

16. Segal, in Berman, ed., *George Segal: Works from the Bible*, 14.

17. Philo, "On Abraham," in *Philo*, trans. F. H. Colson, 9 vols. (London: Heinemann, 1935), 6: 97.

18. "The Northampton *Abraham*" in Norman Davis, ed., *Non-Cycle Plays and Fragments* (London: Early English Text Society, 1970), 38; Philo, "On Abraham," in *Philo*, 6: 97.

19. Philo, "On Abraham," in *Philo*, 6: 97.

20. Moses Maimonides, *The Guide of the Perplexed*, ed. and trans. Shlomo Pines (Chicago: University of Chicago Press, 1963), 500.

21. Jacques Derrida, *The Gift of Death*, trans. David Wills (Chicago: University of Chicago Press, 1995), 58; Martin Luther, *Lectures on Genesis*, trans. George V. Schick, *Luther's Works*, ed. Jaroslav Pelikan and Walter A. Hansen, 55 vols. (Saint Louis: Concordia Publishing House, 1964), 4: 93; John Calvin, *Commentaries on the First Book of Moses, Called Genesis*, ed. and trans. John King, 2 vols. (Grand Rapids, Mich.: William B. Eerdmans, 1948), 1: 562, 560.

22. Luther, *Lectures on Genesis*, *Luther's Works*, 4: 111, 114, 109, 114, 124.

23. Luther, *Lectures on Genesis*, *Luther's Works*, 4: 109, 91.

24. Kierkegaard borrows the term "hard saying" from John 6: 60.

25. Søren Kierkegaard [Johannes de Silentio, pseud.], *Fear and Trembling*, in *Fear and Trembling/Repetition*, ed. and trans. Howard V. Hong and Edna H. Hong (Princeton, N.J.: Princeton University Press, 1843), 72, 88.

26. Ludwig Wittgenstein, *Tractatus Logico-Philosophicus*, trans. D. F. Pears and B. F. McGuinness (London: Routledge and Kegan Paul, 1961), 151. Translation slightly altered.

27. Jean-François Lyotard, *The Inhuman: Reflections on Time*, trans. Geoffrey Bennington and Rachel Bowlby (Stanford, Calif.: Stanford University Press, 1991), 196.

28. Friedrich Nietzsche, *Daybreak: Thoughts on the Prejudices of Morality*, ed. Maudemarie Clark and Brian Leiter, trans. R. J. Hollingdale (Cambridge: Cambridge University Press, 1997), 204.

29. Segal, quoted in Van Der Mark, *George Segal*, 242.

30. Plato, *Republic*, trans. Paul Shorey, *The Collected Dialogues of Plato*, ed. Edith Hamilton and Huntington Cairns (Princeton, N.J.: Princeton University Press, 1961), 630.

31. Paul Spreiregen, "Purpose," in James E. Dalton, ed., *Kent State May 4 Memorial Design Competition* (Kent, Ohio: Kent State University, n. d.), 1.

32. Harriet F. Senie, *Contemporary Public Sculpture: Tradition, Transformation, and Controversy* (New York: Oxford University Press, 1992), 41.

33. Erich Auerbach, *Mimesis: The Representation of Reality in Western Literature*, trans. Willard R. Trask (Princeton, N.J.: Princeton University Press, 1953), 9; Kierkegaard, *Fear and Trembling*, 22.

34. Quoted in Fleischer, "Public Sculpture, Public Debate and the Politics of Commemoration," 113.

35. See the Marquis de Sade, *Justine*, in *The Marquis de Sade: Justine, Philosophy in the Bedroom, and Other Writings*, ed. and trans. Richard Seaver and Austryn Wainhouse (New York: Grove Press, 1965), 553.

36. Quoted in Fleischer, "Public Sculpture, Public Debate and the Politics of Commemoration," 113.

37. Wilfred Owen, "The Parable of the Old Man and the Young," *The Collected Poems of Wilfred Owen*, ed. C. Day Lewis (London: Chatto and Windus, 1966), 42.

38. See, e. g., the fourth-century Aramaic rendering of scripture, *Targum Neofiti 1: Genesis*, ed. and trans. Martin McNamara (Collegeville, Minn.: Liturgical Press, 1992), 118; the seventh- or eighth-century *Targum Pseudo-Jonathan: Genesis*, ed. and trans. Michael Maher (Collegeville, Minn.: Liturgical Press, 1992), 79–80; and the early fifteenth-century York cycle *Sacrifice of Isaac* in Lucy Toulmin Smith, ed., *York Plays* (Oxford: Oxford University Press, 1885), 62–63. Flavius Josephus, the first-century Jewish historian, goes so far as to have Isaac retrospectively condemn his very birth into the world from which Abraham is about to dispatch him. See Josephus, *Judean Antiquities 1–4*, ed. Steve Mason, trans. Louis H. Feldman (Leiden: E. J. Brill, 2000), 92.

39. Antonin Artaud, *Le théatre et son double* (1938), *Oeuvres complètes*, 19 vols. (Paris: Gallimard, 1964), 4: 110.

40. Philo, "On Abraham," in *Philo*, 6: 87.

41. Maher, ed., *Targum Pseudo-Jonathan*, 80.

42. See Maimonides, *The Guide of the Perplexed*, 501.

43. Calvin, *Commentaries on the First Book of Moses*, 1: 569.

44. Kierkegaard, *Fear and Trembling*, 34.

45. Kierkegaard, *Fear and Trembling*, 41.

46. "The Brome *Abraham*" in Davis, ed. *Non-Cycle Plays and Fragments*, 52; *Abraham* in Martin Stevens and A. C. Cawley, eds., *The Towneley Plays*, 2 vols. (Oxford: Early English Text Society, 1994), 1: 55; Origen, *Homilies on Genesis and Exodus*, trans. Ronald E. Heine (Washington, D.C.: Catholic University of America Press, 1982), 139.

47. See Henry Fielding, *The History of the Adventures of Joseph Andrews*, ed. Douglas Brooks-Davies, rev. Thomas Keymer (Oxford: Oxford University Press, 1999), 270.

48. See *Genesis Rabbah*, trans. Jacob Neusner, 3 vols. (Atlanta: Scholars Press, 1985), 2: 884.

49. See Delaney, *Abraham on Trial*, 272 n. 7.

50. See David Lerch, *Isaaks Opferung christlich gedeutet* (Tübingen: J. C. B. Mohr, 1950), 262.

51. See Emmanuel Levinas, "Existence et éthique," *Noms propres* (Paris: Fata Morgana, 1976), 109.

52. See Lerch, *Isaaks Opferung*, 9–11.

53. Josephus, *Judean Antiquities 1–4*, 94 n. 728. In his commentary on this point, the translator refers to the scholarship of Thomas W. Franxman.

54. See Lerch, *Isaaks Opferung*, 223.

55. Luther, *Lectures on Genesis, Luther's Works*, 4: 108.

56. Derrida, *The Gift of Death*, 70.

57. "The Northampton *Abraham*" in Davis, ed., *Non-Cycle Plays and Fragments*, 38.

58. "The Brome *Abraham*" in Davis, ed. *Non-Cycle Plays and Fragments*, 54.

59. On this point and others related to it, see Delaney's feminist analysis in *Abraham on Trial*.

60. "The Northampton *Abraham*" in Davis, ed., *Non-Cycle Plays and Fragments*, 37.

61. "Dublin *Abraham and Isaac*" in R. T. Davies, ed., *The Corpus Christi Play of the English Middle Ages* (London: Faber and Faber, 1972), 410, 417.

62. Quoted in Fleischer, *Public Sculpture, Public Debate and the Politics of Commemoration*, 118.

63. Friedrich Schlegel, "Über die Unverständlichkeit" (1800), *Werke*, ed. Wolfgang Hecht, 2 vols. (Berlin: Aufbau-Verlag, 1980), 2: 206–7. For Kierkegaard's criticism of Schlegel as a representative voice of romantic irony, see Kierkegaard, *The Concept of Irony: With Continual Reference to Socrates* (1841), ed. and trans. Howard V. Hong and Edna H. Hong (Princeton, N.J.: Princeton University Press, 1989), esp. 286–301.

64. Derrida, *The Gift of Death*, 86, 68. For a meditation on the sacrifice of Isaac in relation to the writings of Kierkegaard, Derrida, and Bataille, see Kenneth Itzkowitz, "A Deadly Gift: To Derrida, from Kierkegaard and Bataille," in *Extreme Beauty: Aesthetics, Politics, Death*, ed. James E. Swearingen and Joanne Cutting-Gray (New York: Continuum, 2002), 194–207.

65. Theodor Adorno, *Minima Moralia*, trans. E. F. N. Jephcott (London: Verso, 1978), 111.

66. Philo, "On Abraham," *Philo*, 6: 89–91.

67. It is noteworthy, though, that Derrida is in good company in this respect; Geza Vermes comments, "Rabbinic writings show clearly that sacrifices, and perhaps the offering of all sacrifices, were intended as a memorial of Isaac's self-oblation." See Vermes, *Scripture and Tradition in Judaism: Haggadic Studies*, rev. ed. (Leiden: Brill, 1983), 209.

68. See Segal's comment (quoted in Tuchman, *George Segal*, 95), "Everything in our lives, ultimately, is religious in some way."

69. See Fleischer, "Public Sculpture, Public Debate and the Politics of Commemoration," 107.

Chapter 7. What Is It Like to Be an Artwork?

1. Quoted in Judith Thurman, "The Divine Marquise," *New Yorker* (22 September 2003): 178.

2. Otto Muehl, quoted in Régis Michel, *La peinture comme crime, ou la part maudite de la modernité* (Paris: Réunion des Musées Nationaux, 2001), 262.

3. Gina Pane, quoted in Kathy O'Dell, *Contract with the Skin: Masochism, Performance Art, and the 1970s* (Minneapolis: University of Minnesota Press, 1998), 45.

4. Hannah Wilke, quoted in *Hannah Wilke: A Retrospective*, ed. Thomas H. Kochheiser (Columbia: University of Missouri Press, 1989), 52.

5. Denis Diderot, *Paradoxe sur le comédien*, ed. Jane Marsh Dieckmann, *Oeuvres complètes*, ed. Herbert Dieckmann and Jean Varloot, 25 vols. (Paris: Hermann, 1995), 20. Page numbers are given within the text.

6. Johann Wolfgang Goethe, *Faust*, ed. Gotthard Erler (Berlin: Aufbau-Verlag Berlin und Weimar, 1986), 84.

7. Charles Baudelaire, "Le peintre de la vie moderne" (1863), *Oeuvres complètes*, ed. Y.-G. Le Dantec, rev. Claude Pichois (Paris: Gallimard, 1968), 1160. On the suggestion in the "Paradox of the Actor" that life is "an art-form," see Geoffrey Bremner, *Order and Chance: The Pattern of Diderot's Thought* (Cambridge: Cambridge University Press, 1983), 203.

8. Although I am concerned here with the broader implications of Diderot's paradox, it is noteworthy that, even narrowly construed, it was not unprecedented. In her introductory "Observations au 'Paradoxe' " (Diderot, *Paradoxe sur le comédien*, *Oeuvres complètes*, 20: 8), Dieckmann, among others, has pointed

out that François Riccoboni's *L'Art du théâtre* (1750) anticipated Diderot's arguments; and in his 1758 "Lettre à D'Alembert" Jean-Jacques Rousseau had characterized the actor as one who coolly, with "*sang-froid,*" becomes impassioned. See Rousseau, "*Lettre à D'Alembert,*" ed. Bernard Gagnebin and Jean Rousset, *Oeuvres complètes,* ed. Bernard Gagnebin and Marcel Raymond, 5 vols. (Paris: Gallimard, 1995), 5: 73.

9. Plato, *The Republic,* trans. Paul Shorey, *The Collected Dialogues of Plato,* ed. Edith Hamilton and Huntington Cairns (Princeton, N.J.: Princeton University Press, 1961), 658.

10. Plato, *The Republic,* 659.

11. Orlan, "Virtuel et réel: dialectique et complexité" in *Orlan: Refiguration Self-Hybridations: Série Précolombienne,* ed. Dominque Basqué, Marek Bartelik, and Orlan (Paris: Éditions Al Dante, 2001), 52.

12. Diderot, *Paradoxe sur le comédien, Oeuvres,* 64.

13. Plato, *The Republic,* 772, 736.

14. Plato, *The Republic,* 623.

15. Plato, *The Republic,* 698.

16. Friedrich Nietzsche, *The Will to Power* (1901), ed. Walter Kaufmann, trans. Walter Kaufmann and R. J. Hollingdale (New York: Vintage, 1968), 512–13.

17. Marek Bartelik, "Re-présenter la beauté: notes sur Orlan," in *Orlan: Refiguration Self-Hybridations,* 17n.

18. Orlan, quoted in *Orlan: Refiguration Self-Hybridations,* 18n.

19. Orlan, "Virtuel et réel," 50.

20. See, for example, "Conférence," in Orlan, *Ceci est mon corps . . . Ceci est mon logiciel,* trans. Tanya Augsburg and Michel A. Moos (London: Black Dog Publishing, 1996), 91–3.

21. For the *Star Trek* identifications of Orlan, see Philip Auslander, *From Acting to Performance: Essays in Modernism and Postmodernism* (London: Routledge, 1997), 131. For the reported interest of Cronenberg in her work, see Linda S. Kauffman, "Cutups in Beauty School—and Postscripts, January 2000 and December 2001," in *Interfaces: Women, Autobiography, Image, Performance,* ed. Sidonie Smith and Julia Watson (Ann Arbor: University of Michigan Press, 2002), 128.

22. Linda S. Kauffman, *Bad Girls and Sick Boys: Fantasies in Contemporary Art and Culture* (Berkeley: University of California Press, 1998), 75.

23. Orlan, "Virtuel et réel," 44.

24. Orlan, "Virtuel et réel," 46. For the article in question, see Barbara Rose, "Is it Art? Orlan and the Transgressive Act," *Art in America* 81 (February 1993): 82–87, 125.

25. Orlan, "Carnal Art Manifesto," in *Orlan: 1964–2001,* ed. María José Kerejeta (Alava: Artium/Salamanca and Ediciones Universidad de Salamanca, 2002), 218.

26. Orlan, "Virtuel et réel," 49.

27. Christine Buci-Glucksmann, quoted in "Una Conversaciòn entre Bernard Blistene y Christine Buci-Glucksmann," in *Orlan: 1964–2001,* 115.

28. Orlan, quoted in Michael Enrici and Jean-Noël Bret, "Triumph of the Baroque: Interview with Christine Buci-Glucksmann," trans. Brian Webster and Carsen Irwin, in *Orlan: 1964–2001,* 209.

29. On this topic see Juan Antonio Ramírez, "Frankenstein, Jekyll, Panopticon: Omnipresence of Orlan," trans. Brian Webster and Careen Irwin, in *Orlan: 1964–2001,* 214–18.

30. Parveen Adams, "Opération Orlan," trans. Isabelle Adams, in Orlan, *Ceci est mon corps,* 58. On the relation of Orlan's art to conventional cosmetic surgery and to other feminist practitioners of body art, among other points relevant to my concerns here, see Tanya Augsburg, "Orlan's Performative Transformations of Subjectivity," in *The Ends of Performance,* ed. Peggy Phelan and Jill Lane (New York: New York University Press, 1998), 285–314.

31. Christine Buci-Glucksmann, "Una Conversación entre Bernard Blistene y Christine Buci-Glucksmann," in *Orlan: 1964–2001,* 114.

32. Guillaume Apollinaire, quoted in Jean-François Lyotard, *The Inhuman: Reflections on Time,* trans. Geoffrey Bennington and Rachel Bowlby (Stanford, Calif.: Stanford University Press, 1991), 2.

33. Orlan, "Virtuel et réel," 50. On the uneasy relation between Orlan's art and mainstream feminism, see C. Jill O'Bryan, *Carnal Art: Orlan's Refacing* (Minneapolis: University of Minnesota Press, 2005), 32.

34. On the subject of body art, especially in relation to the issue of gender, see, e. g., Lucy R. Lippard, "The Pains and Pleasures of Rebirth: European and American Women's Body Art," in *From the Center: Feminist Essays on Women's Art* (New York: E. P. Dutton, 1976), 121–38; Rebecca Schneider, *The Explicit Body in Performance* (London: Routledge, 1997); Amelia Jones, *Body Art: Performing the Subject* (Minneapolis: University of Minnesota Press, 1998); O'Dell, *Contract with the Skin;* Amelia Jones and Andrew Stephenson, eds., *Performing the Body/Performing the Text* (London: Routledge, 1999); Lea Vergine, *Orlan: Millenial Female* (Oxford: Berg, 2000); Kate Ince, *Orlan: Millenial Female* (Oxford: Berg, 2000); Smith and Watson, eds., *Interfaces;* and O'Bryan, *Carnal Art.*

35. Marina Abramovic, *Public Body: Installations and Objects, 1965–2001,* trans. Karel Clapshaw and Gino Bernoccho (Milan: Edizioni Charta, 2001), 53–54.

36. Thomas Nagel, "What is it like to be a bat?" (1974) in *Mortal Questions* (Cambridge: Cambridge University Press, 1979). Page numbers are given within the text.

Conclusion: The Necessity of Misanthropy

Epigraph: E. M. Cioran, in a 1992 conversation with Georg Caryat Focke, in *Glossaire, Oeuvres* (Paris: Gallimard, 1995), 1761.

1. Thomas Bernhard, *Old Masters: A Comedy,* trans. Ewald Osers (London: Quartet Books, 1989), 146.

2. Thierry de Duve, *Kant After Duchamp* (Cambridge, Mass.: MIT Press, 1996), 62, 36, 72.

3. Georg Lukács, *The Theory of the Novel: A Historico-Philosophical Essay on the Forms of Great Epic Literature* (1920), trans. Anna Bostock (Cambridge, Mass.: MIT Press, 1971), 72.

4. Bibi Anderson in *Persona* (Bergman) (1963).

5. Lucian, *Timon, or The Misanthrope,* in *Lucian,* ed. and trans. A. M. Harmon, K. Kilburn, and M. D. Macleod, 8 vols. (Cambridge: Harvard University Press, 1953–67), 2: 373.

6. Lucian, *Timon, or The Misanthrope, Lucian,* 2: 365.

7. Percy Bysshe Shelley, *Letters,* ed. Rogert Ingpen, *The Complete Works of Percey Bysshe Shelley,* ed. Roger Ingpen and Walter E. Peck, 10 vols. (New York: Gordian Press, 1965), 10: 124.

8. See Plutarch, "Antony," *Plutarch's Lives,* trans. Bernadotte Perrin, 11 vols. (London: William Heinemann, 1914–26), 9: 299; and William Shakespeare,

Timon of Athens, *The Riverside Shakespeare*, ed. G. Blakemore Evans (Boston: Houghton Mifflin, 1974), 1474.

9. Arthur Schopenhauer, *The World as Will and Representation* (1818), trans. E. F. J. Payne, 2 vols. (New York: Dover, 1969), 1: 390–91.

10. Virginia Woolf, *Mrs. Dalloway* (1952; San Diego: Harcourt, 1981), 102.

11. Georges Bataille, *La part maudite* (1949; Paris: Éditions de Minuit, 1967), 42.

12. Guillaume Budé, in a prefatory commendation quoted in Thomas More, *Utopia*, ed. George M. Logan, Robert M. Adams, and Clarence H. Miller, trans. Robert M. Adams (Cambridge: Cambridge University Press, 1995), 9.

13. Margaret Thatcher, from an interview with Douglas Keay that originally appeared in *Women's Own* (October 3, 1987), as reprinted at http://www.margaretthatcher.org/speeches/displaydocument-asp?docid=106689.

14. Oscar Levant, *The Unimportance of Being Oscar* (New York: Putnam, 1968), 14.

15. Thatcher, from *Women's Own* interview.

16. Petrarch, *The Life of Solitude* (c. 1346–56), ed. and trans. Jacob Zeitlin (Urbana: University of Illinois Press, 1924), 150.

17. Niccolò Machiavelli, *Discourses*, trans. Christian E. Detmold, in The Prince *and the* Discourses (New York: Modern Library, 1940), 247.

18. William Thackeray, *Vanity Fair* (1847–48), ed. John Carey (London: Penguin, 2001), 16.

19. See Jean-Luc Nancy, *The Inoperative Community*, ed. Peter Connor, trans. Peter Connor, Lisa Garbus, Michael Holland, and Simona Sawhney (Minneapolis: University of Minnesota Press, 1991).

20. Before public relations considerations inspired a change to the equally telling, and excruciatingly equivocal, "Operation Enduring Freedom," this was the name given by the Bush administration to their response to the attack on the World Trade Center in 2001.

21. Jonathan Swift, *Gulliver's Travels* (1726), *The Prose Works of Jonathan Swift*, ed. Herbert Davis, 11 vols. (Oxford: Blackwell, 1941), 11: 118–19.

22. Swift, *Gulliver's Travels*, 244.

23. George Gordon, Lord Byron, *Childe Harold's Pilgrimage* (1812), *The Complete Poetical Works*, ed. Jerome J. McGann, 7 vols. (Oxford: Oxford University Press, 1980–93), 2: 39; Bernard Mandeville, *The Fable of the Bees, or Private Vices, Publick Benefits* (1714–28), ed. F. B. Kaye, 2 vols. (Oxford: Oxford University Press, 1924; rep. Indianapolis: Liberty Classics, 1988), 1: 337; and E. M. Cioran, in a 1985 remark to Esther Seligson, *Glossaire, Oeuvres* (Paris: Gallimard, 1995), 1761.

24. Jean-Jacques Rousseau, *Les rêveries du promeneur solitaire, Oeuvres complètes*, ed. Bernard Gagnebin and Marcel Raymond, 5 vols. (Paris: Gallimard, 1959), 1: 999.

25. Martin Heidegger, "The Age of the World Picture," in *The Question Concerning Technology and Other Essays*, trans. William Lovitt (New York: Harper and Row, 1977), 116.

26. Maurice Blanchot, *The Unavowable Community*, trans. Pierre Joris (Barrytown, N.Y.: Station Hill Press, 1988), 48.

27. John Wilmot, Earl of Rochester, "Tunbridge Wells" (c. 1674), *The Complete Poems of John Wilmot, Earl of Rochester*, ed. David M. Vieth (New Haven, Conn.: Yale University Press, 1968), 80.

28. Swift, *Gulliver's Travels*, xxxv.

29. Swift, *Gulliver's Travels*, 270.

30. Joseph Cotton in *Shadow of a Doubt* (screenplay, 1943)

31. Herman Melville, *Moby-Dick*, ed. Hershel Parker and Harrison Hayford, 2nd ed. (New York: W.W. Norton, 2002), 413.

32. Christabel Pankhurst, quoted in E. Sylvia Pankhurst, *The Suffragette Movement: An Intimate Account of Persons and Ideals* (London: Longmans, Green, 1931), 521.

33. Villiers de l'Isle-Adam, *L'Ève-future*, ed. Alan Raitt (Paris: Gallimard, 1993), 321.

34. Thomas Hardy, *Tess of the D'Urbervilles*, ed. Scott Elledge, 3rd ed. (New York: W.W. Norton, 1991), 66.

35. Quoted in Helen Waddell, *The Desert Fathers* (New York: Henry Holt, 1936), 10.

36. Cioran, *Aveux et anathèmes* (1987), *Oeuvres*, 1664.

Index

Acknowledgments

For their reading of this work at various stages of its composition, I'd like to thank Ron Schleifer, Al Shoaf, Tim Murphy, Mary Childers, Eve Bannet, Michelle Lekas, Francesca Sawaya, and Caryl Flinn. I owe special thanks to Len Tennenhouse for his careful reading of the whole, and to Jerry Singerman for his support. To Brandy Kershner, Amitava Kumar, Elizabeth Langland, and Nancy Armstrong goes my gratitude for favors of a professional sort. For their assistance in obtaining images and reproduction permissions, I'd also like to thank Arturo Santos and Jonathan Wells at Sipa Press; John Benicewicz and Humberto DeLuigi at Art Resource; Vivien Adams at the National Gallery; Yaffa Goldfinger at the Tel Aviv Museum of Art; Antje Ananda Müller and Marina Abramovic; Nicole Gordon at the Princeton University Art Museum; Katy Lucas and the ever-generous Chris Burden; Jeanie Deans at Carroll Janis, Inc.; The George and Helen Segal Foundation; Laura Muggeo at Ronald Feldman Fine Arts; Andrea Mihalovic-Lee at VAGA; Nicola Spinosa at Il Polo Museale di Napoli; and Elke Schwichtenberg at the Bildarchiv Preußischer Kulturbesitz. My thanks also to the editors and publishers of *Representations*, *ELH*, and *Common Knowledge*, where earlier or abbreviated versions of the Introduction, Chapter Two, and Chapter Five first appeared under the titles: "To Love to Hate," *Representations* 80 (Fall 2002): 119–38, © 2002 Regents of the University of California; "I Think; Therefore, I am Heathcliff," *ELH* 70 (2003): 1067–88, © 2004 Johns Hopkins University Press; and "Futurism, Nietzsche, and the Misanthropy of Art," *Common Knowledge* 12, 2 (Spring 2006).